Innovation in Multinational Corporations in the Information Age

NEW HORIZONS IN THE ECONOMICS OF INNOVATION

Series Editor: Christopher Freeman, *Emeritus Professor of Science Policy, SPRU – Science and Technology Policy Research, University of Sussex, UK*

Technical innovation is vital to the competitive performance of firms and of nations and for the sustained growth of the world economy. The economics of innovation is an area that has expanded dramatically in recent years and this major series, edited by one of the most distinguished scholars in the field, contributes to the debate and advances in research in this most important area.

The main emphasis is on the development and application of new ideas. The series provides a forum for original research in technology, innovation systems and management, industrial organization, technological collaboration, knowledge and innovation, research and development, evolutionary theory and industrial strategy. International in its approach, the series includes some of the best theoretical and empirical work from both well-established researchers and the new generation of scholars.

Titles in the series include:

Innovation in Multinational Corporations in the Information Age

The Experience of the European ICT Industry

Grazia D. Santangelo

University of Catania - Italy

Edward Elgar

Cheltenham, UK • Northampton, MA, USA

Published by
Edward Elgar Publishing Limited
Glensanda House
Montpellier Parade
Cheltenham
Glos GL50 1UA
UK

Edward Elgar Publishing, Inc.
136 West Street
Suite 202
Northampton
Massachusetts 01060
USA

A catalogue record for this book
is available from the British Library

Library of Congress Cataloguing in Publication Data
Santangelo, Grazia D., 1973–
    Innovation in multinational corporations in the information age : the
    experience of the European ICT industry / by Grazia D. Santangelo
        p. cm.
    Includes index.
    1. International business enterprises—Europe. 2. Information
    technology—Europe. 3. Technological innovations—Europe. I. Title.

    HD2844 .S25 2002
    338'.064—dc21   2002021990

ISBN 1 84064 731 0

Printed and bound in Great Britain by Biddles Ltd *www.biddles.co.uk*

Contents

List of Figures

List of Tables

Acknowledgements

The publishers wish to thank the following who have kindly given permission for the use of copyright material.

Carfax Publishing for article 'Inter-European Regional Dispersion of Corporate ICT Research Activity: the case of German, Italian and UK regions', in *International Journal of Economics of Business*, **7** (3), 2000, pp. 275–95.

Elsevier Science for articles 'The frontier of international technology networks: sourcing abroad the most highly tacit capability', in *Information Economics and Policy*, **11**, 1999, pp. 101–23; 'The Impact of the Information Technology and Communications Technology Revolution on the Internationalisation of Corporate Technology', in *International Business Review*, **10** (6), 2001, pp. 701–26; 'Corporate Strategic Technological Partnerships in the European Information and Communications Technology Industry', in *Research Policy*, **29** (9), 2000, pp. 1015–31.

Imperial College Press for article 'Corporate Technological Specialisation in the European Information and Communications Technology Industry', in *International Journal of Innovation Management*, **2** (3), 1998, pp. 339–66, www.tandf.co.uk.

Springer for articles 'Capitalism, profits and innovation in the new techno-economic paradigm', in *Journal of Evolutionary Economics*, **11** (2), 2000, pp. 131–57.

Preface

It has become very topical to be concerned with innovative activity as a major factor for the competitive strategy of the firm in the information age. This book aims to tackle this topic more precisely by carrying out a consistent analysis of multinational corporations' operations in terms of corporate production and localisation of research and development. The reasons pushing me to work on this book lie in the intention of understanding better the nature of corporate technological development. In fact, new forms of intra- and inter-firm organisation have emerged in order to cope with the fast pace of technological change; corporate geographical dispersion of innovative activity has increased sharply over the last decades; due to the embedded and path-dependent character of technology, this phenomenon has further fed 'virtuous' and 'vicious' cycles in local economies, reinforcing geographical hierarchies.

In the book, the analysis of the process of the firm's production and localisation of technology in the information age is conducted by adopting as theoretical background an evolutionary approach (as articulated and systematised by Nelson and Winter) as well as the resource-based view, originated by the work of Edith Penrose. The focus of the study is the production of technology by multinational corporations worldwide and in Europe especially. By addressing questions related to the management of corporate technological portfolio as well as to the location of corporate research activity, the analysis is carried out in terms of both sectoral specialisation and geographical location of corporate technological development. The findings provide enlightening insights on the changing geographical division of labour within the MNC, the changing boundaries of the international firm and the evolution of corporate learning in a more complex technological system. Evidence on the increasing significance of the region as unit of spatial competition is also proposed.

The book originated in work that I did for my PhD thesis, which I completed in 1999. In developing this analysis, I have been fortunate to have worked at the Economics Department of Reading University, where I benefited from a stimulating atmosphere and had the opportunity to enter in contact with an international research environment both within Reading and from elsewhere tanks to a series of seminars on international topics. During my stay in Reading I especially benefited from regular discussions with John

Cantwell (my PhD supervisor), who is an internationally recognised scholar in the area of the economics of technology and international business. He has made great contributions to the literature and influenced my research providing me with enlightening advice and constructive criticism, which stimulated my intellectual creativeness. The book has also benefited from my active collaboration with John Cantwell to whom I am grateful for providing me with the patent data on which this study is mainly based. I am also grateful to Massimo Colombo for having kindly provided me with the Advanced Research Programme on Agreements (ARPA) data developed at Politecnico di Milano. I have also enjoyed helpful discussions on the work as a whole with John Dunning, Jonathan Michie of Birkbeck College, Bob Pearce from Reading and Nick von Tunzelmann from SPRU who all provided useful comments. In addition, at various times I have received useful comments or ideas from Suma Atrhey, Giovanna Vertova and anonymous referees. I must also thank Mrs Lia Ambrosio who prepared the camera-ready copy of the book. Finally, I am also grateful to Antonio D'Agata, who, although we met when the whole work was already done, has been always supportive of me. The usual qualifying remark applies that none of them is to be responsible for the final contents of the book or any errors that remain.

I gratefully acknowledge the financial support of the Department of Economics of the University of Reading, who awarded me a two-year research grant for the year 1997–99, and the Università degli Studi di Catania (Italy), who provided me with a one-year grant at the start of my research in Reading.

Before beginning it may be useful to make explicit the procedure followed in designing the book. The early chapters deal with the issue of the firm's production and localisation of innovative activity within any industry in a global scenario. The findings provide grounds to frame the issue in the context of the European electronic industry, which is the focus of the second part of the book. The structure of the book may have the advantage that the reader enters into the topic gradually. It first gives the flavour of the issues it deals with in a wider global scenario and then narrows the focus by framing these issues in a geographically and politically defined area.

To Ida

1. Introduction

1.1 AIMS OF THE BOOK

The new techno–socio–economic conditions generated by the information and communications technology (ICT) revolution have promoted major economic transformations embodied in the shift towards a knowledge-based economy. In this overall context there are great implications for the nature of corporate technological development. In order to cope with the complexity of these new streams of knowledge and the new foreseeable technological combinations, multinational corporations (MNCs) need to restructure their internal organisation and locational strategies. New forms of intra- and inter-firm organisation have emerged in order to cope with the fast pace of technological change. On the one hand, intra-firm organisation has seemed to move from top-down hierarchical structures to more heterarchical structures, based on a network of subsidiaries actively involved in the overall corporate development of research activity. The role of subsidiaries concerns more the outsourcing of new complementary knowledge than mere product market supply. On the other hand, inter-firm arrangements seem to be increasingly adopted by MNCs as a means of enhancing the overall value of the firm through fruitful exchange of knowledge. Furthermore, corporate geographical dispersion of innovative activity has increased sharply over the last decades due to the embedded and path-dependent character of technology. Tacitness of some parts of competencies embedded in geographical locations leads to spatial agglomeration and to the geographical dispersion of R&D activities of the firm.

In the light of these fundamental socio–economic transformations, this book investigates the impact of the new pervasive and complex technologies on the nature of corporate technological development. Grounded on the evolutionary tradition, the analysis addresses questions related to the management of corporate technological portfolios as well as to the location of corporate research activity. The empirical investigation is carried out in terms of both sectoral specialisation and geographical location of corporate technology between 1969 and 1995 with the use of patent statistics.

The originality of the book lies in the attempt to provide an analysis of corporate technological development of ICT technologies worldwide and in

Europe over the information age. Both issues seem to be crucial in the new techno–socio–economic conditions in terms of development of economic theory, business strategy and policy-making agenda. Although economic theory has increasingly focused on these issues, a formulated theory of the firm explaining corporate dynamics of knowledge creation and utilisation in sectoral and spatial terms is still lacking. However, this is an important theoretical development given the significance of strategic factors in driving MNCs' behaviour. Similarly, the issues the book deals with are relevant in the making of business strategy. The cumulative generation of technological competencies in firms and their future trajectories seem to be fundamental elements in the firm's capability to generate and implement competitive corporate strategies. The sectoral and spatial aspects of corporate technological development are also a topic linked to high-priority issues on the political agenda due to the path-dependent and embedded character of technology. This is all the more true in the European context. The current global structural change is parallel to an ongoing integration process in Europe, which raises issues linked to corporate competitiveness in a broader socio–economic–political frame. This seems to call for further investigation of the issue discussed above within the European context given the weak technological position of European corporations in the new techno–socio– economic conditions.

Drawing upon the evolutionary framework, the literature on technological change and the 'resource-based view' of the firm, technological specialisation is understood as firm-specific and strictly related to the techno–socio–economic environment in which firms operate. Similarly, corporate internationalisation strategy is seen as firm-specific and closely associated with the embedded, path-dependent and complex character of technology. In investigating both these phenomena, technological and institutional factors are taken into consideration as important elements in the understanding of the ICT-based era. As argued below, technological change implies a restructuring and reorganisation of the institutional set-up of the whole economy.

1.2   THE INFORMATION AGE AND THE NEW CHALLENGES TO MNCs' COMPETITIVENESS

The 1970s technological revolution shift has been characterised by the emergence of technological opportunities in microelectronic technology and computerised systems, on which other technology and related innovations depend. By establishing an information age, the technological shift into ICT has generated a new techno–socio–economic environment and consequent new challenges to corporate competitiveness. The complex and uncertain character of technology accumulation calls for corporate strategies more concerned with technology management (Mitchell, 1986; Dodgson, 1989; Loveridge and Pitt, 1990). Firms need to find new avenues to enhance their 'strategic assets' – understood as non-tradeable, non-imitable and non-substitutable[1] – and consequently their capabilities. The failure in doing so is likely to have serious consequences on the firm's future. Following the evolutionary tradition (Nelson and Winter, 1977, 1982; Kline and Rosenberg, 1986; Nelson, 1992; Cantwell, 1989, 1991a, 1994a; Dosi and Malerba, 1996), there is a constant adjustment through a selection mechanism, which allows successful firms to enter the market and others to leave due to their unsuccessful business performance.

In enhancing their capabilities, firms deal with environmental complexity in two broad domains. First, they face the complexity linked to diversification because of the need to expand corporate capability into new related fields. Second, they face the complexity linked to greater environmental heterogeneity because of the need to expand corporate capabilities geographically. Therefore technological diversification and internationalisation are major constraints in the firm's strategy (McKerm, 1993). None the less, they should be seen as complementary rather than mutually excluding (Cantwell and Piscitello, 1997, 1999, 2000).

Technological diversification refers to the firm's strategy aiming at expanding its technology base into a wider variety of activities. The rise of technological diversification as a phenomenon in technology-based firms prompted the notion of a multi-technology corporation as a corporation diversifying into several technical competence areas (Granstrand and Sjölander, 1990; Granstrand et al., 1992; Granstrand and Oskarsson, 1994; Granstrand, 1996; Granstrand et al., 1997; Patel and Pavitt, 1997). Given the cumulative and complex character of technology, a wide range of technological expertise is nowadays needed in corporate production and organisation. Enhanced technological 'core' competencies enable firms to exploit radically new technologies in order to avoid failures in product development, production, marketing and organisational adaptation (Patel and Pavitt, 1997). Therefore corporate strategy aims at broadening out the firm's technological portfolios in comparison with product portfolios. Firms can compete efficiently in a technologically complex global environment by managing technological competencies larger than their stream of products given the growing process of technological interrelatedness and technological fusion (Kodama, 1992a, 1992b).

To perform efficiently in a highly technologically complex global environment, firms need to adopt geographical international strategies. The globalisation of technological innovation in MNCs refers to the international integration of geographically dispersed and locally specialised activities in order to build effective capabilities of research and development (R&D) abroad (Kuemmerle, 1999, 1997a, 1997b). Corporate strategy, based upon geographically dispersed R&D facilities, aims to tap into local expertises complementary to the firm's technological path. Therefore globalisation of innovative activity by MNCs tends to reinforce and not to dismantle nationally/regionally distinctive patterns of development or national/regional systems of innovation (Cantwell, 1995).

1.3   THE EUROPEAN DIMENSION

This book focuses closely on Europe by investigating the possibility of identifying a specific European pattern of technological specialisation and location in the European ICT industry. The interest in the European situation concerns two orders of reasons.

First, the European integration process, which has been taking place since the 1950s and which has been accelerated by the ambitious targets of the Single European Market (SEM) and the European Monetary Union (EMU), has impacted on how MNCs integrate their intra-bloc operations (Pearce and Tavares, 1998). Similarly, the implementation of the SEM and the EMU together with the launch and the establishment of a European technology policy have led to the prospect of the development of a European System of Innovation (Caracostas and Soete, 1997).

Second, the European integration process is parallel to global structural changes moving towards an international arena fragmented in political and economic regional blocks (as shown by the emergence of the US, Japan and Europe as the leading triad). However, the breakthrough of the information age has clearly highlighted the weakness of the European position within the triad in terms of technological development. Still nowadays, the lagging position of the Union in fields of leading-edge technology (such as ICT) is one of the major concerns of the European Commission (1997). High penetration of foreign companies and low rates of innovation activity were the main characteristics of Europe in electronics and related fields in the early stages of the ICT revolution. After the failure of national procurement policies aimed at supporting national champions (i.e. large firms created through the state-assisted mergers), a Community policy aiming to promote the development of advanced technology started being developed in the 1980s with the launch of the European Strategic Programme for Research in Information Technology (ESPRIT). The European technology policy is nowadays rather articulated and linked to other European actions. Technology policy has been a major instrument of the European integration process, as illustrated by the development of the Framework Programmes for Community Action, aimed at promoting an articulated intervention of the Union in related fields.

1.4   PATENTS AS TECHNOLOGICAL INDICATORS

The empirical evidence provided in this book is mainly based upon patents granted to the world's largest industrial firms in the US between 1969 and 1995. These data are drawn from the University of Reading database (see Appendix A). The use of patenting in a common third country provides a standard for international comparison. The patenting process is monitored by a unique patent office that enforces common screening and legal procedures, thus avoiding problems arising from different legislation. The choice of the USPTO relies on the characteristics of the American market as well as on the structured organisation of the recording activity. The US market is recognised as the largest technologically, where large firms patent and tend to follow stricter pre-patenting screening policies (Archibugi and Pianta, 1992a). Because of these features, patents recorded in the US by non-US firms are more likely to represent significant inventions. Foreign patents (e.g. European) are expected to be of a higher quality than domestic patents (i.e. US) as it is reasonable to assume that only inventions and innovations with highest expected profits will be patented abroad due to the time and cost involved in so doing.[2] Similarly, the structural organisation of the US data offers a unique disaggregation by cross-country, cross-firm structural and historical dimensions, otherwise hardly achievable through other sources.

Following the broad definition of technology adopted by evolutionary theory, there are no direct measures of the tacit component. Patents are alternative indirect measures as they capture the generation of new knowledge and, accordingly, provide some indirect evidence on the establishment of tacit capabilities, which make such knowledge operational (Pavitt, 1985, 1988). Therefore, patent data can be used as a measure of technology creation and a means of innovating diffusion. Technology creation (i.e. innovation) and diffusion (i.e. imitation) are closely linked as the imitation of related technologies supports the cumulative development of the firm's own technology, based upon the tacit capabilities of the company.[3] Therefore, whilst patents represent the results of in-house R&D, they also encompass firms' absorptive capacity (Cohen and Levinthal, 1989, 1990) as being able to use technological knowledge generated outside the firm's presumed in-house development (Cantwell and Barrera, 1998).

A large literature on the use of patent statistics has been growing since the 1960s in an attempt to compare patents with other indicators of innovative activities. A high correlation between patent statistics and R&D expenditures is a common finding of these empirical works, despite the substantial structural differences between patents and R&D data.[4] A major problem with patent statistics concerns the different propensity to patent across firms, industries and countries.[5] In the empirical analysis conducted in this book, this problem is avoided by introducing relative measures as substituted to absolute patent counts.[6] This is the avenue followed in this book by adopting the Revealed Technological Advantage (RTA) index, which is a relative measure of technological specialisation.[7]

For each firm (i), the *RTA* industry is defined as the share of patents granted to a firm (i) in a particular sector (j) divided by the share of patents granted to firm (i) relatively to all firms in the same industry in that sector. Thus, the index can be mathematically formulated as:

$$RTA_{ij} = (P_{ij}/\sum_i P_{ij})/(\sum_j P_{ij}/\sum_{ij} P_{ij}) \tag{1.1}$$

where P_{ij} is the total number of patents granted to firm (i) in a technological sector (j). The numerator ($P_{ij}/\sum_i P_{ij}$) is the patenting share of firm (i) in sector (j), whilst the denominator ($\sum_j P_{ij}/\sum_{ij} P_{ij}$) is the patenting share of firm (i) in sector (j) within the industry. The inter-firm and inter-sectoral differences in the propensity to patent are eliminated by the RTA itself, which is normalised. The numerator accounts for differences in the propensity to patent across firms, whilst the denominator accounts for patenting variation across sectors. Instead the inter-industry differences in the propensity to patent are taken into account by the fact that the index is calculated within industries (e.g. electronic), thus allowing for intra-industry comparison in technological specialisation only. Evidence suggests that the propensity to patent differs more between firms from *different* industries than between firms within the *same* industry (Scherer, 1983). It is assumed that, for instance, electronic companies display the same similar propensity to patent. Therefore the empirical and statistical investigation is conducted through drawing intra- rather than inter-industry comparison between firms. The RTA index varies around 1. If a firm shows a technological disadvantage in a particular technological sector ($RTA < 1$), that means that the firm may still patent in that particular technological sector, but it does not patent as much as the average firm in the same industry. In this sense the RTA index is a comparative measure of technological advantage/ disadvantage, which compares patenting activity of one firm with that of others.

In an analysis focusing on ICT a problem in using patent data might be identified in the fact that software inventions have usually been protected by copyright and software patents have been successfully enforced in the US since the mid-1990s (Merges, 1996).[8] Notwithstanding, this is an issue only in the first part of this book where large aggregates of firms are analysed. However, even there the problem arises with reference to US firms only, which have mainly mastered software technologies. Conversely, Japanese and European companies have lagged behind in the production of this technology (Mowery, 1996; Malerba et al., 1997; Malerba and Torrisi, 1996). Therefore the problems concerning software patenting activity are not a major issue at all in the second part of the book since the empirical analysis narrows down to the European electronic industry.[9]

1.5   OUTLINE OF THE BOOK

The analysis of the new challenges to MNCs' competitiveness in the innovation process is articulated in six core chapters plus a concluding chapter sketching management issues and policy implications related to the findings. These core chapters can be conceptually grouped into two main parts, where the analysis is carried out over the years 1969–95. The reason for focusing on this period lies in the fact that the ICT revolution broke through in the 1970s (Freeman, 1982, 1988; Hall and Preston, 1988). Therefore, in order to provide an understanding of the new information age in terms of corporate technological specialisation profiles, diversification strategies and geographical dispersion of R&D activity, it seems relevant to carry out an analysis of the following 26 years. For the reasons exposed below, the selected period has been broken into three sub-periods:

- 1969–77 (sub-period 1)
- 1978–86 (sub-period 2) and
- 1987–95 (sub-period 3).

This periodisation has a specific meaning in each of the three parts into which the book is articulated. Part One (Chapters 2, 3 and 4) investigates the new techno–socio–economic conditions by providing a general overview of the international geography and specialisation of corporate innovative activity. In this context the years 1969–77 witness the progressive shift from oil-based to computerised technologies as the leading ones. Sub-period 2 is expected to capture the establishment of new technologies and the opening up of new technological opportunities, such as the development of information and communications technologies. The sub-period 1987–95 reflects the latest corporate technological development in the ICT era. Going into the details of the analysis, Chapter 2 measures to what extent the innovation which depends most upon tacit knowledge (in the science-based fields, and in the enhancement of a firm's core competence), tends to remain more agglomerated in the parent company. It is believed that the tacit and locally embedded character of knowledge restricts the ability of firms to combine distant learning processes, and therefore constrains the international location of research activity within the firm. None the less certain firm-specific cases in which the creation of even science-based and industry-specific core technologies is dispersed internationally are analysed in order to identify which are the main factors driving the occasional geographical dispersion of the creation of these kinds of otherwise highly localised technologies. Chapter 3 deals with the relationships between firm size and technological diversification. In line with the most recent 'resource-based view' literature, it is assumed that over time 'smaller' companies are diversifying their technological profiles, whilst giant companies are moving towards an increasing rationalisation of their technological portfolios. A change in the nature of corporate growth is believed to have occurred. Most companies tend to enhance their competitiveness by expanding their competencies in new fields. On the other hand, it is believed that the very largest companies are focusing their efforts on a few more related activities as a result of past over-diversification. Chapter 4 investigates whether the microelectronic revolution has influenced the geographical diversification or internationalisation of firms by accelerating the process of technological interrelatedness through the wide application of ICT as key technology. The increasing geographical dispersion of corporate R&D is a major feature of the current information age, in which many new technological combinations between formerly separate activities are now feasible.

Part Two (Chapters 5, 6 and 7) focuses on the European dimension by framing the issues of corporate technological sectoral and spatial development in the context of the European ICT industry. The empirical analysis surveys the European industry in terms of corporate specialisation at both intra- and inter-firm level. Emphasis is also placed on the geography of this industry across Europe. In this case the three sub-periods are expected to capture the development of the European ICT industry amidst the more general background highlighted in the previous chapters. The years 1969–77 reflect the European weakness in ICT and the launch of national programmes aimed at supporting the development of national companies operating in science-based sectors. The sub-period 1978–86 witnesses the rising of the European technological policy issue and, accordingly, the launch of the first European Community programme (i.e. ESPRIT) promoting the European ICT industry. The latest sub-period is expected to capture technological characteristics specific to the European ICT industry. In more detail, Chapter 5 analyses similar technological characteristics specific to the European ICT industry which emerged over time in terms of large firms' specialisation profiles. It is found that European ICT multinationals came closer together in terms of sectoral specialisation over the period 1969–95. Chapter 6 evaluates the role of corporate technological specialisation factors in the conclusions of intra-European strategic technological partnerships (STPs) in the ICT industry. Following the evolutionary tradition it is held that the increase in technological complexity calls for closer corporate co-operation in order to facilitate the acquisition of new capabilities in related fields. The significance of the cumulativeness and path-dependency in the firm's learning process plays a crucial role in the choice of partners as partners can absorb each other's expertise if they share the same kind of technological commonalties. Chapter 7 investigates the geography of ICT corporate development across European regions. The embedded value added characterising agglomeration economies drive corporate decisions in the location of R&D laboratories in cutting-edge technologies (e.g. ICT).

These two parts are complementary to one another as the former builds (to different extents) the foundations for the analysis developed in the latter. Finally, in Part Three, Chapter 8 provides a forum for discussion of the empirical findings by bringing them together in a broader context, while management issues and policy implications are outlined in Chapter 9.

NOTES

1. The evolutionary theory rooted in the Schumpeterian tradition distinguishes between a public and a private or tacit element of technology. The former, defined as potentially public knowledge, can be codified in patents, blueprint, textbooks, etc. This implies that 'public' technology can be transferred easily and, therefore, traded between firms. The latter is a tacit element embodied in the firm's organisational routines, expertise and skills acquired through a process of learning and takes the shape of a firm-specific set of practises. If the public aspect of technology can be transferred easily, the private element is non-tradable and difficult to transfer as the result of a process of learning-by-using (Rosenberg, 1982). Therefore, tacit knowledge is developed through an internal learning process.

2. The use of US patents as a reliable measure of the geographical dispersion of innovation in international companies is widely acknowledge by Patel and Pavitt (1991a). The reliability of foreign patent data has been shown by Soete and Wyatt (1983). Similarly Basberg (1987) maintained that the propensity to patent in another country is probably related to the perceived potential of the market in that country. In fact the extensive use of foreign patenting in the US as technological indicator is due to the average quality of such data compared to domestic patent statistics. Moreover, Archibugi and Pianta (1992b) have shown that in absolute numbers the USPTO has received by far the largest number of foreign patent applications.

3. Cantwell and Andersen (1996) show empirically that a high rate of technological accumulation is linked to a strong rate of technological innovation and imitation.

4. Unlike the structural limitations of R&D data, patents are available in long and completed time series (Basberg, 1987) and broken down by very detailed technological fields.

Moreover, as pointed out by Archibugi (1992), patent statistics represent the outcome of inventions which are expected to have a business since only inventions anticipating commercial benefits go through the costly and time-consuming patenting process. For this reason, patents appear to be a rather appropriate indicator to capture the proprietary and competitive dimension of technological change. However besides the significance of patent statistics, the large literature on patents has also highlighted limits related to the fact that many inventions are never patented (Basberg, 1987), that firms prefer to protect their innovations with alternative methods such as industrial secrecy (Archibugi, 1992), and that not all inventions which are patented become innovations. None the less, as pointed out by Archibugi (ibid.), if this is true in the case of patents, the same applies to R&D projects since many of them do not result in innovations. In this sense empirical evidence raises some doubts on the model that treats R&D as the "input" and patenting as the measurable "output" (Scherer, 1983; Griliches, 1984). Moreover, problems arise from the different quality of patents, as in the statistics there is no distinction between patents leading to radical technological change or to minor technological improvements. Quantitative methods to assess the value of individual patents (e.g. count of patent citation (Harhoff et al., 1999), estimation of the shifts in the propensity to patent from one to another technological field implying consequent shifts in the pattern of technological opportunities for innovating firms (Cantwell and Andersen, 1996), etc.) confirm the correspondence between patent-based analysis and studies based on other Science and Technological (S&T) indicators (Ernst, 1998; European Commission, 1994).

5. Following Scherer (1983), the different propensity to patent seems to be a more serious problem across industries than across firms within industries since the propensity to patent seems to be higher in some industries (e.g. pharmaceuticals) than in others.

6. The simplest way to avoid this problem may be identified as restricting the analysis to industries (and firms) showing similar degrees of reliance on patent protection and propensity to patent. If this were to be the case for empirical analysis of particular industries, it may be less feasible for cross-sectoral investigations based on larger aggregates. In the latter case, an alternative solution to the one adopted in this book is the introduction of other performance indicators (e.g. market value of firms and industries, companies' accounts, patent citations) or qualitative data (e.g. survey data, company corporate profiles). However, problems of data matching are likely to raise when considering the lowest levels of disaggregation of patent statistics.

7. The RTA index first used by Soete (1987) is based on the Revealed Comparative Advantage (RCA) index of Balassa (1965) by substituting exports with patents. The RTA index has been used extensively as a proxy for technological specialisation controlling variations in the propensity to patent at the firm level (Cantwell, 1993; Cantwell and Fai, 1999a, 1999b; Cantwell and Bachmann, 1998; Cantwell and Barrera, 1998; Cantwell and Santangelo, 2000) at the industry level (Cantwell and Andersen, 1996) and at the country level (Cantwell, 1991b; Archibugi and Pianta, 1992b; Soete and Wyatt, 1983; Vertova, 1998a, 1998b, 1999).

8. The legal debate on the patentability of software concerned the fact that software inventions set out the sequences of steps necessary to perform an activity in terms of functions that are carried out by conventional computer hardware elements. As the novelty mainly relates to the sequences of steps to perform the programme, it took a while to recognise differences in sequences as innovations.

9. As far as the sample of analysis is concerned, while the selection of the samples in the first part of the book will be discussed in each chapter, Appendix B describes the sample of analysis of the second part, concentring the European ICT industry broadly defined.

Appendix A: The University of Reading database

Using a classification scheme derived from the USPTO patent class system, the Reading database classifies each patent by the year in which it was granted and by the type of technological activity with which it is primarily associated. Thus, following the USPTO scheme, all patents recorded are classified into 399 original patent classes. In the Reading database, those patent classes have been allocated to one of 56 technological groups according to related technological fields/sectors. For the purpose of this thesis, patents are counted as belonging to corporate groups according to the information provided in the patent document.[1] Firms have been allocated to one of 14 industries, according to their industrial output, that is the firm's primary field of production (see Table A.1). In turn, as shown in Table A.2, each of these industries has been placed in one of five more broadly defined industrial corporate groups: Chemical, Electronic, Mechanical, Transport and Others (CEMTind).[2] Table A.3 lists all 56 technological sectors by the number of the Reading database classification and the broader industrial group. Table A.4 shows the patent classes sorted by broader industrial technological group (CEMTind classification) and technological sector in order to take into account which technology is included in which technological sector. This allows accounting for the fact that each technological sector contains more than one patent class. It is worth noting that, in the Reading database, the technological classification of each patent is rather distinct from the industrial output classification of the firm to which the patent is granted. While the primary field of technological activity of each patent derives from the US patent class system, each corporate group is allocated to an industry on the basis of its output sales. Most large companies have engaged in at least some development in most of the general spheres of technological activity, regardless of the industry in which they operate.[3]

Births, deaths, mergers and acquisitions as well as the occasional movement of firms between industries (sometimes associated with historical change in ownership) have been taken into account. A consolidation procedure was carried out for the world's largest 792 industrial firms, according to names derived from the listings in Fortune 500 (Dunning and Pearce, 1985). During the entire period 1969–95, patent activity was recorded both for 730 firms of these 792 companies and for a further 54 of the world's largest firms not listed in Fortune 500 and among the most technologically important historically or recently. Patents have been consolidated into corporate groups, initially on the basis of the structure of ownership of groups in 1982. Post-1982 mergers and acquisitions are largely recognised in the data through the practice in most groups of centralising the patent application procedure in the parent company. Accordingly the consolidation of affiliates' research activity into corporate groups does not affect the information recorded in the patent database because of the standardised structure of patent documents. In other important cases of mergers and acquisitions affecting the ultimate ownership of significant numbers of patents, the change in ownership structure is incorporated into the organisation of the data, which involves in some cases the creation of a new corporate group and, in others, the expanded consolidation of groups with newly acquired subsidiaries. To illustrate the former case, the merger between the Swedish ASEA and the Swiss Brown Boveri in 1988 promoted the creation of a new corporate group ABB in which the patent activities of the two partner companies were consolidated. In the latter case, the patenting of the newly acquired affiliates continues to be recorded under their own names.

Recently the University of Reading database has been regionalised. This enables the disaggregation of the patent information concerning the geographical location of the research activity at a lower level than the national does. The sub-national entities identified correspond to the units classified by the European Nomenclature of Territorial Units for Statistics (NUTS) established by Eurostat. By providing a single uniform breakdown of territorial units, this classification is based on the institutional division currently in force in the member states. In each of the EU member states, the NUTS division of the national territory takes into account territorial communities according to the size of population necessary to organise and carry out local economic activity as well as according to historical, cultural and other factors. As the nomenclature is based on institutional division currently in force in the member states, territorial units are classified in a five-level hierarchy (three regional levels and two local levels). Therefore, the NUTS subdivides each member state into a whole number of NUTS 1 regions, each of which is in turn subdivided into a whole number of NUTS 2 regions and so on until the smallest local level is reached. Within the economic territory of the European Union, 77 regions are identified at the NUTS 1 level, 206 regions at NUTS 2 level and 1 301 regions at NUTS 3 level. The local levels (NUTS 4 and 5) are defined only for a selected group of countries.[4] The regionalisation of the Reading patent database has been carried out by attributing a NUTS code (as precise as possible as far as the first three NUTS levels are concerned) to each patent over the period 1969–95. This allows investigation of the geographical and sectoral distribution of MNCs' activities in the EU by taking into consideration intra-border phenomena, which are likely to be neglected in a nation-State analysis (Iammarino and Santangelo, 2000).

NOTES

1. Where patents have been assigned to firms, the inventor is normally directly or indirectly associated with it in some way, but occasionally independent individual inventors choose to assign their patents to firms (Schmookler, 1966). Normally the assignor was a prominent member of a corporate research laboratory or other in-house facility. When patents were assigned to affiliates of a parent company, they were consolidated in a common corporate group.
2. This broader level of aggregation will be referred to as CEMTind level from hereafter, where 'C' stands for Chemical, 'E' for Electronic, 'M' for Mechanical, 'T' for Transport and 'ind' for industries, thus dropping 'Others' including non-industrial corporate groups.
3. An overall picture of the classification scheme adopted in the University of Reading database is drawn in Figure A.1.
4. The NUTS 4 level is only defined for Finland, Greece, Ireland, Luxembourg, Portugal and the United Kingdom. The NUTS 5 level consists of 98 433 communes or their equivalent (Eurostat, 1995).

Table A.1 – List of firms by 14 broadly defined industries

	Chapter 2 (case studies)	Chapter 3	Chapter 4	Chapters 5, 6 and 7
	1969—95	1969—77 1987—95	1969—77 1978—86 / 1978—86 1987—95	1969—77 1978—86 1987—95

Chemical industrial group

Chemicals n.e.s. and Pharmaceuticals

Firm	Chapter 2	Chapter 3	Chapter 4	Chapters 5, 6 and 7
DOW CHEMICAL (US)	X		X	
UNION CARBIDE (US)	X			
3M (US)	X		X	
MONSANTO (US)	X			
ALLIED (US)	X			
W R GRACE (US)	X		X	
AMERICAN CYANAMID (US)	X			
PPG INDS (US)	X	X		
CELANESE (US)	X		X	
HERCULES (US)	X		X	
SCM (US)	X			
SHERWIN WILLIAMS (US)	X		X	
ROHM & HAAS (US)	X	X	X	
OLIN (US)	X			
INT MINERALS & CHEMICALS (US)	X			
STAUFFER CHEMICALS (US)	X	X		
ETHYL (US)	X			
AIR PRODUCTS AND CHEMICALS (US)	X	X	X	
NATIONAL DISTILLERS AND CHEMICALS (US)	X	X		
PENNWALT (US)	X			
LUBRIZOL (US)	X			
ICI (UK)	X		X	
BOC GROUP (UK)	X		X	
MITSUBISHI CHEMICAL INDUSTRIES (JP)	X	X	X	
ASAHI CHEMICAL INDUSTRIES (JP)	X	X		
SUMITOMO CHEMICAL INDS (JP)	X	X	X	
UBE INDUSTRIES (JP)	X		X	
FUJI PHOTO FILM (JP)	X	X		
MITSUI TOATSU CHEMICALS (JP)	X		X	
DAINIPPON INK & CHEMICAL (JP)	X	X	X	
SHOWA DENKO (JP)	X	X	X	
MITSUBISHI PETROCHEMICALS (JP)	X			
MITSUI PETROCHEMICAL (JP)	X			
MITSUBISHI GAS CHEMICAL (JP)	X			
DENKI KOGAKU KOGYO (JP)	X			
KYOWA HAKKO KOGYO (JP)	X			
TOYO SODA MANUFACTURING (JP)	X			
LION (JP)	X			
DAICEL CHEMICAL INDS (JP)	X		X	
HOECHST (G)	X	X	X	
BAYER (G)	X		X	

	Chapter 2 (case studies)	Chapter 3	Chapter 4		Chapters 5, 6 and 7		
	1969—95	1969—77 1987—95	1969—77 1978—86	1978—86 1987—95	1969—77	1978—86	1987—95
BASF (G)		X	X	X			
CHEMISCHE WERKE HULS (G)		X	X	X			
DSM (NL)		X					
AKZO (NL)		X	X				
CIBA-GEIGY (SZ)		X		X			
MONTEDISON (IT)		X	X	X			
RHÔNE-POULENC (FR)	X	X	X	X			
CHARBONNAGES DE FRANCE (FR)		X	X	X			
L'AIR LIQUIDE (FR)		X	X	X			
SOLVAY (BE)		X					
CANADA DEVELOPMENT CORP (CA)		X	X	X			
PROCTER & GAMBLE (US)		X	X	X			
JOHNSON & JOHNSON (US)		X	X				
COLGATE PALMOLIVE (US)		X		X			
AMERICAN HOME PRODUCTS (US)		X		X			
BRISTOL MYERS (US)		X	X	X			
PFIZER (US)		X	X	X			
WARNER LAMBERT (US)		X		X			
MERCK (US)		X		X			
AVON PRODUCTS (US)		X	X	X			
SMITH KLINE BEECHAM (US)		X					
ELI LILLY (US)		X	X	X			
ABBOTT LABS (US)		X	X	X			
REVLON (US)		X	X				
UPJOHN (US)		X	X				
SCHERING PLOUGH (US)		X	X	X			
STERLING DRUG (US)		X					
SQUIBB (US)		X					
CHESEBROUGH PONDS (US)		X		X			
BEECHAM GROUP (UK)		X					
GLAXO (UK)		X	X	X			
WELLCOME FOUNDATION (UK)		X					
SYNTEX (US)		X		X			
ROCHE/SAPAC (SZ)		X					
SANDOZ (SZ)		X					
TAKEDA CHEMICAL (JP)		X	X	X			
SHIONOGI (JP)		X					
HENKEL (G)		X	X	X			
SCHERING (G)		X	X	X			
BOEHRINGER INGELHEIM (G)		X					
L'OREAL (FR)		X	X	X			
DEGUSSA (G)		X					
FLICK (G)		X					
DU PONT (US)		X					
GAF (US)		X					
MORTON THIOKOL (US)		X		X			
INTERNATIONAL FLAVORS & FRAGRANCES (US)		X					
E. MERK (G)		X					
BOEHRINGER MANNHEIM (G)		X	X	X			
ASTRA (SE)		X	X	X			
AB PHARMACIA (SE)		X					
Textiles and clothing							
BURLINGTON INDUSTRIES (US)		X	X				
TORAY INDUSTRIES (JP)		X	X	X			

	Chapter 2 (case studies)	Chapter 3	Chapter 4		Chapters 5, 6 and 7		
	1969—95	1969—77 1987—95	1969—77 1978—86	1978—86 1987—95	1969—77	1978—86	1987—95
KANEBO (JP)		x					
TEIJIN (JP)		x	x	x			
TOYOBO (JP)		x					
UNITIKA (JP)		x	x	x			
MITSUBISHI (JP)		x	x	x			
Coal and petroleum products							
EXXON (US)		x					
MOBIL (US)		x	x	x			
TEXACO (US)		x					
ST. OIL OF CALIFORNIA (US)		x					
STANDARD OIL INDIANA (US)		x	x	x			
ATLANTIC RICHFIELD (US)		x	x				
OCCIDENTAL PETROLEUM (US)		x	x				
PHILLIPS PETROLEUM (US)		x					
TENNECO (US)		x		x			
UNION OIL OF CALIFORNIA (US)		x		x			
ASHLAND OIL (US)		x	x	x			
KERR-McGEE (US)		x					
DIAMOND SHAMROCK (US)		x	x				
PENN CENTRAL (US)		x					
CABOT (US)		x	x	x			
WITCO (US)		x					
DU PONT (US)			x				
SHELL (UK/NL)	x	x		x			
BP (UK)		x					
ENI (IT)		x	x				
ELF AQUITAINE (FR)		x	x	x			
INSTITUT FRANCAIS DU PETROL (FR)		x					

Electrical industrial group

Electrical equipment n.e.s. and Office equipment

	Chapter 2	Chapter 3	Chapter 4		Chapters 5, 6 and 7		
GENERAL ELECTRIC (US)		x		x			
ITT (US)		x					
WESTINGHOUSE ELECTRIC (US)		x		x			
TRW (US)		x		x			
TEXAS INSTRUMENTS (US)		x		x			
MOTOROLA (US)		x	x	x			
EMERSON ELECTRIC (US)		x	x	x			
ALLEGHENY INDUSTRIES (US)		x					
SINGER (US)		x					
WHIRLPOOL (US)		x		x			
GOULD (US)		x	x				
HARRIS (US)		x	x	x			
GENERAL SIGNAL (US)		x					
JOHNSON CONTROLS (US)		x					
AMP (US)		x		x			
ZENITH RADIO (US)		x		x			
NATIONAL SEMICONDUCTOR (US)		x	x	x			
SQUARE D (US)		x	x	x			
GENERAL INSTRUMENT (US)		x	x	x			
INTEL (US)		x	x	x			
GENERAL ELECTRIC CO (UK)		x		x	x	x	x
THORN EMI (UK)		x	x		x	x	x

	Chapter 2 (case studies)	Chapter 3	Chapter 4		Chapters 5, 6 and 7		
	1969—95	1969—77 1987—95	1969—77 1978—86	1978—86 1987—95	1969—77	1978—86	1987—95
BICC (UK)		x	x	x	x	x	x
PLESSEY (UK)		x		x	x	x	x
RACAL ELECTRONICS (UK)		x	x	x	x	x	x
STANDARD TELEPHONES AND CABLES (UK)					x	x	x
HITACHI (JP)		x	x	x			
MATSUSHITA ELECTRIC INDS (JP)		x	x	x			
TOSHIBA (JP)		x	x	x			
MITSUBISHI ELECTRIC (JP)		x		x			
NIPPON ELECTRIC (JP)		x	x	x			
SONY (JP)		x	x	x			
SANYO ELECTRIC (JP)		x	x				
SHARP (JP)		x	x	x			
PIONEER ELECTRONIC (JP)		x	x	x			
TDK (JP)		x	x				
TOKYO SANYO ELECTRIC (JP)		x		x			
SIEMENS (G)		x		x	x	x	x
AEG-TELEFUNKEN (G)		x		x	x	x	x
BOSCH-SIEMENS HAUSGERATE (G)					x	x	x
COMPAGNIE GENERALE D'ELECTRICITE (FR)		x	x	x	x	x	x
THOMSON-BRANDT (FR)		x	x	x	x	x	x
SAGEM (FR)							x
PHILIPS (NL)	x	x		x	x	x	x
ELECTROLUX (SE)		x	x	x	x	x	x
LM ERICSSON (SE)	x	x	x	x	x	x	x
BROWN BOVERI (SZ)		x	x		x		
NORTHERN TELECOM (CA)		x	x	x			
ZANUSSI GROUP (IT)					x	x	
IBM (US)		x		x			
XEROX (US)		x		x			
HONEYWELL (US)		x					
LITTON (US)		x		x			
CONTROL DATA (US)		x	x	x			
HEWLETT PACKARD (US)		x	x	x			
DIGITAL EQUIP (US)		x		x			
NCR (US)		x		x			
PITNEY BOWES (US)		x	x	x			
FUJITSU (JP)		x	x	x			
RICOH (JP)		x	x	x			
OLIVETTI (IT)		x			x	x	x
ICL (UK)		x	x	x	x	x	x
CII-HONEYWELL BULL (FR)		x	x	x	x	x	x
NIXDORF COMPUTER (G)					x	x	x
AT&T (US)		x	x				
RCA (US)		x					
GTE (US)		x					
BELL & HOWELL (US)		x					
ASEA BROWN BOVERI (ABB) (SZ+SE)	x						x
UNISYS (US)		x	x	x			

Mechanical industrial group

Food

DART AND KRAFT (US)		x					
BEATRICE FOODS (US)		x		x			
GENERAL FOODS (US)		x					

	Chapter 2 (case studies)	Chapter 3	Chapter 4		Chapters 5, 6 and 7		
	1969—95	1969—77 1987—95	1969—77 1978—86	1978—86 1987—95	1969—77	1978—86	1987—95
NABISCO BRANDS (US)		X	X	X			
GENERAL MILLS (US)		X					
BORDEN (US)		X					
CPC INTERNATIONAL (US)		X		X			
QUAKER OATS (US)		X	X				
AJINOMOTO (JP)		X					
UNILEVER (UK/NL)		X	X	X			
NESTLE (SZ)		X	X	X			
R J REYNOLDS (US)		X		X			
PHILIP MORRIS (US)		X	X	X			
BAT INDS (UK)		X	X	X			

Metals and Mechanical engineering

	Chapter 2 (case studies)	Chapter 3	Chapter 4		Chapters 5, 6 and 7		
US STEEL (US)		X					
ARMCO (US)		X	X				
BETHLEHEM STEEL (US)		X					
LTV (US)		X					
CONTINENTAL GROUP (US)		X					
McDERMOTT (US)		X	X	X			
ALUMINIUM CO OF AMERICA (US)		X	X	X			
NATIONAL STEEL (US)		X					
REYNOLDS METALS (US)		X		X			
NORTHWEST INDUSTRIES (US)		X					
GILLETTE (US)		X		X			
ENGELHARD (US)		X	X	X			
FOSTER WHEELER (US)		X	X	X			
STANLEY WORKS (US)		X	X	X			
BALL (US)		X	X	X			
MASCO (US)		X	X	X			
RIO TINTO-ZINC (UK)		X	X	X			
METAL BOX (UK)		X	X	X			
JOHNSON MATTHEY (UK)		X	X	X			
NIPPON STEEL (JP)		X	X	X			
NIPPON KOKAN (JP)		X					
SUMITOMO METAL INDS (JP)		X		X			
KOBE STEEL (JP)		X	X	X			
SUMITOMO ELECTRIC INDS (JP)		X		X			
FURUKAWA ELECTRIC (JP)		X		X			
MITSUBISHI METAL (JP)		X					
SANDVIK GROUP (SE)		X	X	X			
THYSSEN (G)		X	X	X			
KRUPP (G)		X	X	X			
MANNESMANN (G)		X	X	X			
METALLGESELLSCHAFT (G)		X	X	X			
DEGUSSA (G)			X	X			
KLOCKNER-WERKE (G)		X	X	X			
W C HERAEUS (G)		X	X	X			
PECHINEY UGINE KUHLMANN (FR)		X					
ALCAN (CA)		X	X	X			
NORANDA MINES (CA)		X	X	X			
VOEST-ALPINE (AU)		X	X				
ALUSUISSE (SZ)		X	X	X			
CATERPILLAR TRACTORS (US)		X					
INTERNATIONAL HARVESTOR (US)		X					
DEERE (US)		X	X	X			
DRESSER (US)		X					

	Chapter 2 (case studies)	Chapter 3	Chapter 4		Chapters 5, 6 and 7		
	1969—95	1969—77 1987—95	1969—77 1978—86	1978—86 1987—95	1969—77	1978—86	1987—95
COMBUSTION ENGINEERING (US)		X					
FMC (US)		X					
TELEDYNE (US)		X	X	X			
INGERSOLL-RAND (US)		X		X			
BAKER INTERNATIONAL (US)		X	X				
COOPER INDUSTRIES (US)		X	X	X			
NL INDUSTRIES (US)		X					
EMHART (US)		X	X				
HUGHES TOOLS (US)		X	X				
WHEELABRATOR-FRYE (US)		X					
BLACK & DECKER (US)		X	X	X			
PARKER-HANNIFIN (US)		X		X			
SMITH INTERNATIONAL (US)		X	X				
DOVER (US)		X	X	X			
REXNORD (US)		X		X			
HAWKER SIDDELEY (UK)		X	X	X			
VICKERS (UK)		X	X	X			
IHHI (JP)		X	X	X			
KAWASAKI HEAVY INDS (JP)		X	X	X			
KOMATSU (JP)		X	X	X			
GUTEHOFFNUNGSHUTTE (G)		X	X				
KHD (G)		X	X				
LINDE (G)		X	X				
ASEA (SE)	X	X				X	
SKF (SE)		X	X				
ALFA-LAVAL (SE)		X	X	X			
SULZER BROS (SZ)		X	X	X			
GEORG FISCHER (SZ)		X					
VALMET (FN)		X	X	X			
SCHNEIDER (FR)		X	X	X			
TH GOLDSMITH (G)		X		X			
VARIAN (US)		X	X	X			
HALLIBURTON (US)		X					
SCHUBERT & SALZER (G)		X		X			
RHEINMETAL (G)		X		X			

Paper products n.e.s. and Printing and publishing

	Chapter 2	Chapter 3	Chapter 4		Chapters 5, 6 and 7		
GEORGIA PACIFIC (US)		X	X	X			
WEYERHAESER (US)		X	X	X			
INTERNATIONAL PAPER (US)		X		X			
KIMBERLEY CLARK (US)		X		X			
MEAD (US)		X	X	X			
JIM WALTER (US)		X					
WESTVACO (US)		X	X	X			
AB TETRA PAK (SE)		X					

Non-metallic mineral products

	Chapter 2	Chapter 3	Chapter 4		Chapters 5, 6 and 7		
OWENS CORNING FIBREGLASS (US)		X	X				
AMERICAN STANDARD (US)		X		X			
ARMSTRONG WORLD INDUSTRIES (US)		X	X				
NORTON (US)		X		X			
LIBBEY-OWENS-FORD (US)		X	X	X			
ANCHOR HOCKING (US)		X					
PILKINGTON BROS (UK)		X		X			
SAINT-GOBAIN (FR)		X		X			

	Chapter 2 (case studies)	Chapter 3	Chapter 4		Chapters 5, 6 and 7
	1969—95	1969—77 1987—95	1969—77 1978—86	1978—86 1987—95	1969—77 1978—86 1987—95
ASAHI GLASS (JP)		X		X	
SEKISUI CHEMICAL (JP)		X			
YOSHIDA KOGYO (JP)		X	X	X	
Professional and scientific instruments					
EASTMAN KODAK (US)		X		X	
BAXTER TRAVENOL LABS (US)		X	X	X	
POLAROID (US)		X			
TEKTRONIX (US)		X	X	X	
BECTON DICKINSON (US)		X	X	X	
PERKIN ELMER (US)		X	X	X	
CANON (JP)		X	X	X	
KONISHIROKU PHOTO INDS (JP)		X	X	X	
CITIZEN WATCH (JP)		X	X		
CARL-ZEISS-STIFTUNG (G)		X	X	X	
INCENTIVE (SE)		X	X	X	
OLUPMPUS OPTICAL (JP)		X	X	X	
MINOLTA CAMERA (JP)		X	X	X	
NIPPON KOGAKU (JP)		X			
Other manufacturing					
GULF & WESTERN (US)		X			
OWENS ILLINOIS (US)		X			
KIDDE (US)		X			
CORNING GLASS WORKS (US)		X		X	
AMF (US)		X			
MATTEL (US)		X		X	
BRUNSWICK (US)		X		X	
RUHRKOHLE (G)		X	X		
SCHLUMBERGER (NL/AN)		X		X	
OERLIKON-BUHRLE (SZ)		X	X	X	
NIPPON GAKKI (JP)		X			
CANADIAN PACIFIC (CA)		X	X	X	

Transport industrial group

Motor vehicles

	Chapter 2 (case studies)	Chapter 3	Chapter 4		Chapters 5, 6 and 7
GENERAL MOTORS (US)		X		X	
FORD MOTOR (US)		X		X	
CHRYSLER (US)		X		X	
BENDIX (US)		X			
BORG-WARNER (US)		X			
EATON (US)		X		X	
DANA (US)		X	X	X	
NISSAN MOTOR (JP)		X	X	X	
TOYOTA MOTOR (JP)		X	X	X	
MITSUBISHI HEAVY INDUSTRIES (JP)		X	X	X	
HONDA MOTOR (JP)		X	X	X	
TOYO KOGYO (JP)		X		X	
NIPPONDENSO (JP)		X	X	X	
YAMAHA MOTOR (JP)		X	X	X	
AISIN SEIKI (JP)		X	X	X	
DAIMLER-BENZ (G)		X		X	
VW (G)		X	X		
BOSCH (G)		X	X	X	

	Chapter 2 (case studies) 1969—95	Chapter 3 1969—77 1987—95	Chapter 4 1969—77 1978—86	Chapter 4 1978—86 1987—95	Chapters 5, 6 and 7 1969—77	1978—86	1987—95
ZAHNRADFABRIK FRIEDRICHSHAFEN (G)		x	x	x			
MTU (G)		x		x			
RENAULT (FR)		x	x				
PEUGEOT (FR)		x					
FIAT (IT)		x	x				
VOLVO (SE)		x	x	x			
SAAB-SCANIA (SE)		x	x	x			
GKN (UK)		x					
LUCAS (UK)		x					
AUTOMOTIVE PRODUCTS (US)		x	x	x			
Aircraft							
UNITED TECHNOLOGIES (US)		x	x	x			
BOEING (US)		x	x	x			
ROCKWELL INTERNATIONAL (US)		x					
McDONNELL DOUGLAS (US)		x	x				
GENERAL DYNAMICS (US)		x					
LOCKHEED (US)		x					
RAYTHEON (US)		x	x				
SIGNAL COMPANIES (US)		x					
MARTIN MARIETTA (US)		x					
TEXTRON (US)		x					
NORTHROP (US)		x					
GRUMMAN (US)		x					
SUNDSTRAND (US)		x	x	x			
BRITISH AEROSPACE (UK)		x	x	x			
ROLLS ROYCE (UK)		x	x	x			
AEROSPATIALE (FR)		x	x	x			
SNECMA (FR)		x					
MBB (G)		x	x	x			
ALLIED SIGNAL (US)		x		x			
HUGHES AIRCRAFT (US)		x	x	x			
Other transportation equipmen							
MITSUI SHIPBUILDING & ENGINEERING (JP)		x	x				
Rubber and plastic products							
GOODYEAR TIRE AND RUBBER (US		x					
FIRESTONE TIRE AND RUBBER (US)		x	x				
BF GOODRICH (US)		x		x			
UNIROYAL (US)		x	x	x			
MICHELIN (FR)		x	x	x			
PIRELLI (IT)		x	x	x			
BRIDGESTONE TIRE (JP)		x	x	x			
Total	6	376	194	231	20	21	19

Notes:
Bold x denotes the sample of analysis of Chapter 7.
n.e.s. = Not elsewhere specified.
Country Code: Austria: AU; Belgium: BE; Canada: CA; Finland: FN; France: FR; Germany: G; Japan: JP ; Italy: IT; The Netherlands: NL; Neitherlands Antilles: AN; Sweden: SE; Switzerland: SZ; U.S.A.: US; U.K.: UK.

Source: Author's elaboration on University of Reading database.

Table A.2 – Industries sorted by five more broadly defined industrial corporate groups

---

Chemical industrial group
> Chemicals n.e.s. and Pharmaceuticals
> Textiles and clothing
> Coal and petroleum products

Electronic industrial group
> Electrical equipment n.e.s. and Office equipment

Mechanical industrial group
> Food products
> Metals and Mechanical engineering
> Paper products n.e.s. and Printing and publishing
> Non-metallic mineral products
> Professional and scientific instruments
> Other manufacturing

Transport industrial group
> Motor vehicles
> Aircraft
> Other transport equipment
> Rubber and plastic products

Note:
n.e.s. = Not elsewhere specified.

Source: Author's elaboration on University of Reading database.

Table A.3 – List of the 56 technological sectors

1	Food and tobacco products	(Mechanical)
2	Distillation processes	(Chemical)
3	Inorganic chemicals	(Chemical)
4	Agricultural chemicals	(Chemical)
5	Chemical processes	(Chemical)
6	Photographic chemistry	(Chemical)
7	Cleaning agents and other compositions	(Chemical)
8	Disinfecting and preserving	(Chemical)
9	Synthetic resins and fibres	(Chemical)
10	Bleaching and dyeing	(Chemical)
11	Other organic compounds	(Chemical)
12	Pharmaceuticals and biotechnology	(Chemical)
13	Metallurgical processes	(Mechanical)
14	Miscellaneous metal products	(Mechanical)
15	Food, drink and tobacco equipment	(Mechanical)
16	Chemical and allied equipment	(Mechanical)
17	Metal working equipment	(Mechanical)
18	Paper making apparatus	(Mechanical)
19	Building material processing equipment	(Mechanical)
20	Assembly and material handling equipment	(Mechanical)
21	Agricultural equipment	(Mechanical)
22	Other construction and excavating equipment	(Mechanical)
23	Mining equipment	(Mechanical)
24	Electrical lamp manufacturing	(Mechanical)
25	Textile and clothing machinery	(Mechanical)
26	Printing and publishing machinery	(Mechanical)
27	Woodworking tools and machinery	(Mechanical)
28	Other specialised machinery	(Mechanical)
29	Other general industrial equipment	(Mechanical)
30	Mechanical calculators and typewriters	(Electrical)

31	Power plants	(Mechanical)
32	Nuclear reactors	(Other)
33	Telecommunications	(Electrical)
34	Other electrical communication systems	(Electrical)
35	Special radio systems	(Electrical)
36	Image and sound equipment	(Electrical)
37	Illumination devices	(Electrical)
38	Electrical devices and systems	(Electrical)
39	Other general electrical equipment	(Electrical)
40	Semiconductors	(Electrical)
41	Office equipment and data processing systems	(Electrical)
42	Internal combustion engines	(Transport)
43	Motor vehicles	(Transport)
44	Aircraft	(Transport)
45	Ships and marine propulsion	(Transport)
46	Railways and railway equipment	(Transport)
47	Other transport equipment	(Transport)
48	Textile, clothing and leather	(Other)
49	Rubber and plastic products	(Transport)
50	Non-metallic mineral products	(Mechanical)
51	Coal and petroleum products	(Chemical)
52	Photographic equipment	(Electrical)
53	Other instruments and controls	(Mechanical)
54	Wood products	(Other)
55	Explosive compositions and charges	(Chemical)
56	Other manufacturing and non-industrial	(Other)

Source: University of Reading database.

Table A.4 – Patent classes sorted by technological sector

M	1	sugar, starch and carbohydrates
M	1	tobacco
M	1	food or edible material: processes, compositions and products
C	2	distillation: processes, thermolityc
C	2	distillation: processes, separatory
C	3	chemistry of inorganic compounds
C	4	chemistry: fertilisers
C	5	chemistry: physical processes
C	5	abrading
C	5	gas separation
C	5	refrigeration
C	5	cleaning and liquid contact with solids
C	5	adhesive bonding and miscellaneous chemical manufacture
C	5	chemistry: electrical and wave energy
C	5	liquid purification or separation
C	5	coating processes
C	5	heating
C	5	chemistry: Fischer-Tropsch processes, or purification or recovery or products thereof
C	6	radiation imagery chemistry: processes, composition or product thereof
C	7	compositions: coating or plastic
C	7	compositions
C	7	perfume compositions
C	8	chemical apparatus and process disinfecting, deodorising, preserving or sterilising
C	9	chemistry of carbon compounds
C	9	synthetic resins or natural rubber
C	9	ion exchange resins, cellular products
C	9	resins prepared by wave energy
C	9	resins with nonreactive additives
C	9	resins with nonreactive additives
C	9	mixed synthetic resins, block or graft copolymers
C	9	resins by reaction zone features
C	9	polymers from specialised reactants
C	9	resins condensates
C	10	bleaching and dyeing, fluid treatment and chemical modification of textiles and fibres
C	11	carbocylic or acyclic
C	11	natural resins or derivatives, peptides or proteins, lignins
C	11	noble gas, radioactive or rare earth metal
C	11	carbohydrates
C	11	heterocyclic compounds, seven or more ring members
C	11	six-membered ring with more than one hetero nitrogen
C	11	six-membered ring with one hetero nitrogen
C	11	five-, four-, or three-membered ring
C	11	hetero sulfur or oxygen
C	11	azides, triphenylmethanes
C	11	heavy metal, aluminum or silicon containing
C	11	esters
C	11	esters
C	11	organic acids, acid halides, acid anhydrides, selenium or tellurium compounds
C	11	urea adducts, amino nitrogen compounds
C	11	boron, phosphorus, sulfur or oxygen compounds

C	11	halogen containing
C	12	drug, bio-affecting and body treating compositions
C	12	chemistry: molecular biology and microbiology
C	12	chemistry: analytical and immunological testing
C	12	drug, bio-affecting and body treating compositions
C	12	multicellular living organism and unmodified parts thereof
M	13	metal treatment
M	13	metal founding
M	13	metal fusion bonding
M	13	metal working (rolls)
M	13	powder metallurgy processes
M	13	alloys or metallic compositions
M	13	specialised metallurgical processes
M	14	baths, closets, sinks and spittoons
M	14	compound tools
M	14	bolt, nail, nut, rivet and screw making
M	14	miscellaneous hardware
M	14	buckles, buttons, clasps, etc.
M	14	undertaking
M	14	cutlery
M	14	moveable or removable closures
M	14	jewellery
M	14	locks
M	14	horizontally supported planar surfaces
M	14	safes, bank protection or a related device
M	14	mechanical guns and projectors
M	14	toilet
M	14	tent, canopy, umbrella and cane
M	14	pipes and tubular conduits
M	14	purses, wallets and protective covers
M	14	flexible or portable closures, partitions or panels
M	14	fire escapes, ladders or scaffolds
M	14	trunks and hand-carried luggage
M	14	special receptacle or package
M	14	supports: racks
M	14	bottles and jars
M	14	receptacles
M	14	deposit and collection receptacles
M	14	supports
M	14	fences
M	14	spring devices
M	14	amusement and exercising devices
M	14	chucks or sockets
M	14	pipe joints or couplings
M	14	closure fasteners
M	14	supports: cabinet structures
M	14	flexible bags
M	14	joints and connections
M	14	expanded, threaded, driven, headed, tool-deformed or lock-threaded fastener
M	14	rotary shafts, gudgeons, housing and flexible couplings for rotary shafts
M	14	prosthesis (i.e. artificial body members), parts thereof or aids and accessories thereof
M	15	foods and beverages: apparatus

M	15	sugar, starch and carbohydrates
M	15	tobacco
M	16	drying and gas or vapour contact with solid
M	16	abrading
M	16	gas separation
M	16	textiles, fluid treating apparatus
M	16	coating apparatus
M	16	cleaning and liquid contact with solid
M	16	adhesive bonding and miscellaneous chemical manufacture
M	16	concentrating evaporators
M	16	mineral oil: apparatus
M	16	distillation: apparatus
M	16	classifying, separating and assorting solids
M	16	liquid purification or separation
M	16	gas and liquid contact apparatus
M	16	agitating
M	16	chemical apparatus and process disinfecting, deodorising, preserving or sterilising
M	16	imparforate bowl: centrifugal separators
M	16	catalyst, solid sorbent, or support thereof, product or process
M	16	record receiver having plural leaves or a colourless colour former
M	17	chain, staple and horseshoe making
M	17	metal deforming
M	17	metals tools and implements, making
M	17	tools
M	17	turning
M	17	cutting
M	17	needle and pin making
M	17	metal founding
M	17	tool driving or impacting
M	17	severing by tearing or breaking
M	17	metal fusion bonding
M	17	selective cutting
M	17	metallurgical apparatus
M	17	work holders
M	17	bearing
M	17	cutters for shaping
M	17	cutting by use of rotating axially moving tool
M	17	gear cutting, milling or planing
M	17	sheet metal container making
M	17	endless belt power transmission systems or components
M	18	package making
M	18	paper making and fiber preparation
M	18	envelopes, wrappers and paperboard boxes
M	18	manufacturing container or tube from paper
M	19	glass manufacturing
M	19	solid material comminution or disintegration
M	19	static moulds
M	20	merchandising
M	20	elevators
M	20	conveyors, chutes, skids, guides and ways
M	20	conveyors, power-driven
M	20	traversing hoists

M	20	package and article carriers
M	20	advancing material of indeterminate length
M	20	winding and reeling
M	20	implements or apparatus for applying pushing or pulling forces
M	20	railway mail delivery
M	20	sheet feeding or delivering
M	20	handling: hand and hoist-line implements
M	20	binder device releasably engaging aperture or notch of sheet
M	20	conveyors: fluid corrent
M	20	freight accommodation on freight carrier
M	20	material or article handling
M	21	harvesters
M	21	planting
M	21	earth working
M	21	land vehicles: animal draft appliances
M	21	crop threshing or separating
M	22	excavating
M	22	unearthing plants or buried objects
M	22	road structure: process or apparatus
M	23	wells
M	23	boring or penetrating the earth
M	23	mining or in situ disintegration of hard material
M	24	electrical lamp or space discharge component or device manufacturing
M	25	boot and shoe making
M	25	textiles: fiber preparation
M	25	textiles: cloth finishing
M	25	textiles: manufacturing
M	25	textiles: ironing or smoothing
M	25	textiles: spinning, twisting and twining
M	25	textiles: knitting
M	25	leather manufactures
M	25	textiles: braiding, netting and lace making
M	25	sewing
M	25	textiles: weaving
M	25	apparel apparatus
M	26	printing
M	26	type casting
M	26	sheet-material associating
M	26	typesetting
M	26	books, strips and leaves
M	26	manifolding
M	26	printed matter
M	26	bookbinding: process and apparatus
M	27	wood turning
M	27	woodworking
M	28	brushing, scrubbing and general cleaning apparatus
M	28	cutlery
M	28	button making
M	28	ventilation
M	28	presses
M	28	signals and indicators
M	28	wireworking

M	28	fluent material handling, with receiver or receiver coating means
M	28	coopering
M	28	wheelwright machines
M	28	fire extinguishers
M	28	check-actuated control mechanisms
M	28	article dispensing
M	28	dispensing
M	28	elongated-member-driving apparatus
M	28	implements or apparatus for applying pushing or pulling forces
M	28	joint packing
M	28	track sanders
M	28	brush, broom and mop making
M	28	coating implements with material supply
M	28	plastic article or earthenware shaping or treating: apparatus
M	28	coin handling
M	29	gas: heating and illuminating
M	29	motors: expansible chamber type
M	29	expansible chamber devices
M	29	furnaces
M	29	liquid heaters and vaporisers
M	29	stoves and furnaces
M	29	fluid handling
M	29	heat exchange
M	29	lubrication
M	29	motors: spring, weight or animal powered
M	29	brakes
M	29	clutches and power-stop control
M	29	heating system
M	29	fluid sprinkling, spraying and diffusing
M	29	valves and valve actuation
M	29	fluid pressure brake and analogous systems
M	29	rotary kinetic fluid motors or pumps
M	29	fluid reaction surfaces
M	29	pumps
M	29	rotary expansible chamber devices
M	29	combustion
M	29	heating
E	30	registers
E	30	typewriting machines
M	31	power plants
Oth	32	induced nuclear reactions; processes, systems and elements
E	33	*telegraphy*
E	33	*demodulators*
E	33	*modulators*
E	33	*communications, electrical: acoustic wave systems and devices*
E	33	*multiplex communications*
E	33	*pulse or digital communications*
E	33	*telephonic communications*
E	33	*telecommunications*
E	34	*communications: electrical*
E	34	*coded data generation or conversion*
E	**34**	***selective visual display systems***

E	34	*image analysis*
E	35	*communications: directive radio wave systems and devices*
E	35	*communications: radio wave antennas*
E	36	*music*
E	36	*acoustics*
E	36	*pictorial communication: television*
E	**36**	**television**
E	36	*electrical audio signal processing systems and devices*
E	37	electrical lamp and discharge devices
E	37	electrical lamp and discharge devices: consumable electrodes
E	37	electrical lamp and discharge devices: systems
E	37	illumination
E	38	electricity: conductors and insulators
E	38	electricity: circuit makers and breakers
E	38	electrical transmission or interconnection systems
E	38	electricity: power supply or regulation systems
E	38	miscellaneous electron space discharge device systems
E	38	amplifiers
E	38	oscillators
E	38	wave transmission lines and networks
E	38	tuners
E	38	electricity: magnetically operated switches, magnets and electromagnets
E	38	inductor devices
E	38	electricity: electrothermally or thermally actuated switches
E	38	electrical resistors
E	38	electricity: electrical systems and devices
E	38	electric power conversion systems
E	38	coherent light generators
E	38	electrical connectors
E	38	superconductor technology: apparatus, material, process
E	39	refrigeration
E	39	batteries: thermoelectric and photoelectric
E	39	chemistry: electrical and wave energy
E	39	electric heating
E	39	automatic temperature and humidity regulation
E	39	prime-mover dynamo plants
E	39	electrical generator or motor structure
E	39	electricity: motive power systems
E	39	electricity: battery and condenser charging and discharging
E	39	electricity: single generator systems
E	39	electricity: electrical systems and devices: capacitors
E	39	industrial electric heating furnaces
E	39	electricity: motor control systems
E	39	electric resistant heating devices
E	39	chemistry: electrical current producing apparatus, product and process
E	39	semiconductor device manufacturing: process
E	40	*electrical transmission or interconnection systems*
E	**40**	**electrical digital logic circuitry**
E	40	*active solid state devices (eg. transistor, solid state diodes)*
E	41	*register*
E	41	*dynamic magnetic information storage or retrieval*
E	41	*electrical computers and data processing systems*

E	41	*static information storage and retrieval*
E	41	*dynamic information storage and retrieval*
E	41	*error detection/correction and fault detection/recovery*
E	41	*electrical pulse counters, pulse dividers or shift registers circuits and systems*
E	**41**	***information processing system organisation***
E	41	*electronic funds transfer*
T	42	internal combustion engines
T	43	motor vehicles
T	43	land vehicles: bodies and tops
T	44	aeronautics
T	45	ships
T	45	marine propulsion
T	45	buoys, rafts and aquatic devices
T	46	railways
T	46	railway rolling stock
T	46	railway draft appliances
T	46	railways: surface track
T	46	railway switches and signals
T	47	electricity: transmission to vehicles
T	47	land vehicles
T	47	vehicle fenders
T	47	railway wheels and axles
T	47	land vehicles: dumping
T	47	land vehicles: wheels and axles
T	47	wheel substitutes for land vehicles
Oth	48	apparel
Oth	48	boots, shoes and leggings
Oth	48	wire fabrics and structure
Oth	48	knots and knot tying
Oth	48	foundation garments
T	49	resilient tires and wheels
T	49	plastic and non-metallic article shaping or treating: processes
M	50	static structures
M	50	glass manufacturing
M	50	stone working
M	50	bottles and jars
M	50	solid material comminution or disintegration
M	50	stock material or miscellaneous articles
M	50	compositions: ceramics
C	51	fuel and related compositions
C	51	mineral oils: processes and products
C	51	chemistry of hydrocarbon compounds
E	52	photography
E	52	photocopying
M	53	geometrical instruments
M	53	measuring and testing
M	53	machine element or mechanism
M	53	surgery
M	53	weighing scales
M	53	elevators (sub class 29)
M	53	registers
M	53	radiant energy

M	53	electricity: measuring and testing
M	53	recorders
M	53	optics: systems (including communication) and elements
M	53	optics: eye examining, vision testing and correcting
M	53	optics: motion pictures
M	53	optics: image projectors
M	53	optics: measuring and testing
M	53	horology: time measuring systems or devices
M	53	thermal measuring and testing
M	53	x-ray or gamma ray systems or devices
M	53	dentistry
M	53	planetary gear transmission systems or components
M	53	surgery
M	53	surgery
M	53	surgery
Oth	54	beds
Oth	54	wooden receptacles
Oth	54	chairs and seats
C	55	explosive and thermic compositions or charges
Oth	56	bridges
Oth	56	card, picture or sign exhibiting
Oth	56	firearms
Oth	56	fishing, trapping and vermin destroying
Oth	56	plant husbandry
Oth	56	harness
Oth	56	ammunition and explosive-charge making
Oth	56	ordnance
Oth	56	ammunition and explosive devices
Oth	56	ships
Oth	56	animal husbandry
Oth	56	farriery
Oth	56	whips and whips apparatus
Oth	56	aeronautics
Oth	56	amusement devices: games
Oth	56	cryptography
Oth	56	road structure: process or apparatus
Oth	56	hydraulic and earth engineering
Oth	56	education and demonstration
Oth	56	amusement devices: toys
Oth	56	bee culture
Oth	56	butchering

Source: University of Reading database.

Note:
Italics indicate ICT patent classes. ***Bold italics*** indicate patent classes added in the sub-period 1987-1995 as a consequence of a post-1990 reclassification.

399 original patent classes
(as classified by the USPTO)

56 technological sectors/fields

14 broadly defined industries

5 more broadly defined industrial groups

Source: Author's elaboration on University of Reading database.

Figure A.1 – Classification scheme adopted in the University of Reading database

Appendix B: The European sample of analysis

The European ICT industry refers to all European firms classified in the broad electrical industrial group in the University of Reading database. In Chapters 5, 6 and 7, their profiles of specialisation are analysed at the level of the ICT original patent classes, which are those corresponding to the technological sectors 'telecommunications', 'other electrical communications systems', 'special radio systems', 'image and sound equipment', 'semiconductors' and 'office equipment and data processing systems' in the Reading database and listed in *italics* in Table A.4. Due to a post-1990 reclassification of the data, the ICT technological patent classes are 26 in the first and second sub-periods considered and 30 in the years 1987–95. The patent class 'electronic funds transfer' is dropped from the analysis because of the absence of patenting activity by the firms in the sample in all three sub-periods. The four patent classes added in the last sub-period as a consequence of the post-1990 reclassification are reported in ***bold italics*** in Table A.4.

De facto, the sample of analysis concerns all European electronic firms active in ICT patent classes in the period considered. This determines the exclusion from the analysis of Grundig and the Finnish firm Nokia. None of them seems to have been active in these classes over the period 1969–95. Moreover, in each of the three sub-periods, other European electrical firms are furthermore dropped from the analysis on the grounds of null values in their total patenting activity in the ICT patent classes considered. The outcome is the consequent variation in the number of firms in the sample from one sub-period to another. As listed in Table A.1, 20 firms are examined in the sub-period 1969–77, whilst 21 and 19 are taken into account in the two later sub-periods respectively. It should be mentioned that ASEA AB is taken into account in the analysis in the second and third sub-period because of the merger with Brown Boveri. ABB (ASEA Brown Boveri) – an equally owned company – is the result of the 1988 merger between the Swedish ASEA AB and the Swiss Brown Boveri. In focusing on the European ICT industry, the analysis of the second part of this thesis considers ABB as a Swiss company as its inherited corporate patenting activity across the ICT patent classes is mainly due to the Swiss partner

Brown Boveri rather than to the Swedish ASEA AB. However, in the first part of the book (Chapter 2), ABB is considered as a Swedish company since its inherited corporate patenting activity in the specific technological sectors analysed before 1988 is mainly due to the Swedish partner rather than the Swiss.

PART ONE

Location, Innovative Activity and MNCs

2. The geography of innovation and local embeddedness: tacit versus codified knowledge

2.1 INTRODUCTION

This chapter opens Part One which analyses the sectoral and spatial technological patterns followed in the development of corporate technology over the ICT-based era. The analysis carries on throughout Chapters 3 and 4. The present chapter examines the geographical implications of the closer linkages between science and technology in the information age. As some technological knowledge becomes more codified, international knowledge flows rise and research communities cross national boundaries, but this may be accompanied by the agglomeration of at least some kind of technological development in centres of excellence (Jaffe et al., 1993; Audretsch and Feldman, 1994; Frost, 1996; Almeida and Kogut, 1997). The aim is to identify which types of technology are becoming most locationally concentrated, and most dependent upon local linkages with the indigenous science base in the sites in question; and in which other areas cross-border flows of knowledge allow innovation to be co-ordinated more easily across geographically dispersed locations.

The phenomenon of generation, transmission and diffusion of technology has been increasingly internationalised over the last decade (Archibugi and Michie, 1995). The rise of 'techno-globalism' has promoted corporate strategies based upon an internationally integrated approach to technological development (Dunning, 1994, 1996b; Amin and Thrift, 1995; Dunning and Wymbs, 1999; Zander, 1997c; Zander and Sölvell, 1997). The evolution of this process has been characterised by the geographical dispersion of MNCs' R&D facilities according to indigenous technological specialisation (Cantwell and Harding, 1998; Cantwell and Janne, 1999). As argued elsewhere (Santangelo, 2001), in the ICT era, the phenomenon of globe-standing networks of MNCs has greatly increased partly as a result of a rise in ICT specialisation. The intensity of this phenomenon has amplified the interaction between multinationals' affiliates and the local (national and regional) systems. The incentive to organise affiliate specialisation is the desire to tap into a locationally specific and differentiated stream of innovation in each centre. If this is true in production, it is also true in the development of technology. In both cases, the international dispersion of corporate activity creates the necessary conditions for the MNC to exploit local capabilities or tacit knowledge. In this global–local interplay, the affiliate's role goes beyond the mere supply of the local market. The new generation of overseas subsidiaries interplays more with their own respective local dimensions in both the creation and application of technology (Kuemmerle, 1996; Maskell, 1996; Pearce and Papanastassiou, 1996; Florida, 1997; Gooderham and Heum, 1997; Pearce, 1997a; Zander, 1997b; Blanc and Sierra, 1999). Such entrepreneurial subsidiaries, which also tend to have either world (or regional) product mandates (Papanastassiou and Pearce, 1994; Pearce, 1997b), adopt operations which enable the parent company to tap into a much wider range of resources as an integrated part of its global activity.[1] Foreign units seem to develop world mandate for groups of technologies in which they have provided their technological excellence. In this sense, globalisation is understood as the establishment and development of internationally integrated intra- and inter-firm technological networks in part through the co-ordination of geographically dispersed R&D activities.

Globalisation is a concept broader than internationalisation since it implies the establishment and development of international integrated intra- and inter-firm technological networks and, accordingly, the co-ordination of geographically dispersed R&D activities. Globalisation of technology can be understood as a process involving 'new modes of interactions across borders (such as foreign direct investment – FDI – and inter-firm corporate agreements) as well as the active intervention of new economic agents, such as multinational corporations' (Svetličič, 1996). None the less these two terms are used synonymously with reference to the definition provided above. Great attention has been paid to this phenomenon as a consequence of the increasing share of technological activity located abroad by leading multinationals. The dimensions of this process have been evaluated in a rather controversial way. The argument of an effective impact of such a process in economic life (Dunning, 1993, 1996a; Howells and Wood, 1993; Cantwell, 1995, 1998a; Humbert, 1995; Cantwell and Piscitello, 2000; Howells and Michie, 1997b; Archibugi and Iammarino, 2000) faces the sceptical view about the dimensions of globalisation in empirical terms (Patel and Pavitt, 1991b; Patel, 1995). It should, however, be pointed out that the sceptics seem to criticise mainly the idea of a stateless corporation. Indeed few firms have lost the central role played by their home base, even if they now interact with other geographically dispersed centres.

As an outcome of the globalisation of technology, the new corporations' strategy is increasingly worldwide rather than multi-state based.

In this direction Cantwell (1995) demonstrates empirically that the phenomenon of techno-globalism is complementary to national (regional) specialisation rather than conflictual (as also argued by Archibugi and Pianta, 1992b; Archibugi and Michie, 1997; Howells and Michie, 1997a; Kitson and Michie, 1996). The local (national and regional) system of innovation is the institutional network of each country/region that supports the initiation, modification and diffusion of new technologies (Freeman, 1987, 1995; Saxenian, 1994; Florida, 1995; Storper and Scott, 1995). What makes each system unique is the particular sectoral patterns of tacit capability that have been developed in private firms in each location over time (Nelson, 1993; Patel and Pavitt, 1994). In this sense the creation of tacit capability has a location-specific as well as a firm-specific dimension. Thus globalisation and local (national and regional) specialisation/de-specialisation are mutually reinforced by virtuous and vicious circles. Multinationals increase their technological competitiveness by exploiting local expertise, which is, in turn, strengthened by foreign corporate activities. If this cumulative causation mechanism promotes corporate technological diversification through the establishment of newly integrated technological systems across borders, it also fosters the narrowing down of technological specialisation of countries (regions) (Cantwell, 1992). On the one hand, MNCs locate their international operations in locations characterised by suitably specialised fields complementary to their own major strengths and which they therefore wish to access to enjoy localised spillovers from dynamic host (national or regional) systems of innovation. On the other hand, the comparative advantage in innovation of the local system is enhanced over time through the presence of able foreign-owned affiliates (Cantwell, 1991c). Therefore in the evolutionary view technological change is localised and differentiated (Nelson and Winter, 1982) and thus, in general, technological competition engenders healthy variety rather than wasteful duplication (Saviotti, 1996; Metcalfe, 1998).

As emphasised by evolutionary theory (Nelson and Winter, 1982), the cumulative and path-dependent character of innovation (Rosenberg, 1976, 1982) explains the embeddedness of tacit knowledge in social organisations. None the less it has been argued (Breschi, 2000) that the different degrees of geographical agglomeration depend on the different structure and organisation of innovative activity. The creation of technology may be locationally concentrated or dispersed according to the degree of complexity embedded in it (Cantwell and Santangelo, 2000). Some kinds of technologies are easily dispersed geographically, whilst the uncodified character of others makes cross-border learning within and across organisations much more difficult. Thus, although multinationals have recently shown a greater internationalisation of their R&D facilities, it depends upon the type of technological activity involved. The more that knowledge is tacit, the more innovations tend to cluster together as knowledge transmission becomes more complex both within and across different organisations (Winter, 1987). Tacitness requires a greater intensity of face-to-face interaction, thus implying higher and more closely complementary technological competencies on the part of co-operating teams. This is the case of science-based sectors, in which knowledge is highly context-dependent. In these sectors innovative activity is developed to a much greater extent by a narrower group of firms primarily in the associated science-based industries (i.e. electronics and chemicals), and more concentrated in centres of excellence (Cantwell and Santangelo, 1999). Instead the development and transmission of traditional engineering-based sectors is more based on regular codified knowledge, thus facilitating its co-ordination and dispersion over greater geographical distances and between a greater number of centres of innovation. None the less exceptions do exist, as shown by Cantwell and Santangelo (ibid.).

Following this evolutionary perspective, this chapter argues that the technological fields that have continued to be relatively concentrated are those in which tacitness is greatest and linkages with a local science base (and the face-to-face interaction that this entails) are most significant. In such cases, MNCs are likely to locate the development of technology which is mainly outside the core of their main fields of competence abroad. The geographical concentration of development is all the more true for the science-based technologies as well for industry-specific core technologies. For firms of all industries (even those that are not science-based), the creation of technologies in which tacit knowledge carries a greater weight is harder to co-ordinate across longer distances. However, within the science-based industries firms may generate abroad some technologies which are heavily dependent on tacit knowledge, but normally in fields that lie outside their own core technological competencies. Thus it may sometimes still be the case that science-based and firm- and industry-specific core technologies are dispersed internationally. In this chapter these exceptions are taken into account in the later part of the analysis by adopting a case study approach. The analysis focuses on the global dispersion of technological development in six of the world's largest companies across technological sectors and host locations. It is argued that the dispersion of complex kinds of technology may be due to a need to access locationally specific expertise in some specialised field of activity that is lacking at home, or it may be the result of a corporate strategy that rests upon an ability to organise an especially complex form of cross-border network for technological development. In the former case, the increasing internationalisation of corporate innovation will require at least some investment in co-ordination across borders. In the latter, it may be part of a more global corporate strategic approach in which the international corporate network has an even more central role than in the M-form.

The chapter is organised into seven sections. The following section describes the econometric methodology by shedding some light on the measures and the regression model adopted. Section 2.3 draws an overview of the globalisation trends in the information age. Section 2.4 provides empirical evidence on the tacit and codified nature of knowledge across industries. This distinction is further investigated in section 2.4 by adopting a case study approach, where electronic and non-electronic corporations are distinguished. Section 2.6 investigates the host country dimension on corporate dispersion of science-based technologies. Section 2.7 summarises some conclusions.

2.2   METHODOLOGICAL NOTES

In this chapter, the degree of international dispersion of different kinds of technology is investigated with a cross-sectional regression analysis over the period 1969–95 as a whole in order to provide an overall picture of technological globalisation in the information age.

To evaluate the extent of the geographical dispersion of technology creation, the regression analysis takes into account different degrees of internationalisation (i.e. country- and industry-level) as well as specialisation patterns of national groups of firms across industries. Differences in the degree of internationalisation, which are attributable to the country of ownership or the industry of the firm, are accounted for by adopting different levels of data consolidation. Patent data are consolidated by home country of the parent company and by broadly defined industrial group. In the former case each patent is assigned to one of the ten technologically most important national groups of firms (by nationality of ownership) (as listed in Table 2.1).[2] In the latter, each patent is placed in one of 14 broadly defined industries on the basis of the primary field of production of the corporate group in question (as listed in Table 2.2). In both cases, a further distinction is made as to whether the research facilities responsible for the relevant inventions are located in the parent's home country or abroad. Focusing on the inventions attributable to research facilities located abroad, the foreign patent share (*FS*) is calculated. Following other empirical studies (Pearce, 1983; Cantwell and Piscitello, 1997, 1999, 2000; Cantwell and Harding, 1998; Cantwell and Janne, 1998, 1999, 2000; Cantwell and Santangelo,

1999, 2000), *FS*, calculated across the usual 56 technological sectors, is used as a proxy for the degree of geographical agglomeration/dispersion. The foreign share is given by the share of US patents of the world's largest national groups of firms, which are attributable to research in foreign locations. *FS* is then defined as

$$FS_{ijk} = (FP_{ijk}/P_{ijk}) \tag{2.1}$$

where P_{ijk} denotes the number of US patents granted in a sectoral activity (j) to a national group of firms (i) in a particular industry (k), whilst FP_{ijk} indicates only the number of US patents granted for research conducted outside the home country of the parent firm to the same national group (i) in the same sectoral activity (j) in the industry in question (k). Country-specific locational factors were taken into account through the use of the foreign share calculated across the ten technologically largest home countries considered (*FSH*). Thus *FSH* can be written as

$$FSH_i = \Sigma_{jk}FP_{ijk}/\Sigma_{jk}P_{ijk} \tag{2.2}$$

The foreign patent share calculated across 14 industries (FSI) is, instead, employed to control for industry-specific location factors:

$$FSI_k = \Sigma_{ij}FP_{ijk}/\Sigma_{ij}P_{ijk} \tag{2.3}$$

In both equations (2.2) and (2.3), the subscript (i), (j) and (k) have the same meaning as in equation (2.1).

In addition, the specialisation patterns of national groups of firms across industries were considered through the use of the RTA index (see section 1.4). For each national group of parent companies the RTA is calculated across the 14 industries. Thus

$$RTA_{ik} = (P_{ik}/\Sigma_i P_{ik})/(\Sigma_k P_{ik}/\Sigma_{ik} P_{ik}) \tag{2.4}$$

where P_{ik} denotes the number of US patents granted in industry (k) to a national group of firms (i) in the industry in question. In this chapter the RTA index is exceptionally calculated for national industrial groups of firms rather than for single companies. Inter-industry differences in the propensity to patent are taken into account by the numerator, whilst the denominator accounts for inter-country differences. As explained in section 1.4, by relating the technological advantage in a particular spectrum of activity of each national group of firms to that of other national groups in the same industry, the RTA is a relative measure of technological specialisation.

The extent of the corporate geographical dispersion of technological activity is, then, analysed with a cross-section linear regression model of the following form:

$$FS_{ijk} = \alpha + \beta_1 FSH_i + \beta_2 FSI_k + \beta_3 RTA_{ik} + \beta_4 D_{ic} + \beta_5 D_{ooc} + \beta_6 D_{tcl} + \beta_7 D_{wp} + \beta_8 D_{bmpe} + \varepsilon_I \quad (2.5)$$

where D_{ic}, D_{ooc}, D_{tcl}, D_{wp} and D_{bmpe} are four sectoral dummy variables ('sector' j here being used to mean types of technological activity as defined by the US patent class system, and not the industries of corporate groups k), which refer to 'inorganic chemicals', 'other organic compounds', 'textiles, clothing and leather', 'wood products' and 'building material processing equipment' respectively. These dummy variables are introduced to account for sectoral dispersion patterns. The selection of these technological sectors is based on the statistical significance of the relevant sets of residuals of the model (when run initially without any such dummy variables).

2.3 GLOBALISATION TRENDS IN THE INFORMATION AGE

Before investigating the geographical implications of the closer linkages between science and technology in the information age, the trends in the internationalisation of corporate technology creation by national and industrial groupings respectively are briefly described, as shown in Tables 2.1 and 2.2. It is worth investigating in which cases knowledge creation is most likely to be a locationally dispersed process which crosses national boundaries, and in which cases instead activities are most likely to agglomerate in centres of excellence. In both Tables, the period 1969–95 is divided into six sub-periods:

- 1969–72,
- 1973–77,
- 1978–82,
- 1983–86,
- 1987–90 and
- 1991–95.

This periodisation enables a detailed evolution of the trend in internationalisation of corporate technology over time to be followed.

For each national group of the world's technologically largest firms, Table 2.1 records the share of US patents attributable to research conducted outside the home country of the parent company.

Table 2.1 – Share of US patents of the world's largest firms attributable to research in foreign locations (outside the home country of the parent company), organized by the nationality of parent firm, 1969–95 (%)

Nationality of the Parent Company	1969–72	1973–77	1978–82	1983–86	1987–90	1991–95
USA	4,96	5,89	6,40	7,53	7,91	8,62
Germany	12,77	11,05	12,07	14,47	17,05	20,72
UK	43,08	41,24	40,47	47,09	50,42	55,79
Italy	13,39	16,03	13,85	12,59	11,14	16,47
France	8,16	7,74	7,17	9,19	18,17	33,17
Japan	2,63	1,88	1,22	1,26	0,92	1,08
The Netherlands	50,40	47,37	47,65	53,99	53,96	55,69
Belgium and Luxembourg	50,36	51,11	49,28	58,15	47,53	53,25
Switzerland	44,36	43,63	43,78	41,59	42,99	52,47
Sweden	17,82	19,90	26,20	28,94	30,60	42,42
Canada	41,19	39,30	39,49	35,82	40,12	43,96
Others	28,21	22,22	26,37	30,34	7,54	3,94
Total (including Japan)	10,04	10,53	10,50	10,95	11,28	11,27
Total (excluding Japan)	10,52	11,59	12,25	13,87	15,76	16,53

Source: Cantwell and Santangelo (2000).

These figures show a slight increase in the total average of the share of overseas research activity from 10.04 per cent to 11.27 per cent between the late 1960s and the early 1990s. However, in assessing the pattern of total corporate patenting activity attributable to foreign research, it is worth mentioning the compositional shift in the make-up of total patenting across firms, involving an increase in the share of patenting accounted for by Japanese and Korean firms. As these firms are on average little internationalised in their technological development, this leads, in turn, to a downward pull on the global average foreign share. This argument is illustrated by the figures reported for Japanese firms as well as companies in the category labelled as 'others', in which the share of Korean corporate patenting has risen over time. Japan and 'others' are, indeed, the only national groups of firms showing an overall decline in foreign share since the late 1960s. Over the whole period 1969–95 the internationalisation of research activity grew from 10.52 per cent to 16.53 per cent when excluding Japanese companies. Moreover the internationalisation of the US firms is understated by this measure because of their higher propensity to patent in their own home market from domestically located research. The increase in the internationalisation of corporate technological activity occurred mainly in the mid- and late-1980s as a result of a growth in the overseas R&D of German, British, French, Swedish and Canadian firms. This internationalisation was achieved in large part through foreign mergers.

In Table 2.2, the pattern of the internationalisation of corporate R&D is, instead, analysed in terms of the industrial group of the parent company.

The overall increase in the internationalisation of technological activity was greatest in 'Food products', 'Paper products n.e.s. and Printing and publishing', 'Non-metallic mineral products' and 'Other manufacturing', whilst in science-based industrial sectors the increase in the geographical dispersion of R&D was more contained, although it remained at a level well above average in 'Chemicals n.e.s. and Pharmaceuticals', and in petrochemicals ('Coal and petroleum products'). Instead in the 'Electrical equipment n.e.s. and Office equipment' industrial sector foreign research was slightly below average, and only marginally more geographically dispersed over the period as a whole (from 9.15 per cent to 10.23 per cent). As will be further argued below, this pattern might be explained by the fact that much science-based technology embodies a greater degree of tacit competencies, which are more difficult to transmit or utilise over longer geographical distances.

2.4　TACIT AND CODIFIED KNOWLEDGE: CROSS-INDUSTRY DIFFERENCES

To analyse which types of technology continue to remain most locationally concentrated, and most dependent upon local linkages with an indigenous science base, variations in the extent of world-wide location/dispersion of different types of technology are investigated, controlling for country- and industry-specific locational factors in the period 1969–95.

As shown in Table 2.3, this exercise allows us to indicate technological fields in which the geographical location of activity is the most concentrated or dispersed, having controlled for established firm-level variation in internationalisation across countries and industries.

Table 2.3 suggests that the 'inorganic chemicals' and 'other organic compounds' sectors are the most geographically concentrated, whilst 'textiles, clothing and leather', 'wood products' and 'building material processing equipment' are the most internationalised, having allowed for the fact that, for example, chemical firms have a relatively high degree of internationalisation of technological development, while textile companies are relatively little internationalised. Whilst the regression model selects the strongest cases of either geographically concentrated or dispersed technological fields, somewhat weaker (but still relevant) cases are taken into account in Tables 2.4 and 2.5 ranked by the average residual of each sector.

Table 2.2 – Share of US patents of the world's largest firms attributable to research in foreign locations (outside the home country of the parent company), organised by the industrial group of the parent firm, 1969–95 (%)

Industrial Group of the Parent Company	1969–72	1973–77	1978–82	1983–86	1987–90	1991–95
Food products	16,85	20,72	23,43	24,73	23,70	25,40
Chemicals n.e.s. and Pharmaceuticals	12,07	13,72	13,60	13,34	14,49	16,22
Metals and Mechanical engineering	11,14	9,93	11,81	12,61	13,49	11,70
Electrical equipment n.e.s. and Office equipment	9,15	9,61	9,07	10,21	10,38	10,23
Motor vehicles	4,56	5,11	5,25	6,95	7,13	4,75
Aircraft	1,93	2,01	2,28	2,93	2,47	2,69
Other transport equipment	9,66	3,52	8,23	5,24	6,54	3,09
Textiles and clothing	6,45	8,49	7,10	4,31	3,10	2,40
Paper products n.e.s. and Printing and publishing	6,66	9,05	8,03	13,26	16,08	16,06
Rubber and plastic products	7,04	7,46	6,73	6,20	9,12	10,49
Non-metallic mineral products	7,68	8,75	10,73	13,12	14,94	18,38
Coal and petroleum products	18,02	15,21	15,04	16,08	20,32	20,36
Professional and scientific instruments	6,28	4,07	2,97	2,72	1,99	3,61
Other manufacturing	6,86	10,75	13,06	14,14	15,42	20,34
Total	**10,04**	**10,53**	**10,50**	**10,95**	**11,28**	**11,27**

Note:
n.e.s. = Not elsewhere specified.

Source: Cantwell and Santangelo (2000).

Table 2.3 – Results of the regression in equation 3.5

	Coefficient	Standard Error	t-Ratio
Intercept	–9,590	1,161	–8,259**
FSH_i	0,893	0,024	36,906**
FSI_k	0,752	0,088	8,547**
RTA_{ik}	2,014	0,310	6,494**
organic chemicals dummy (D_j for $j = oc$)	–6,816	3,082	–2,212*
other organic compounds dummy (D_j for $j = ooc$)	–6,698	3,231	–2,073*
textiles, clothing and leather dummy (D_j for $j = tcl$)	12,549	3,642	3,445**
wood products dummy (D_j for $j = wp$)	8,379	3,464	2,419*
building material processing equipment dummy (D_j for $j = bmpe$)	7,001	3,370	2,077*
R^2	0,341		
Adjusted R^2	0,339		
No. of observations	3,353		

Notes:
** significant at 1% level.
* significant at 2 % level.

Source: Cantwell and Santangelo (2000).

Table 2.4 lists a selection of geographically more concentrated technological sectors. For these technologies (selected values of j), FS_{ijk} was on average 3.02 per cent lower than expected from the model, thus implying a relatively low degree of internationalisation. In contrast, Table 2.5 lists a selection of geographically more dispersed technological sectors j, which show a FS_{ijk} on average 4.26 per cent higher than expected from the model. The composition of sectors appears to suggest that at least some core science-based and research-grounded technologies (such as chemicals and computing) are among the geographically most concentrated, whilst those shown in Table 2.5 suggest that mature technologies are to a greater extent geographically more dispersed. This finding might be explained by the fact that the spatial pattern followed by science-based technologies is highly influenced by the more pronounced tacit character of knowledge in these fields. The more tacit knowledge is, the more spatially concentrated it is expected to be. Since tacitness implies localisation of development and greater context-specificity, and requires greater intensity of face-to-face interaction, knowledge transmission becomes more complex both within and across different organisations (Winter, 1987). The transmission and absorption of knowledge takes on an informal and experimental character, thus requiring higher and more closely complementary technological competencies on the part of co-operating teams. This is the case, for instance, for many computer-based technologies. As argued by Cantwell and Harding (1998), the research strategies of computing multinationals are fairly internationalised, and hence computer technology tends to be so too, since much of it is developed within these specialist companies. In the exercise carried out in this chapter, having taken into account the overall internationalisation of computer and electronic equipment firms at the industry level (i.e. FSI_k), computer technology tends to be locationally concentrated at home across the firms of various industries that are involved in its development. Conversely the transmission of some mature technologies (such as 'food and tobacco products' and 'textile and clothing machinery') is based on more regularly codified knowledge. This allows for simpler and less context-dependent channels of transmission, thus allowing for the co-ordination of creative efforts over greater geographical distances and, therefore, the spatial dispersion of innovation.

Table 2.4 – A selection of geographically more concentrated technological sectors, by average residuals, 1969–95

Technological Sectors	Average Residuals
Internal combustion engines	−5,76
Power plants	−4,73
Disinfecting and preserving	−4,05
Office equipment and data processing systems	−3,36
Cleaning agents and other compositions	−3,06
Chemical processes	−2,76
Bleaching and dyeing	−2,50
Other electrical communications systems	−2,24
Distillation processes	−2,14
Coal and petroleum products	−1,45
Semiconductors	−1,15
Total average	**−3,02**

Source: Cantwell and Santangelo (2000).

Table 2.5 – A selection of geographically more dispersed technological sectors, by average residuals, 1969–95

Technological Sectors	Average Residuals
Agricultural equipment	7,86
Woodworking tools and machinery	7,83
Food and tobacco products	5,26
Paper making apparatus	3,88
Mining equipment	3,49
Non-metallic mineral products	2,82
Printing and publishing	2,65
Other specialised machinery	2,37
Textile and clothing machinery	2,22
Total average	**4,26**

Source: Cantwell and Santangelo (2000).

Following Breschi (2000), it is possible to distinguish between two groups of technological sectors, according to the different structure and organisation of innovative activity. A first group is represented by traditional and engineering-based sectors, in which innovative activity is geographically more dispersed and is widely developed across the firms of most industries. A second group includes, instead, science-based sectors (e.g. 'office equipment and data processing systems', 'semiconductors', 'chemical processes', 'coal and petroleum products', and 'other electrical communications systems'). These are characterised by geographically more concentrated innovative activity and are developed to a much greater extent by a narrower group of firms primarily in the associated science-based industries.

Of course, beyond the average tendencies revealed by the econometric results, it might still be argued that in some instances even science-based technologies are developed over greater geographical distances, despite their higher tacitness. For this reason in Table 2.6, the analysis focuses on the principal outlying combinations of home country and industry within the spatially more concentrated technological sectors identified in Table 2.4. For each sector, the most extreme cases of either positive or negative residuals are taken into account. This allows one to distinguish between the groups which are most representative of a high degree of spatial concentration of these activities, and other less representative groups which have managed to develop a high degree of internationalisation of even these kinds of mainly tacit branches of technological development.

The figures clearly reveal that British multinationals prefer to retain their R&D activity at home in the science-based industries. Both UK chemicals and electronics companies show an above-average degree of geographical concentration, having controlled for either industry- and country-specific factors (including the 'British'-specific and the 'chemicals'- or 'electronics'-specific). Conversely, controlling for the same factors, Dutch electronics corporations (e.g. Philips) seem to follow a different R&D locational strategy by dispersing their research activity abroad to an above-average extent, whilst the technological activity of the Dutch chemical industry appears to be spatially concentrated. Instead, the experience of the Swedish science-based industries is less clear cut in the sense that the geographical dispersion/ concentration of research activity varies across the selected fields of technological development.

Therefore in certain cases the development of science-based technology is dispersed contrary to the trend towards greater concentration, even taking into account industry- and country-specific factors. However, in such cases MNCs seem to locate abroad the development of technology only outside the core of their main activity. To illustrate the point, in the electronics industry R&D is more likely to be dispersed in the chemical or mechanical fields, and not in the electrical equipment and computing technologies themselves. Thus in this industry Dutch firms have dispersed innovation in 'bleaching and dying processes', 'distillation processes', and 'internal combustion engines', while Swedish firms have done likewise in 'distillation processes' and 'power plants', and Italian firms in 'chemical processes'. Conversely, in the chemicals industry when R&D is more dispersed it tends to occur outside the chemical technologies. This is the case for French chemical companies (e.g. Rhône Poulenc), which locate intensively abroad their research in 'office equipment and data processing systems', the high locational dispersal of innovation in 'semiconductors' by German and Swiss chemical firms, and in power plants by Swedish and Belgian chemical companies.

Thus the trend is that MNCs dispersed the development of some science-based technologies only when they lay outside the core of their technology base. However, there are exceptions even to this generalisation. In Table 2.6 the three exceptions are the Swiss chemical industry, which heavily locates innovation in the core technology 'disinfecting and preserving' abroad; the Swedish electronic industry, which strongly disperses R&D abroad in 'semiconductors'; the Belgian chemical firms, which highly disperse the development of 'bleaching and dying processes' geographically. It is worth noting that all these groups of firms are from small countries. As argued by Walsh (1988), companies from small countries adopt *ad hoc* technological

Table 2.6 – The largest individual residuals from the geographically more concentrated technological sectors, by nationality of the parent company and industry, 1969–95*

Geographically More Concentrated			Geographically More Dispersed		
Internal combustion engines			**Internal combustion engines**		
UK	Food products	-57,54	UK	Textiles	61,69
The Netherlands	Chemicals and Pharmaceuticals	-48,33	The Netherlands	Metals and mechanical engineering	54,00
UK	Chemicals and Pharmaceuticals	-43,74	Netherlands	Electrical equipment and Computing	42,67
UK	Non-metallic mineral products	-41,99	US	Non-metallic mineral products	41,86
Switzerland	Metals and mechanical engineering	-38,28	UK	Metals and mechanical engineering	30,74
power plants			**power plants**		
UK	Food products	-57,54	German	Textiles	91,99
UK	Rubber and plastic products	-39,57	Sweden	Chemicals and Pharmaceuticals	73,53
Switzerland	Chemicals and Pharmaceuticals	-37,22	Sweden	Electrical equipment and Computing	46,34
UK	Electrical equipment and Computing	-34,54	Belgium and Luxembourg	Chemicals and Pharmaceuticals	35,36
UK	Aircraft	-30,58	US	Scientific and professional instruments	32,67
Disinfecting and preserving			**Disinfecting and preserving**		
Belgium and Luxembourg	Chemicals and Pharmaceuticals	-64,64	Switzerland	Chemicals and Pharmaceuticals	49,19
Sweden	Paper products and Publishing	-38,62	UK	Food products	42,46
Sweden	Metals and mechanical engineering	-33,55	UK	Oil	32,13
Sweden	Electrical equipment and Computing	-23,87	Switzerland	Food products	30,61
France	Oil	-21,73	US	Non-metallic mineral products	16,86

Table 2.6 – continued

Geographically More Concentrated			Geographically More Dispersed		
Office equipment and data processing systems			**Office equipment and data processing systems**		
The Netherlands	Metals and mechanical engineering	–46,00	France	Chemicals and Pharmaceuticals	55,78
UK	Other manufacturing	–42,01	Switzerland	Food products	50,61
UK	Paper products and Publishing	–41,55	UK	Textiles	49,19
UK	Food products	–40,87	*Belgium and Luxembourg*	*Metals and mechanical engineering*	36,67
UK	Scientific and professional instruments	–33,84	France	Non-metallic mineral products	35,66
Cleaning agents and other compositions			**Cleaning agents and other compositions**		
Switzerland	Other manufacturing	–44,67	France	Textiles	90,98
UK	Other manufacturing	–42,01	Italy	Metals and mechanical engineering	87,95
UK	Rubber and plastic products	–39,57	Sweden	Rubber and plastic products	78,26
UK	Motor vehicles	–38,05	Switzerland	Non-metallic mineral products	60,68
Belgium and Luxembourg	Oil	–31,71	UK	Paper products and Publishing	33,45
Chemical processes			**Chemical processes**		
The Netherlands	Food products	–53,70	Germany	Textiles	75,33
Belgium and Luxembourg	Metals and mechanical engineering	–52,22	France	Food products	61,68
UK	Other manufacturing	–42,01	France	Textiles	40,98
UK	Other transport equipment	–36,98	UK	Oil	32,57
UK	Aircraft	–34,75	Italy	Electrical equipment and Computing	22,11
Bleaching and dyeing processes			**Bleaching and dyeing processes**		
UK	Non-metallic mineral products	–41,99	UK	Paper products and Publishing	58,45
UK	Electrical equipment and Computing	–39,54	Italy	Oil	46,33
UK	Chemicals and Pharmaceuticals	–38,62	The Netherlands	Electrical equipment and Computing	44,53
Sweden	Paper products and Publishing	–38,62	UK	Oil	39,71
Sweden	Metals and mechanical engineering	–33,55	*Belgium and Luxembourg*	*Chemicals and Pharmaceuticals*	35,36

Other electrical communications systems

The Netherlands	Metals and mechanical engineering	−46,00
UK	Other manufacturing	−42,01
UK	Paper products and Publishing	−41,55
UK	Rubber and plastic products	−39,57
UK	Other transport equipment	−36,98

Distillation processes

Switzerland	Chemicals and Pharmaceuticals	−46,65
The Netherlands	Metals and mechanical engineering	−46,00
UK	Other manufacturing	−42,01
UK	Chemicals and Pharmaceuticals	−34,22
Belgium and Luxembourg	Chemicals and Pharmaceuticals	−31,31

Coal and petroleum products

UK	Other manufacturing	−42,01
UK	Electrical equipment and Computing	−39,54
UK	Chemicals and Pharmaceuticals	−28,70
UK	Food products	−24,21
Sweden	Metals and mechanical engineering	−22,44

Semiconductors

Switzerland	Other manufacturing	−44,67
UK	Motor vehicles	−38,05
UK	Aircraft	−34,75
Sweden	Metals and mechanical engineering	−33,55
UK	Metals and mechanical engineering	−29,01

Other electrical communications systems

Italy	Oil	79,66
UK	Textiles	61,69
Sweden	Paper products and Publishing	44,72
Belgium and Luxembourg	Metals and mechanical engineering	36,67
UK	*Oil*	*33,01*

Distillation processes

Sweden	Scientific and professional instruments	81,15
Sweden	Electrical equipment and Computing	76,13
Sweden	Metals and mechanical engineering	66,45
The Netherlands	Electrical equipment and Computing	50,78
UK	Metals and mechanical engineering	32,66

Coal and petroleum products

France	Non-metallic mineral products	80,11
Sweden	Paper products and Publishing	61,38
US	Non-metallic mineral products	41,86
Belgium and Luxembourg	Metals and mechanical engineering	36,67
UK	Metals and mechanical engineering	32,66

Semiconductors

Germany	Other manufacturing	85,71
Switzerland	Chemicals and Pharmaceuticals	53,35
Germany	Chemicals and Pharmaceuticals	52,78
Sweden	*Electrical equipment and Computing*	*35,39*
UK	*Oil*	*33,80*

Note:
Italics denotes consideration of national industrial groups dispersing technological sectors on average geographically more concentrated investigated in the case study analysis.

Source: Cantwell and Santangelo (1999).

strategies (e.g. niche specialisation and increased internationalisation) to cope with the domestic resource constraints. Closer attention is paid to these occasional exceptions to the rule in the next sub-section.

2.5   A CASE STUDY APPROACH: ELECTRONIC VERSUS NON-ELECTRONIC CORPORATIONS

The results of the regression analysis show that mature technologies are geographically dispersed to a greater extent. Conversely, science-based technologies are more spatially concentrated because of the more pronounced tacit character of knowledge in these fields. However, the analysis showed that there are extreme cases of national industrial groups of firms, which dispersed geographically even these kinds of mainly tacit branches of technological development. This appeared to be more likely when these science-based technologies lie outside the core of the multinational's technology base. The point is illustrated in Table 2.6, which reports each national industrial group that achieved a high spatial dispersal of development within the technological sectors that on average are geographically more concentrated. From a first glance at the figures, it is possible to see that French, Swiss and German chemical and pharmaceutical companies dispersed non-core technologies in ICT fields (i.e. 'Office equipment and data processing systems', and 'Semiconductors') abroad. The Dutch electronic firm (i.e. Philips) located R&D related to 'Bleaching and dyeing processes' outside The Netherlands. The trend also seems to be confirmed in the case of the Italian and British oil multinationals, which develop ICT technologies (i.e. 'Other electrical communications systems' and 'Semiconductors') outside their home country. Conversely Belgian chemical and pharmaceutical, and Swedish electronic firms have managed to internationalise their R&D activity in certain core technologies. Swedish electronic firms carry out research activity abroad in a core technology such as 'Semiconductors'. Similarly, the Belgian chemical companies dispersed R&D development in 'Bleaching and dyeing processes', as did some Italian and British oil firms.

The analysis moves further by investigating these exceptions to the average trend towards greater concentration in science-based activities. For this purpose, the focus is on any national industrial group of firms dispersing electronic technologies as well as any national electronic group of firms dispersing any technology. In each of the geographically more dispersed technological sectors listed in Table 2.6, for each of the national group selected, the analysis narrows at the firm level. Firms are selected by imposing a minimum number of corporate patents in the relevant sectors.

The threshold chosen is that firms have to have at least ten patents in the selected technologies in the period 1969–95. Therefore, geographical dispersion of research activity is analysed in the technological sectors:

- 'internal combustion engines',
- 'office equipment and data processing systems',
- 'bleaching and dyeing processes',
- 'other electrical communications systems' and
- 'semiconductors'.

Within these technological sectors, the national industrial groups analysed are:

- Chemicals n.e.s. and Pharmaceuticals,
- Metals and Mechanical engineering,
- Electrical equipment n.e.s. and Office equipment and
- Coal and petroleum products.

For each of these industrial groups the firms analysed, organised by broadly defined industrial group, are listed in Table A.1. For the selected industrial groups of parent companies, Table 2.7 illustrates the foreign share of US patents of the world's largest firms, which is attributable to research in foreign locations. Therefore in this case

$$FS_{jk} = \Sigma_i FP_{ijk} / \Sigma_i P_{ijk} \tag{2.6}$$

where the subscripts (i), (j), (k) have the same meaning as in equation 2.1.

The detailed analysis for selected industries helps to illustrate the previous findings on the sectoral internationalisation of technology. The 'Chemicals n.e.s. and Pharmaceuticals' industrial group seems to have located research activity abroad mainly among mature technologies, and to retain R&D in its core science-based technologies at home. In the industry in question, ICT technologies (e.g. 'special radio systems') and more general electronic technologies (e.g. 'electrical devices and systems') show a degree of geographical dispersion above both the industry total average (14.0 per cent) and 'All Industries' sectoral averages (8.3 per cent and 9.6 per cent respectively). However, there are some exceptions in which the development of core science-based technologies is dispersed. This is the case in 'disinfecting and preserving' and 'pharmaceuticals and biotechnology', in which the industry appears to show a degree of geographical dispersion (22.8 per cent and 19.8 per cent respectively) above the total industry average and slightly above 'All Industries' sectoral averages. None the less it is worth noting that these are only partial exceptions in the sense that these fields of activity are highly dispersed in general in all industries. From the last column in Table 2.7 ('All Industries'), it is possible to elicit that 'disinfecting and preserving' and 'pharmaceuticals and biotechnology' are among the most internationalised technological sectors (18.2 per cent and 18.8 per cent respectively). In the case of pharmaceuticals, for example, this may be because national regulatory regimes require the presence of some local R&D in return for access to the local market.

Table 2.7 – Share of US patents of the world's largest firms attributable to research in foreign locations as a proportion of total US patents assigned to the firms in question, by industrial group of the parent company, 1969–95 (%)*

Technological Sectors	Chemicals n.e.s. and Pharmaceuticals	Metals and Mechanical engineering	Electrical Equipment n.e.s. and Office Equipment	Coal and Petroleum Products	All Industries
Food and tobacco products	10,1	15,1	1,5	7,1	13,6
Distillation processes	5,9	11,0	15,2	18,3	10,3
Inorganic chemicals	9,9	7,8	4,7	17,4	10,1
Agricultural chemicals	9,9	13,9	21,1	14,1	10,8
Chemical processes	12,0	8,8	7,2	22,4	10,2
Photographic chemistry	16,0	7,5	14,2	20,0	11,6
Cleaning agents and other compositions	15,3	7,0	6,8	12,6	13,8
Disinfecting and preserving	22,8	12,9	0,0	11,7	18,2
Synthetic resins and fibres	12,0	7,3	5,2	24,7	12,2
Bleaching and dyeing	*12,3*	*4,8*	*13,9*	*21,5*	*12,0*
Other organic compounds	14,6	8,9	7,6	18,8	14,2
Pharmaceuticals and biotechnology	19,8	11,2	11,9	16,8	18,8
Metallurgical processes	13,1	9,1	6,3	25,9	8,0
Miscellaneous metal products	13,7	16,0	14,6	12,0	12,7
Food, drink and tobacco equipment	10,7	28,1	10,7	18,2	17,6
Chemical and allied equipment	10,4	12,8	6,9	19,3	11,2

Technological Sectors	Chemicals n.e.s. and Pharmaceuticals	Metals and Mechanical Engineering	Electrical Equipment n.e.s. and Office Equipment	Coal and Petroleum Products	All Industries
Metal working equipment	10,1	14,2	7,4	21,7	11,4
Paper making apparatus	16,0	22,0	10,2	7,7	15,5
Building material processing equipment	9,1	21,7	8,5	30,4	15,1
Assembly and material handling equipment	16,4	14,6	9,3	18,4	11,8
Agricultural equipment	8,0	15,4	23,8	5,1	20,2
Other construction and excavating equipment	11,1	4,4	5,3	23,3	6,5
Mining equipment	9,4	6,1	6,2	17,7	13,2
electrical lamp manufacturing	9,1	0,0	7,9	28,6	7,5
Textile and clothing machinery	25,1	34,3	11,0	4,1	19,2
Printing and publishing machinery	7,5	5,9	12,5	0,0	13,0
Woodworking tools and machinery	28,6	23,8	13,3	5,9	19,6
Other specialised machinery	14,1	19,0	11,8	16,5	13,8
Other general industrial equipment	20,3	10,9	10,8	21,8	10,4
Mechanical calculators and typewriters	5,1	4,4	11,2	4,3	9,8
Power plants	10,5	5,6	8,3	10,5	5,2
Nuclear reactors	29,4	1,6	9,1	8,6	7,8
Telecommunications	8,9	8,2	13,7	12,1	12,5
Other electrical communication systems	*12,3*	*9,6*	*11,7*	*11,2*	*10,0*
Special radio systems	14,3	3,8	12,1	7,4	8,3
Image and sound equipment	5,8	8,1	12,1	5,6	9,1
Illumination devices	8,3	5,9	10,5	6,9	9,0
Electrical devices and systems	19,5	9,1	10,3	11,7	9,6

Technological Sectors	Chemicals n.e.s. and Pharmaceuticals	Metals and Mechanical Engineering	Electrical Equipment n.e.s. and Office Equipment	Coal and Petroleum Products	All Industries
Other general electrical equipment	11,4	13,1	7,3	20,5	7,9
Semiconductors	*10,3*	*2,6*	*9,7*	*14,8*	*8,9*
Office equipment and data processing systems	*10,4*	*6,4*	*8,4*	*11,9*	*7,7*
Internal combustion engines	*6,3*	*7,5*	*6,0*	*7,9*	*4,6*
Motor vehicles	21,1	11,0	8,7	6,3	7,8
Aircraft	4,8	6,2	3,0	0,0	2,6
Ships and marine propulsion	6,7	11,4	9,5	20,4	8,2
Railways and railway equipment	5,1	9,4	10,9	25,0	8,4
Other transport equipment	18,7	11,2	27,6	8,9	11,4
Textiles, clothing and leather	12,0	21,1	38,7	40,9	19,2
Rubber and plastic products	12,6	10,7	7,0	20,4	10,6
Non-metallic mineral products	8,5	12,5	6,8	22,3	9,1
Coal and petroleum products	5,8	5,0	9,0	11,0	8,6
Photographic equipment	7,5	15,1	7,1	20,0	4,4
Other instruments and controls	13,7	9,0	11,6	15,0	9,7
Wood products	18,2	19,1	26,2	26,1	10,5
Explosive compositions and charges	17,0	4,7	27,8	15,6	13,7
Other manufacturing and non-industrial	10,7	8,6	11,6	25,8	10,7
Total	**14,0**	**11,6**	**9,9**	**17,3**	**10,8**

Notes:
Italics are used for the spatially more concentrated technologies drawn from Table 2.4, having controlled for country and industry effects.
n.e.s.= Not elsewhere specified.

Source: Cantwell and Santangelo (1999).

The 'Metals and Mechanical engineering' industry conforms to the general pattern in the sense that this industrial group does not disperse science-based technologies abroad. Chemical and ICT technologies are mainly retained at home as shown by the sectoral foreign shares well below average relative to the industry as a whole as well as to 'All industries' sectoral values.

The trend towards greater geographical dispersion of non-core technologies is fully confirmed in the case of the 'Electrical equipment n.e.s. and Office equipment' industry, which seems to locate R&D activity in mature and in chemical technological sectors abroad. In the latter case the point may be illustrated by 'agricultural chemicals' technologies, which are shown to be highly dispersed (21.1 per cent) in comparison with the industry and the total sectoral averages. Instead core technologies (e.g. 'semiconductors' and 'office equipment and data processing systems') are rather concentrated in home locations. It is worth pointing out that computing technologies are slightly more concentrated than communications technologies, this suggesting a relatively higher degree of embeddedness of knowledge in their development. The overall similarity in the degree of dispersion of computing and communications technologies may be interpreted as a result of the process of technological convergence within the ICT fields. It has been argued that ICT technologies are likely to converge into digital technology. This argument is based upon the increasing extent to which digitalisation would prove to be a technological commonality (von Tunzelmann, 1999). The debate on technological convergence is open in the literature. However, as argued in Chapter 3, a common view seems to have emerged in the sense that wider and wider ranges of technologies are involved and combined into producing specific products (Granstrand and Sjölander, 1990; Granstrand et al., 1997; Patel and Pavitt, 1997).

When the analysis turns into the 'Coal and petroleum products' industrial group, it seems that oil companies disperse geographically some chemical technologies such as 'synthetic resins and fibres'. 24.7 per cent of the companies research activity in this sector is carried out outside their home countries in comparison with the 17.3 per cent of the industry total foreign R&D and the 12.2 per cent of 'All industries' sectoral technological activity. However, the industry foreign share in 'Coal and petroleum products' (11.0 per cent) is below the total industry average, thus confirming the trend of concentration of core technologies.

In the case of 'All industries' it is worth underlining that ICT technologies are on average more concentrated. This may be explained by their role as core pervasive technologies in the current techno–economic conditions (Freeman and Perez, 1988; von Tunzelmann, 1995). After having discussed the general features of the above listed industries, the analysis turns to the case studies of companies selected on the ground of the criterion exposed in section 2.4. For the sake of exposition, electronic and non-electronic (i.e. chemical and oil) companies are analysed separately in what follows.

Table 2.8 shows the foreign share calculated across the 56 technological sectors for selected companies. For each of the four electronic firms considered, FS is then defined as in equation 2.6.

It should be mentioned that LM Ericsson is included in the analysis as a point of comparison with the other Swedish companies, since it belongs to the group of Swedish electronic firms active in semiconductor research (Table 2.6). None the less, the company seems to conform fully to the general trend by geographically concentrating its R&D activity in ICT technologies, while dispersing it in non-core (e.g. chemicals) and mature technologies. The point may be illustrated by LM Ericsson's foreign share in 'semiconductors' (0.0 per cent), which is below both the company's total average (8.9 per cent) and the industry's sectoral average (9.7 per cent). Conversely the development of 'chemical processes' technologies is geographically relatively dispersed (33.3 per cent).

ASEA's foreign research activity is taken into account as one of the forerunners of ABB, which company appears to be to some extent an exception. ABB shows high percentages of its research located outside Sweden in ICT technologies such as 'other electrical communications systems' (100 per cent), 'semiconductors' (88.6 per cent) and 'office equipment and data processing systems' (75.0 per cent). However it should also be noted that the R&D activity of ABB appears highly internationalised in general. As illustrated in Table 2.8, 79.8 per cent of the research activity of this company is carried out outside Sweden. Yet, as will be better illustrated below, a relevant percentage of this research is located in Switzerland, which is the home country of the other parent (i.e. Brown Boveri).

Philips' internationalisation of corporate research activity is consistent with the industry trend. The Dutch company seems to locate a large part of its R&D in chemicals and mature technologies abroad. The former case is illustrated by the geographical dispersion in the development of 'distillation processes' (100 per cent) and 'bleaching and dyeing' (93.8 per cent) technologies. Table 2.8 shows also a high spatial dispersion of mature technologies in the case of 'food and tobacco products' and 'internal combustion engines'.

Table 2.8 – Share of US patents of the selected electrical firms attributable to research in foreign locations as a proportion of total US patents assigned to the firm in question, by technological sector, 1969–95 (%)

Technological Sectors	Philips	LM Ericsson	ASEA	ABB	Industry Average
Food and tobacco products	100,0	n.a.	n.a.	n.a.	1,5
Distillation processes	100,0	n.a.	n.a.	100,0	15,2
Inorganic chemicals	57,1	n.a.	50,0	100,0	4,7
Agricultural chemicals	12,5	n.a.	n.a.	n.a.	21,1
Chemical processes	49,6	33,3	21,8	75,0	7,2
Photographic chemistry	42,9	n.a.	n.a.	n.a.	14,2
Cleaning agents and other compositions	38,7	0,0	0,0	n.a.	6,8
Disinfecting and preserving	n.a.	n.a.	n.a.	n.a.	0,0
Synthetic resins and fibres	37,5	n.a.	n.a.	100,0	5,2
Bleaching and dyeing	*93,8*	*n.a.*	*n.a.*	*n.a.*	*13,9*
Other organic compounds	26,9	n.a.	100,0	n.a.	7,6
Pharmaceuticals and biotechnology	29,7	n.a.	n.a.	n.a.	11,9
Metallurgical processes	40,9	16,7	7,7	70,5	6,3
Miscellaneous metal products	45,4	0,0	5,6	61,5	14,6
Food, drink and tobacco equipment	50,0	n.a.	n.a.	0,0	10,7
Chemical and allied equipment	63,0	0,0	19,8	88,9	6,9
Metal working equipment	35,6	33,3	3,6	63,6	7,4
Paper making apparatus	44,4	n.a.	16,7	n.a.	10,2
Building material processing equipment	50,0	n.a.	0,0	n.a.	8,5
Assembly and material handling equipment	56,8	11,1	5,6	20,0	9,3
Agricultural equipment	0,0	n.a.	n.a.	n.a.	23,8
Other construction and excavating equipment	n.a.	n.a.	n.a.	n.a.	5,3
Mining equipment	n.a.	n.a.	0,0	n.a.	6,2
Electrical lamp manufacturing	31,1	n.a.	0,0	n.a.	7,9
Textile and clothing machinery	32,0	0,0	72,7	n.a.	11,0
Printing and publishing machinery	71,4	n.a.	n.a.	100,0	12,5
Woodworking tools and machinery	n.a.	n.a.	n.a.	n.a.	13,3
Other specialised machinery	55,3	30,0	10,6	0,0	11,8
Other general industrial equipment	49,3	25,0	2,6	79,6	10,8

Technological Sectors	Philips	LM Ericsson	ASEA	ABB	Industry Average
Mechanical calculators and typewriters	86,9	0,0	n.a.	n.a.	11,2
Power plants	22,7	n.a.	3,8	73,3	8,3
Nuclear reactors	64,3	n.a.	2,5	21,3	9,1
Telecommunications	60,4	12,1	0,0	84,6	13,7
Other electrical communication systems	*57,5*	*10,0*	*0,0*	*100,0*	*11,7*
Special radio systems	62,7	7,4	n.a.	n.a.	12,1
Image and sound equipment	51,3	0,0	0,0	66,7	12,1
Illumination devices	38,6	0,0	0,0	100,0	10,5
Electrical devices and systems	52,8	5,0	24,9	64,4	10,3
Other general electrical equipment	57,4	0,0	10,3	88,2	7,3
Semiconductors	*62,2*	*0,0*	*0,0*	*88,6*	*9,7*
Office equipment and data processing systems	*43,6*	*8,1*	*0,0*	*75,0*	*8,4*
Internal combustion engines	*91,9*	*n.a.*	*n.a.*	*n.a.*	*6,0*
Motor vehicles	100,0	n.a.	0,0	n.a.	8,7
Aircraft	61,5	n.a.	n.a.	n.a.	3,0
Ships and marine propulsion	100,0	n.a.	0,0	n.a.	9,5
Railways and railway equipment	76,9	0,0	0,0	33,3	10,9
Other transport equipment	85,7	n.a.	0,0	n.a.	27,6
Textiles, clothing and leather	100,0	n.a.	n.a.	n.a.	38,7
Rubber and plastic products	50,0	25,0	0,0	75,0	7,0
Non-metallic mineral products	36,5	0,0	20,0	71,4	6,8
Coal and petroleum products	66,7	n.a.	50,0	n.a.	9,0
Photographic equipment	51,7	n.a.	n.a.	n.a.	7,1
Other instruments and controls	61,6	5,7	7,7	75,7	11,6
Wood products	62,5	n.a.	n.a.	n.a.	26,2
Explosive compositions and charges	100,0	n.a.	n.a.	n.a.	27,8
Other manufacturing and non-industrial	85,8	0,0	0,0	n.a.	11,6
Total	**51,9**	**8,9**	**12,4**	**79,8**	**9,9**

Notes:

Italics are used for the spatially more concentrated technologies drawn from Table 2.4, having controlled for country and industry effects.

n.a. = Not available.

Source: Cantwell and Santangelo (1999).

The same case study analysis was conducted for the 'Chemicals n.e.s. and Pharmaceuticals', and 'Coal and petroleum products' industries in Table 2.9. Table 2.9 lists the foreign shares across the 56 technological sectors of Rhône-Poulenc and Shell as defined in equation 2.6.

Table 2.9 – Share of US patents of selected large non-electrical firms attributable to research in foreign locations as a proportion of total US patents assigned to the firm in question, by technological sector, 1969–95 (%)

Technological Sectors	Rhône-Poulenc	Chemical Industry Average	Shell	Oil Industry Average
Food and tobacco products	32,0	10,1	100,0	7,1
Distillation processes	0,0	5,9	100,0	18,3
Inorganic chemicals	3,2	9,9	98,8	17,4
Agricultural chemicals	58,9	9,9	56,6	14,1
Chemical processes	9,2	12,0	95,5	22,4
Photographic chemistry	10,0	16,0	100,0	20,0
Cleaning agents and other compositions	11,3	15,3	93,1	12,6
Disinfecting and preserving	50,0	22,8	100,0	11,7
Synthetic resins and fibres	2,3	12,0	98,5	24,7
Bleaching and dyeing	*0,0*	*12,3*	*100,0*	*21,5*
Other organic compounds	9,3	14,6	87,3	18,8
Pharmaceuticals and biotechnology	24,6	19,8	58,2	16,8
Metallurgical processes	11,1	13,1	97,1	25,9
Miscellaneous metal products	65,6	13,7	87,7	12,0
Food, drink and tobacco equipment	n.a.	10,7	n.a.	18,2
Chemical and allied equipment	3,2	10,4	98,1	19,3
Metal working equipment	0,0	10,1	100,0	21,7
Paper making apparatus	18,2	16,0	100,0	7,7
Building material processing equipment	0,0	9,1	n.a.	30,4
Assembly and material handling equipment	14,7	16,4	100,0	18,4
Agricultural equipment	n.a.	8,0	100,0	5,1
Other construction and excavating equipment	n.a.	11,1	100,0	23,3

Technological Sectors	Rhône-Poulenc	Chemical Industry Average	Shell	Oil Industry Average
Mining equipment	0,0	9,4	99,1	17,7
Electrical lamp manufacturing	n.a.	9,1	n.a.	28,6
Textile and clothing machinery	11,1	25,1	80,0	4,1
Printing and publishing machinery	0,0	7,5	n.a.	0,0
Woodworking tools and machinery	n.a.	28,6	n.a.	5,9
Other specialised machinery	8,3	14,1	84,9	16,5
Other general industrial equipment	10,5	20,3	93,0	21,8
Mechanical calculators and typewriters	n.a.	5,1	100,0	4,3
Power plants	n.a.	10,5	100,0	10,5
Nuclear reactors	n.a.	29,4	100,0	8,6
Telecommunications	n.a.	8,9	98,9	12,1
Other electrical communication systems	*66,7*	*12,3*	*90,0*	*11,2*
Special radio systems	n.a.	14,3	n.a.	7,4
Image and sound equipment	0,0	5,8	100,0	5,6
Illumination devices	0,0	8,3	100,0	6,9
Electrical devices and systems	13,3	19,5	95,0	11,7
Other general electrical equipment	5,4	11,4	89,7	20,5
Semiconductors	*n.a.*	*10,3*	*100,0*	*14,8*
Office equipment and data processing systems	*80,0*	*10,4*	*97,1*	*11,9*
Internal combustion engines	*0,0*	*6,3*	*53,8*	*7,9*
Motor vehicles	n.a.	21,1	n.a.	6,3
Aircraft	n.a.	4,8	n.a.	0,0
Ships and marine propulsion	n.a.	6,7	93,9	20,4
Railways and railway equipment	n.a.	5,1	n.a.	25,0
Other transport equipment	n.a.	18,7	n.a.	8,9
Textiles, clothing and leather	0,0	12,0	100,0	40,9
Rubber and plastic products	16,7	12,6	87,3	20,4
Non-metallic mineral products	5,1	8,5	92,9	22,3
Coal and petroleum products	7,7	5,8	97,8	11,0
Photographic equipment	0,0	7,5	100,0	20,0

Technological Sectors	Rhône-Poulenc	Chemical Industry Average	Shell	Oil Industry Average
Other instruments and controls	0,0	13,7	91,4	15,0
Wood products	0,0	18,2	100,0	26,1
Explosive compositions and charges	n.a.	17,0	100,0	15,6
Other manufacturing and non-industrial	0,0	10,7	99,0	25,8
Total	**11,6**	**14,0**	**92,9**	**17,3**

Notes:
Italics are used for the spatially more concentrated technologies drawn from Table 2.4, having controlled for country and industry effects.
n.a. = Not available.

Source: Cantwell and Santangelo (1999).

The French company seems to follow the trend of the industry in the sense that it dispersed abroad some ICT technologies such as 'other electrical communications systems' (66.7 per cent) and 'office equipment and data processing systems' (80.0 per cent).

When the analysis turns to the oil industry, Shell's corporate research activity appears heavily internationalised overall (92.9 per cent). This trend is also confirmed at the sectoral level when comparing the company's with the industry's sectoral figures. The oil company confirms the trend of geographical dispersion of non-core technologies as illustrated by its foreign shares in 'other electrical communications systems' (90.0 per cent) and 'semiconductors' (100.0 per cent). However Shell's overall trend can be better understood from the perspective of its propensity since the 1930s to locate the bulk of its research close to its extractive facilities in the US, rather than in Britain or The Netherlands, as discussed further below.

2.6   THE SIGNIFICANCE OF THE HOST COUNTRY DIMENSION

The analysis of the geography of technological activity in the selected industries and companies is further developed by focusing on the host location of the companies' R&D activity in these unusually spatially dispersed technologies reported in italics in Table 2.6. For each of the six corporate case studies, Table 2.10 reports the share of US patents attributable to research located in all relevant locations as a proportion of the total US patents assigned to the firm in question in the sector in question.

Table 2.10 – Share of US patents of selected firms attributable to research in specific locations as a proportion of the total US patents assigned to the firm in question, for selected technologies, 1969–95 (%)

Internal combustion engines

Host country	Philips
France	5,4
The Netherlands	8,1
Sweden	2,7
US	83,8

Office equipment and data processing systems

Host country	Rhône-Poulenc
France	20
Switzerland	10
US	70

Bleaching and dyeing processes

Host country	Philips
France	12,5
The Netherlands	6,3
US	81,3

Other electrical communication systems

Host country	Shell
Japan	10
The Netherlands	10
UK	10
US	70

Semiconductors

Host country	ASEA	LM	Shell	ABB
Germany				5,7
Sweden	100,0	100,0		11,4
Switzerland				54,3
US			100,0	28,6

Source: Cantwell and Santangelo (1999).

Table 2.10 shows that most of the European firms under analysis in the international location of R&D facilities tend to be US oriented. Although Dutch companies' strategies in other fields of activity are substantially based on corporate European integration (Cantwell and Janne, 1998), here it seems that Philips locates its R&D investments mainly in the US. Both in 'bleaching and dyeing processes' and 'internal combustion engines', high percentages of Philips' research activity are concentrated in the US (81.3 per cent and 83.8 per cent respectively), and to a lesser extent in France (12.5 per cent and 5.4 per cent respectively) and in The Netherlands (6.3 per cent and 8.1 per cent respectively). This pattern may well be sector-driven in the sense that in the above mentioned technologies US sites provide access to indigenous technological expertise. This is consistent with the argument of the context-dependent and cumulative nature of technology. The Dutch company is able to gain access to complementary paths of technological development as well as to exploit local capabilities in these particular technologies by investing in the US. It is worth pointing out that the technologies in question represent chemicals and transport fields, in which giant US companies have been highly competitive since 1945.

In contrast, Rhône-Poulenc is consistent with a greater significance of US investments for French companies (Cantwell and Janne, 2000). In 'office equipment and data processing systems' the French chemical multinational locates 70 per cent of its R&D in the US and just 10 per cent in Switzerland, while retaining 20 per cent at home. The US also seems to be the most appealing location in the case of Shell's research activity in both 'semiconductors' and 'other electrical communications systems' technologies. This is less likely to be attributable to sector-specific factors. In the study referred to above, Cantwell and Janne (ibid.) found that British company technological investments are heavily US oriented. Yet, in any event, Shell has always located most of its R&D in all sectors in the US, quite apart from the British contribution to its ownership (Cantwell and Barrera, 1998). In 'semiconductors', Shell's research activity is fully located in the US. In the case of 'other electrical communications systems', 70 per cent of the oil company's R&D is absorbed by the US and the remaining 30 per cent is equally located in the UK, The Netherlands and Japan.[3] The choice of Japan as host location for research in an ICT technology may be due to the opportunities to exploit tacit knowledge in the host location in the sector in question. This seems to confirm the Japanese technological strength in the current techno–economic situation (Freeman, 1987; Cantwell and Andersen, 1996).

Conversely, in 'semiconductors' the Swedish companies show a more home-oriented trend as illustrated by the figures of ASEA and LM Ericsson. In the ABB pattern of geographical dispersion of technological activity, the

1988 merger between ASEA and Brown Boveri seems to play a major role in the sense that 54.3 per cent of the company's R&D activity in semiconductors since 1988 is now carried out in Switzerland. This may be due to a corporate reorganisation subsequent to the merger, which promoted a relocation of company technological activity according to the specialisation of the two merging partners. Indeed the Swiss Brown Boveri was more involved in electronics than was its Swedish partner ASEA. It is worth noting that also in this case the US emerged as one of the most attractive locations for the company's technological activity. This confirms the role of the US as a dynamic technological base for new sourcing in this field.

Yet, of all the firms considered, ABB is the only one that has developed an international division of labour in a core science-based field which is genuinely and widely geographically dispersed, and which requires the ability to organise an international network as part of a broader global strategy. It is well known in other contexts that ABB is a special case in terms of its particularly pronounced ability to develop an organisational heterarchy (Hedlund, 1986; Hedlund and Rolander, 1990; Hedlund and Ridderstråle, 1995). The company has been described by the literature as an example of the new corporate form of organisation defined as N-form. Unlike the M-form (of multiple divisions) based on hierarchical organisation and functional division, the N-form (of internal network) logic is built upon the concept of multiplication and functional combination (Hedlund, 1992). Following Ridderstråle (1996, 359), the ultimate aim is 'not so much to minimise transaction costs, or to optimise information-processing capacity, as it is to maximise the knowledge-creation capability'. In a new global environment characterised by an increasing degree of economic and political interdependence, the heterarchical or holographic (Ridderstråle, 1992) logic promotes an efficient intra-firm organisational form. The heterarchical form enables the MNC to achieve this goal by promoting flexible managerial roles and developing an interdependent intra-firm network. In this 'neterarchy', the interaction between companies/affiliates and the local environment goes beyond merely market bidding imperatives, and instead focuses on knowledge creation aspects.

In this new corporate organisational scenario ABB is renowned for its global matrix organisation. Built on decentralisation and responsibility, and individual accountability, the success of this structure lies in organising the company activities into business segments across geographical locations. This means that, for each business segment, there are as many operating companies/affiliates as there are geographical locations in which the corporation operates. The headquarters monitors and co-ordinates this network of activities. Therefore, the competitive advantage of the company lies in the ability to learn and share information effectively across its units under the single ABB umbrella (Holmström and Roberts, 1998). Brandes and Brege (1993) remark on the importance of the role played by top managers in the strategic turnaround of ABB. In the words of the ABB director Percy Barnevik, this corporate structure makes the company 'global, local, big and small, radically decentralised with centralised reporting control' (Bartlett and Ghoshal, 1995). The global matrix structure allows each company/affiliate a certain degree of enterpreneurship in its geographical location, which is chosen on the grounds of local embedded competencies. In this sense, Zander (1998) argues that the gradual and revolutionary internationalisation of ABB's advanced technological capabilities has provided the company with access to new growth opportunities. Zander (ibid.) emphasises the enhanced flexibility which the integrated growing number and diversity of knowledge bases within the multinational network has promoted. The location of ABB's R&D activity in 'semiconductors' fits this logic. The profile of technological expertise of Brown Boveri seems to have driven ABB's decision to locate research facilities in the field in question in Switzerland, while its international network strategy encouraged a dispersion and sourcing of this area of activity from other suitable locations as well.

2.7   CONCLUSIONS

This chapter shows that the geographical dispersion of innovation tends to be achieved more readily in some fields than others; the creation of some technologies remains more highly concentrated in local centres of excellence. Although firms are increasingly dispersing their R&D facilities over greater geographical distances, the internationalisation of their activity is likely to be sector-specific. Technologies embodying a greater extent of tacit and uncodified knowledge require as a rule a closer face-to-face interaction. The technological fields that have continued to be relatively concentrated are those in which tacitness is greatest and linkages with a local science base (and the face-to-face interaction that this entails) are most significant. This was found to be the case in both science-based (i.e. electronics and chemicals) and science-based related technological activity, as well as in each industry's and firm's core technologies. Conversely, mature and non-core technologies appear less context-dependent, and are thus easier to transfer across borders. Part of the reason for this is that the science-based technologies are developed primarily by firms in the science-based industries (chemicals and electronics) and, although these firms have certainly internationalised their innovation activity, they have tended to retain the generation of their core technologies at home, while dispersing other related R&D efforts abroad (Cantwell and Santangelo, 1999). Yet the other consideration is simply that for firms in all industries (even those that are not science-based), the creation of technologies in which tacit knowledge carries a greater weight is harder to co-ordinate across longer distances. Furthermore, the results show that in the exceptional cases in which the development of science-based technologies has been locationally dispersed, this is usually attributable to firms in the science-based industries developing a few non-core technologies over distance – chemical firms that develop some electronic technologies abroad, or electronic equipment companies that innovate in chemical technologies over a greater geographical distance.

This trend is confirmed in the company-case study approach adopted here. The analysis explores further by examining the host locations over which the companies selected disperse the development of science-based technologies. The results seem to suggest that the reason for dispersing R&D facilities in particular locations may be due to the need to access locally embedded sectoral specialisation. In this cumulative process government support of science and technology (S&T) is crucial in sustaining a local dynamic environment (Dunning, 1993; Archibugi and Iammarino, 1999; Iammarino and Michie, 1998). By supporting education and training as well as public research, governments indirectly encourage firms to invest in their own R&D to be able to tap into a more extensive external network of research, including complementary expertise in fields in which local companies are not specialised. In this sense the host location is likely to provide the new generation of multinational subsidiaries with a technologically specialised and dynamic environment, thus enhancing its comparative advantage (Tavares and Pearce, 1998). Furthermore, firms increase the returns on their own R&D through suitably adapting their underlying tacit capability so that they can absorb and apply knowledge more intensively in their own internal learning process. This is especially pertinent for MNCs developing technology in more than one location, as potential opportunities for cross-border learning have been enhanced by an increased take-up of ICT technologics (Santangelo, 2001). The reason lies in the more sophisticated modern system of production as well in the more intensive linkages between science and technology in the information age, which relies on flexibility through computerisation and diversity through new combinations drawing upon a wider range of disciplines. ICT specialisation seems to amplify the firm's technological flexibility by enabling it to fuse together a wider range of formerly separate technologies. In this sense in the current ICT-based era government intervention is better geared towards the support of S&T institutions and to the promotion of cross-firm and cross-border knowledge flows, rather than to provisions to protect the monopolistic and separate exploitation of knowledge by those that have independently invested in its creation.

However, the choice of the host country can exceptionally be dictated by firm-specific global strategies in a case such as ABB, in which as with a few other Swedish and Swiss companies a particular capability has grown up to manage an especially geographically complex international network for technological development (Cantwell and Piscitello, 1999). As argued above, the companies considered are influenced by at least one of these two main considerations when dispersing their research facilities in highly tacit lines. This is consistent with the view that R&D units which are strongly embedded in the local environment and maintain close and frequent contacts with local partners are more innovative than others (Håkanson and Nobel, 1998b). In line with other studies on R&D dispersion (Cantwell and Janne, 1998) it was also possible to distinguish between US- and European-oriented corporate strategic approaches to the choice of location. Yet, these results seem to support the argument that governments may need to encourage cross-border knowledge flows, unlike in the past when their perspective was one of enabling local firms to capture a full 'rent' on knowledge created at home, the use of which would then be strictly controlled by firms located in the home country. Following Nelson (1995), government technology policy should have a broad focus, and avoid trying to fund research on a firm-by-firm basis. Moreover to facilitate cross-border learning governments may have to improve domestic absorptive capacity to access relevant complementary knowledge created abroad, and to support the organisational efforts of domestically-owned MNCs to establish more complex international networks to follow the lead of companies that have pioneered the combine development of technologies over distance, and certain Swiss and Swedish firms in particular. This is illustrated by the case of ABB, which has developed its international operations by establishing geographically dispersed centres of excellence within its overall portfolio of technologies (Zander, 1998). The successful organisational development of ABB towards more heterarchical forms of technology management is also in line with the findings of Håkanson and Nobel (1998a). Using evidence on the internationalisation of R&D in Swedish-owned MNCs, they show that certain aspects of tacitness may facilitate the internal transfer of tacit knowledge within the MNC. Affiliate networks are increasingly used to source new technology. Accordingly, global learning has become an important mechanism for corporate technological renewal within MNCs. This phenomenon raises the issue of the different R&D units. Nobel and Birkinshaw's (1998) study on a sample of 110 international R&D units from 15 multinationals confirms the emergence of new alternative organisational forms. As emphasised by Kogut (1990) the corporate advantage of these new organisational forms, based on established multiple subsidiaries throughout the world, lies in the co-ordination of the multinational network.

On the grounds of these findings concerning corporate internationalisation of technology in the ICT era, the analysis moves further by investigating the pattern followed by corporate technological specialisation in the period under analysis in the next chapter.

NOTES

1. In a study on the technological diversification of 24 leading Swedish multinationals, Zander (1997a) confirms that foreign units are becoming increasingly engaged in the local integration of several technologies.
2. The technological significance of these national groups of firms is established on the grounds of their number of patents abroad. Each of them holds more than 700 patents abroad over the period 1969–95. In Table 2.1, Canadian and 'other' firms are listed for comparative purposes, but they are not included in the econometric analysis.
3. It is should be borne in mind that Shell is a British–Dutch jointly owned company.

3. The management of corporate technological portfolios: rationalisation versus diversification

3.1   INTRODUCTION

If in spatial terms the significance of the tacit component of technology is confirmed over the new techno–socio–economic conditions by the statistical results of Chapter 2, there is a need to investigate the patterns followed by MNCs in terms of technological specialisation. This chapter examines how corporate technological diversification has been adapted across firms in recent years in response to the opportunities opened up for innovation by rising technological interrelatedness. The hypothesis tested is that technological diversification cannot be explained only in terms of size. It is suggested that this phenomenon occurs as technology becomes more complex and interrelated over time.

Following Edith Penrose's work (1959) and the resource-based view derived from it, the firm is understood as a collection of competencies developed through an internal learning process in the form of evolutionary experimentation. In order to strengthen these capabilities, the firm has to extend them into new activities and new geographical locations (Loasby, 1991). Leaving aside the latter issue (already developed in Chapter 2), the former implies that the firm has to accumulate strategic stocks by choosing appropriate technological paths over a period of time (Dierickx and Cool, 1989). As corporate learning is specific to some extent to the firm's particular facilities, each firm tends to follow its distinctive path in developing its own core capabilities. The resource-based view emphasises the accumulation of more sophisticated technological competencies through technology creation rather than exchange. For firms operating in other technological fields, specialisation in key technologies (e.g. ICT) may be a better alternative than exchange since transaction costs are likely to prove costly. Knowledge creation generated by an R&D department is more valuable to its own firm than to any other corporation. Any new item of knowledge is more valuable for alternative processes of learning and innovation if it is the outcome of the firm's own R&D rather than one of exchange. Therefore the concept of technological diversity refers to the distributed technological competencies of the firm across new technological fields.

Due to the tacit aspect of technology, in this learning process, the firm-specific history plays a critical role, the result being stability over time in its specialisation pattern (Cantwell and Andersen, 1996; Cantwell and Fai, 1999a). As illustrated by the history of successful MNCs, the diversification process enables them to accumulate new competencies and furthermore widen their market. This cumulative process refers to 'similar' as well as 'complementary' activities (Richardson, 1972). The former are defined as 'activities which require the same capabilities' (ibid., 888), whilst the latter concern 'activities which represent different phases of production and require to be co-ordinated' (ibid., 889). The issue of co-ordination is related to the size of the firm, which, in turn, impacts upon organisation. Large firms generate more innovative activity by taking advantage of the wide range of skills and specialised knowledge available through the greater division of labour. Although size can be a drawback as activities can be much harder to co-ordinate at high levels of bureaucratic organisation, large firms are then expected to show a greater technological diversity. However, in recent years, large firms seem to have reduced their diversification, whilst 'smaller' firms show a more diversified portfolio (Markides, 1995a, 1995b). In this context there is a need to distinguish more carefully between technological diversification (i.e. the diversification of competence) and business diversification (i.e. the diversification of product). The former refers to the trajectories that firms follow in accumulating competencies which are firm-specific by incorporating diversity of sources of learning in order to raise their innovative potential. The latter concerns the exploitation of the firm's established competence to better effect by serving diverse product markets. However, it is worth noting that the corporate capacity to generate new products and to diversify or differentiate an existing product underlies the corporate capacity to create and redefine new products and process, which lies in the cumulative generation of technological competence in firms (Cantwell and Fai, 1999a). Accordingly technological diversification seems to be rising, while business diversification is falling (Granstrand and Oskarsson, 1994; Granstrand, 1996; Granstrand et al., 1997; Patel and Pavitt, 1997). This may be attributed to the new nature of international competition and technological advance in the current ICT era. Similarly the growing pressures of international competition imply that in a dynamic (as opposed to a static) setting, surviving firms must be increasingly committed to the continuous upgrading of their own capability base, and hence to technological improvement.

In the information age, the linkages between science, education and technology have been further increased, and the potential fusion between formerly unrelated technologies has created major new opportunities for innovation based upon corporate technological diversification. In this context ICT operates as an integrator of diverse and hence flexible production systems (Freeman, 1987) reliant on more collective types of organisational forms (Lazonick, 1992). ICT and ICT-based technologies can be applied in various different ways to make many different products (von Tunzelmann, 1995). In this sense it has been argued that communications and computing technology is a facilitator of new combinations or a fusion (Kodama, 1992a, 1992b) between formerly separate economic activities within or between firms. To illustrate the point, within the same broad industry computing technology involves not only technological knowledge about semiconductors, but also knowledge about software, optic fibres, displays, etc. Similarly, between different industries, microchips are a good example of the current technological interdisciplinary as they can be installed in a wide range of products. Accordingly this increase in technological fusion and interrelatedness creates the need for technological portfolios broader than product portfolios (Granstrand and Oskarsson, 1994; Granstrand, 1996; Granstrand et al., 1997; Patel and Pavitt, 1997). Therefore while corporate technological specialisation widens over time, corporate product specialisation follows an inverse path.

The increased technological interrelatedness and areas of potential fusion often made feasible in the current techno–socio–economic conditions by ICT provide fresh opportunities for new technological combinations. In turn, this new technological environment encourages companies to adapt their profiles of internal technological diversification accordingly. Dosi et al. (1992) argue that the enhanced technological opportunities offered by the ICT era promote the diversity process and its direction. In some cases this may mean simply broadening corporate diversification into new (as yet unexplored or little explored) fields; while in other cases it may mean a more intensive effort in certain newly interconnected branches of technology in which the firm has already been engaged (Cantwell and Santangelo, 2000). Such areas of research may well have been kept largely separate previously (perhaps being the responsibility of different divisions in the M-form firm), yet can now be beneficially brought together to exploit new economies of scope. In the general growth of corporate diversification (Granstrand et al., 1997; Cantwell and Fai, 1999b; Cantwell and Piscitello, 2000), firms following 'coherent' directions of diversification seem to outperform less 'coherent' corporations in the long-run (Teece et al., 1994). The concept of 'coherence' refers to the ability of the firm to allocate common characteristics across corporate related lines of business (ibid.) by generating, exploring and combining synergies.

Therefore, in the case of both firms diversifying in new fields and firms strengthening connections between branches of technologies where they are already engaged, path-dependency, firm capabilities and technological opportunities are key factors (ibid.). However in the latter case the consolidation of the firms' corporate profiles may have promoted a move towards corporate forms of organisation alternative to the M-form. If the M-form supported a corporate growth strategy based upon size-driven diversification (Chandler, 1990), the rise of a related-diversification growth strategy (Cantwell and Fai, 1999b) calls for more decentralised or heterarchical forms of corporate organisation. Organisation capability is an important factor in corporate management. The adoption of a related diversification strategy appears to call for greater co-ordination across internationally dispersed networks that may be better implemented through organisational forms alternative to the M-form. The management of multi-market and multi-technology firms seems to move towards new forms of organisations. Increasingly independent networks of geographically dispersed subsidiaries seem to be the main characteristic of these new organisational forms as argued in Chapter 2. Therefore if corporate internal capabilities are a central factor in order to restructure the MNC's organisation, inter-firm relationships have become a great source of access to complementary but dissimilar capability difficult to control within the company. Thus, for example, the new wave of strategic alliances between MNCs has been far more oriented towards joint technological development and inter-firm co-operation in learning, and has been relatively less motivated by the joint exercise of market power, in comparison with the international cartels of the interwar years (Hagedoorn and Schakenraad, 1990; Cantwell and Barrera, 1998).

This chapter argues that corporate growth is no longer pursued through diversification, but diversification opens up new opportunities for long-run incremental growth. In the past firms also over-diversified in unrelated areas, aiming mainly at an increase in corporate size. In this case firms over-estimated the extent to which their capabilities could be stretched, thus incurring organisational problems. In recent years, firms' strategy appears to be more concerned with diversification in corporate similar and complementary areas. In what remains, evidence on diversification of corporate technology is examined. In investigating the role of the recent increase in technological interrelatedness and with it corporate technological diversification, the chapter is organised into four sections. Section 3.2 explains the measures adopted and the regression model. The section also sheds some light on the sample of firms analysed. Section 3.3 discusses the empirical results. In section 3.4 some general conclusions are drawn.

3.2 METHODOLOGICAL NOTES

In the light of the apparent rise in the degree of inter-relatedness between formerly distinct fields of technology in the information age, the relationship between technological diversification and firm size is examined. To do so, the form and extent of the shift in the relationship between firm size and diversification is investigated over time.

A minimum firm size for inclusion was imposed to ensure meaningful indicators of corporate technological diversification across fields of activity. The threshold chosen is that firms had to have at least 60 patents in each of the three sub-periods under consideration. However, to allow for an adequate lapse of time in which to observe changes in the pattern of technological diversification at the level of individual firms, the econometric analysis of this chapter focuses on two out of the three usual sub-periods listed in section 1.5. The two sub-periods under analysis are:

- 1969–77 (sub-period 1) and
- 1987–95 (sub-period 3).

Therefore the firms in the sample of analysis are listed in Table A.1. As shown in the table, the firms are classified into 14 industrial groups according to their industrial output (see also Appendix A). This allows an inter-industry comparison of the diversification–size relationship. However, only industrial groups counting more than 20 firms, which meet the selection criteria above, are taken into account in order to ensure meaningful results. Therefore the analysis focuses on five industrial groups:

- Chemicals n.e.s. and Pharmaceuticals,
- Metals and Mechanical engineering,
- Electrical equipment n.e.s. and Office equipment,
- Coal and petroleum products and
- Motor vehicles.

Yet, before exposing the regression model, the measures adopted must be presented. The total accumulated patent stock (Patot) of each firm (i) is used as a proxy for the company's technological size. The use of the patent stock is consistent with the theoretical notion of technological accumulation, which is analogous to capital accumulation and which follows from the view that technological change is a cumulative, incremental and path-dependent process. For each firm (i), the firm's degree of diversification is estimated by the coefficient of variation (CV) of the RTA distribution across the usual 56 technological sectors, as described in Appendix A. Therefore,

$$CV_{RTAi} = \sigma_{RTAi}/\mu_{RTAi} * 100 \qquad (3.1)$$

where, σ_{RTAi} is the standard deviation and μ_{RTAi} is the mean value of the RTA distribution for each firm (i). CV measures concentration of technological activity among sectors for a firm in any particular time period. This measure has some advantage over the simple standard deviation for two reasons. First, it takes into account possible changes in the mean over time, thus embodying a relative concept of dispersion. Second, it is related to the Herfindahl Index (H), which has frequently been used as a measure of concentration/dispersion across sectors within a firm (see Hart and Prais, 1956).[1] As CV is a positive measure of concentration and, therefore, an inverse measure of diversification, 1/CV is used as direct measure of diversification, for ease of exposition. Therefore:

- high values of 1/CV indicate wide dispersion of a firm's profile of specialisation across many technological sectors. This implies that the RTA values across the 56 technological sectors are very similar among them and very close to the mean. Thus the firm diversifies its specialisation across sectors;
- low values of 1/CV indicate high concentration of a firm's profile of specialisation into a few technological sectors. This implies that a firm shows very high RTA values in same particular technological sectors and very low RTA values in others. Thus the firm concentrates its specialisation in those technological sectors with very high RTA values.

As the diversification–size relationship is investigated over time, it should be borne in mind that a rise of 1/CV indicates increasing technological diversification and a fall indicates increasing technological concentration.

To assess the relationship between size and diversification, the following linear regression model is run:

$$1/CV_i = \alpha + \beta \ln Patot_i + \varepsilon_i \qquad (3.2)$$

where $\ln Patot_i$ is the natural logarithm of the patent stock ($Patot_i$), which is used to normalise the exponential distribution of the cumulative patent stock. In equation 3.2 $1/CV_i$ and $\ln Patot_i$ are considered for each firm (i) at the same point in time. This regression is run for each of the five industrial groups of firms listed above in both the two sub-periods under analysis.

3.3   MNCs AND THE 'OPTIMAL' BALANCE OF TECHNOLOGICAL DIVERSIFICATION

For each of the five industrial groups, the regression lines estimated are reported separately in both sub-periods in Figures 3.1, 3.2, 3.3, 3.4 and 3.5. Each chart also reports the regression equations and the mean values of the estimated variables. Two main findings seem to emerge from the regression analysis.

First, the point emerging from the Figures is the apparent 'convergence' in overall level of technological diversification across large firms. In the science-based industries (i.e. 'Chemicals n.e.s. and Pharmaceuticals', 'Electrical equipment n.e.s. and Office equipment', 'Coal and petroleum products') and in 'Motor vehicles', it seems that, whilst many relatively smaller firms have diversified, 'giant' firms have on average rationalised the extent of their technological dispersion. As illustrated in Figures 3.1, 3.3, 3.4 and 3.5, in all these industries it is possible to observe a rotational shift of the regression line from the first sub-period analysed to the second, thus confirming an average diversification of 'smaller' firms and on average the rationalisation of technological specialisation by 'giant' companies.

This pattern is less clear in Figure 3.2, in that, although there is also a rotational shift in the 'Metals and Mechanical engineering' industrial group, a greater diversification occurred only at the very lower end of the size categories. These inter-industry differences in the diversification pattern over time may be attributed to differences in the strength and source of technological opportunities (Klevorick et al., 1993; Cantwell and Andersen, 1996). The fast-growing rate of technological advance in science-based and related ('Motor vehicles'[2]) industries enables firms to diversify in order to explore new technological opportunities, while promoting a rationalisation of the technological corporate portfolio for already large diversified firms. Conversely, in mature industries (e.g. 'Metals and Mechanical engineering') the rate of overall development is slower, thus calling for less 'catching-up' strategies through diversification by 'smaller' firms. Cantwell and Andersen (1996) demonstrate empirically that there is a linkage between innovation diffusion among firms and a rapid rate of technological development. In industries showing a fast growth of technological activity 'smaller' companies tend to catch up with the leading pioneers. Instead technologically mature industries seem to show a more concentrated pattern of technological development. In these industries the slower growth rate of technological opportunities appears to call for corporate consolidation of technological profiles.

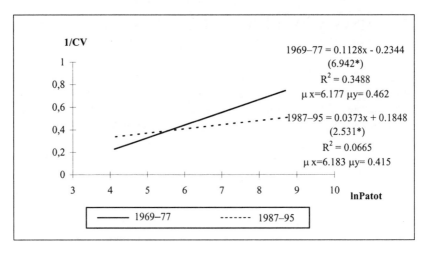

Source: Cantwell and Santangelo (2000).

Figure 3.1 – Estimated regression lines for the Chemicals n.e.s. and Pharmaceuticals industry, 1969–77, 1987–95

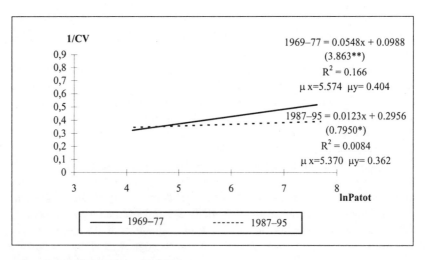

Source: Cantwell and Santangelo (2000).

Figure 3.2 – Estimated regression lines for the Metals and Mechanical engineering industry, 1969–77, 1987–95

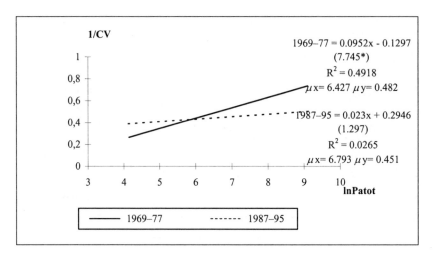

Source: Cantwell and Santangelo (2000).

Figure 3.3 – Estimated regression lines for the Electrical equipment n.e.s. and Office equipment industry, 1969–77, 1987–95

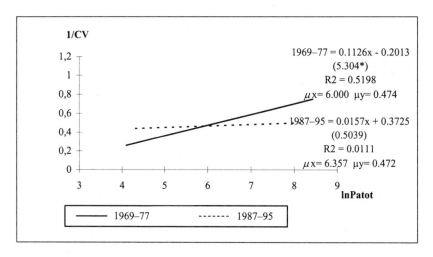

Source: Cantwell and Santangelo (2000).

Figure 3.4 – Estimated regression lines for the Motor vehicles industry, 1969–77 and 1987–95

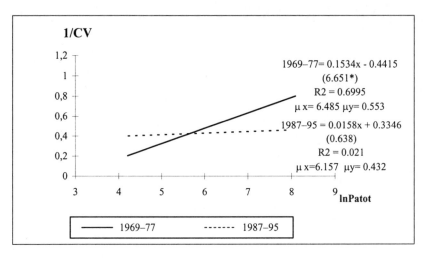

Source: Cantwell and Santangelo (2000).

Figure 3.5 – Estimated regression lines for the Coal and petroleum products industry, 1969–77, 1987–95

In more dynamic technological environments (e.g. science-based and related industries), 'smaller' firms have been obliged not merely to internationalise their technology base, but for similar reasons to exploit new areas of technological interrelatedness through corporate technological diversification (Cantwell and Piscitello, 1999). Greater interrelatedness between formerly distinct fields of technology and the process of technological fusion (Kodama, 1992a, 1992b) may have been a source of pressure for greater diversification. Technological fusion enables companies to establish new and closer technological complementarities between different fields of innovation to cope with the increasing technological complexity and shortening life cycles. The importance of a technological profile broader than the corporate product profiles has been argued in the literature (Granstrand and Oskarsson, 1994; Granstrand, 1996; Granstrand et al., 1997; Patel and Pavitt, 1997) as a multi-product firm needs to be multi-technology. Growing firms are increasing diversifying in order to develop competencies 'distributed' across a large number of fields. Granstrand and Sjölander (1990) demonstrate that technological diversification is positively associated with product diversification, thus corporations need to have broader technological competencies in comparison to their range of products. As von Tunzelmann (1995) points out, technological knowledge must be shared between fields to produce a single product. This is especially true in the modern techno–economic conditions grounded in information and communications technology, computerisation, and flexible (more complex) production systems, in which the local linkages between science and technology have become more intensive than they were in the past, and increasingly run across a wide range of formerly separate disciplines. A broader technological diversity is likely to lead firms to explore new technological opportunities by enhancing their 'core' competencies. Thus, in addition to 'core' or 'distinctive' technological competencies, a multi-technology corporation should develop competencies, which are distributed across a largely increasing number of technical fields in its geographically dispersed locations, and around its strategic targets (Granstrand et al., 1997). In this sense the overall move towards diversification of 'smaller' and hence initially less diversified firms might be explained as a result of technological 'fusion' between formerly unrelated technologies. In this process ICT has been both an agent and a catalyst by establishing new areas of technological interconnectedness in the way the capital good sector did in the mechanisation era of the past (Rosenberg, 1976). Technological fusion facilitated in the current techno–economic conditions by ICT has created new opportunities for diversification for firms that were relatively little diversified before. This enables 'smaller' firms to experiment with a greater 'coherence' of technological combinations by rationalising their technological profiles.

As far as 'larger' firms are concerned, the findings of a move towards greater consolidation of technological profiles are consistent with Markides' analysis (1995a, 1995b). The author argues that during the 1960s–1980s large conglomerates diversified beyond their limits. However since the 1980s overdiversified firms have refocused[3] whilst the undiversified firms have increased their diversification. Markides also finds a relationship between the likelihood of refocusing and the firm's R&D intensity. Every firm has an intrinsic limit to how much it can diversify, which depends on its resources. Therefore large firms that diversify beyond their 'limits' into unrelated areas are most likely to run into some forms of diseconomies (e.g. managerial diseconomies of scale). In the analysis of this trend, von Tunzelmann's argument (1995) on the difference between product and technology diversification should be taken into account. Over time, product diversification seems to narrow in comparison with the expansion of technological diversification. The cause of this phenomenon is identified in the increasing technological fusion and interrelatedness. Andersen (1998) demonstrates that the new information age governing the evolution paths of technological trajectories builds to a greater extent on inter-group complementarity and interrelatedness rather than more isolated individual channels of development. This new technological environment enables companies to consolidate their technological profiles in the recent period. By taking advantage of the new possible technological combinations, firms expand in related areas. A firm is more likely to be successful if it efficiently co-ordinates interrelated assets and activities (Penrose, 1959). That is, if it follows a 'coherent' diversification. Evidence has been provided by the literature about purposive (Scott and Pascoe, 1987) and 'coherent' (Montgomery and Hariharan, 1991; Teece et al., 1994; Piscitello, 1998; Silverman, 1999) diversification. Cantwell and Andersen (1999) demonstrate empirically that a firm's technological position in space changes only in a path-dependent manner. Accordingly Foss and Christensen (1996) have argued that complementarity may determine sustained competitive advantage. In the overall refocusing of larger companies, the greater technological interrelatedness between formerly separated branches of technology and the process of technology fusion should be taken into account. Technological fusion encourages a greater focus of effort in the largest firms, in and around those sectors which have become most closely interrelated to one another and to the core strengths of the firm. Thus giant companies show greater 'coherence' by moving into new related activities over time. In refocusing on their core competencies, they are now exploring technological paths more related to their corporate expertises.

The findings of these two different groups of firms seem to be consistent with the second major result of the regression analysis. A 'target' degree of diversification can be identified from the plots of the regression lines. For each industrial group analysed, Table 3.1 reports the average values of 1/CV and lnPatot in each of the sub-periods considered. Focusing on the average value of 1/CV over time, across the industries analysed the degrees of diversification seem to converge on average.

Across all five industries there seems to be a clear 'target' degree of technological diversification in the later period, to which most firms aspire and which can be identified as occurring at an average value of around 0.43 per cent. Thus 0.43 per cent is the total average diversification value in 1987–95 across industrial groups. This value represents the optimal balance between diversification and consolidation, which firms strive to maintain across industries. Similarly Bachmann (1998) finds a corporate convergence towards an 'industrial optimum' of technological diversification in the case of the British and German pharmaceutical industry. The author argues that 'smaller' firms have not yet reached their 'optimal' balance of diversification, thus continuing to diversify, while larger corporations appear to have been consolidating their technological competencies to a persistent level of specialisation. A similar cross-company convergence in the level of technological diversification has also been found recently by Piscitello (1998), and by Cantwell and Bachmann (1998) in the case of the pharmaceutical industry. This seems to suggest that firms aim at a level of diversification specific to the industry in which they operate and the target level of diversification converges across industrial groups. Graphically, this argument can be illustrated by considering the intersection point between the two regression lines in Figures 3.1, 3.2, 3.3, 3.4 and 3.5. Firms lying on the left of the intersection point have diversified and still need to diversify towards the industrial optimum level. Companies lying to the right of this point show a more concentrated specialisation pattern as a result of an over-diversification in the past. As reported in Table 3.1, the mean values of the 1/CV and the log of technological size lie just to the right of the intersection point, thus supporting this interpretation of the co-existence of one group of firms with increasing diversification (below size), and another with a greater concentration of effort (above the mean size). The former have not yet reached the industrial 'optimal' balance of technological diversification, and thus continue to diversify. The latter appear to have been consolidating their technological competencies to a persistent level of specialisation.

Table 3.1 – The mean values of the regressand variables in the industries analysed

Industry	Average $1/CV_{(1969-77)}$	Average $1/CV_{(1987-95)}$	Average $lnPatot_{(1969-77)}$	Average $lnPatot_{(1987-95)}$
Chemicals n.e.s. and Pharmaceuticals	0.46	0.42	6.18	6.18
Metals and Mechanical engineering	0.40	0.36	5.57	5.37
Electrical equipment n.e.s. and Office equipment	0.48	0.45	6.43	6.79
Motor vehicles	0.47	0.47	6.00	6.36
Coal and petroleum products	0.55	0.43	6.49	6.16
Total average	0.48	0.43	6.13	6.17

Source: Cantwell and Santangelo (2000).

In the current more integrated technological system, the achievement of a balanced portfolio between greater concentration and dispersion of technological capabilities may enable firms to exploit new, fresh technological opportunities. The new trend toward a balanced technological portfolio between consolidation and diversification may have marked the end of the conventional R&D laboratory by creating the need for an overall corporate management of technology to pursue synergy and corporate 'coherence' (Christensen, 1998). This change in technology management is reflected by the move in corporate organisation from a 'pure' M-form to a more decentralised M-form (Markides, 1995a) or more extreme heterarchical N-forms (Hedlund, 1992, Ridderstråle, 1992) (see Chapter 2). The 'pure' M-form is consistent with a strategy of unrelated diversification in order to realise financial economies, but not with related diversification (Christensen, 1998). The latter strategy requires a degree of central co-ordination and internationalisation, which can be better provided in more decentralised, if not heterachical, forms of organisation (Argyres, 1996).

3.4   CONCLUSIONS

This chapter reaches two main results. First of all, it confirms that the size–diversification relationship, although still valid, has changed in its nature. As demonstrated empirically by Cantwell and Fai (1999b), diversification may be increasingly associated with technological interrelatedness rather than with size in the most recent period. This finding challenges the Chandlerian concept of growth (1990). Over time, firms pursued competitiveness by adopting business which appeared to have great potential growth, although involving competencies sometimes unrelated to their own capabilities (Chandler, 1992). Empirical evidence from the recent period seems to show that firms are more concerned about diversifying in related fields in order to use the existing capabilities to attain economies of scope (Piscitello, 1998). This trend is here explained by the changes in the technological environment.

Following Andersen (1998), historically it is possible to identify a shift away from intragroup technological diversification and the formation of a structure of specialised engineering and science-based fields towards more integrated technological diversification (i.e. inter-group diversification). In the most recent period, the author finds that the gap between the science-based technologies (i.e. chemicals and electronic) and the engineering-based and non-industrial technologies has been widening less quickly. Technological 'convergence' in corporate technological diversification across large firms is facilitated by the now common spread in the use of information and communication technologies as integrators of formerly separate technological systems. The integration of previously disparate technologies does not refer only to computers and communications, but to mechanical industries and electronics ('mechatronics') or to 'robochemistry', the science of applying computerisation to drug molecule research, which according to some accounts is leading to a new age in medicine (Teece,

1998). This development leads 'smaller' firms to diversify in order to enhance their technological and product advantage. Conversely, the increased technological complexity in the information age leads giant firms to consolidate activity around those technologies that have become most interrelated (Cantwell and Santangelo, 2000). The former case is consistent with the corporate need to expand technologically in new areas to perform better in product specialisation. The latter case is mainly due to the fact that large firms have pushed their resources' limit too far by moving into unrelated areas. This has forced them to refocus on their core business and pursue technological paths more 'coherent' with their resource portfolio. Unrelated diversification may affect corporate organisation by creating managerial co-ordination problems. The lack of both organisational and technological capabilities is likely to affect the firm's market and technological performance.

The distinction between smaller diversifying firms and large rationalising corporations seems to follow a cross-industry pattern as this distinction is found in science-based (e.g. Chemicals n.e.s. and Pharmaceuticals, Electrical equipment n.e.s. and Office equipment, Coal and petroleum products) and related (e.g. Motor vehicles), but lacking in mature industries (Metals and Mechanical engineering). The latter is identified with mechanical industries characterised by relative technological ease of entry, and mechanical continuous erosion in competitive and technological advantages of established firms. The former is identified with science-based industries characterised by relevant barriers to entry for new innovators and continuous innovative leadership of few firms based on their cumulative technological capabilities. In the mature industries, the features of the industrial structure as described by Malerba and Orsenigo (1996, 1997) and the slower rate of technological opportunities (Cantwell and Andersen, 1996) shape a more concentrated path of technological development according to firm size. Conversely, in science-based industries, the industrial structure (Malerba and Orsenigo, 1996, 1997) and the faster rate of technological opportunities (Cantwell and Andersen, 1996) promote paths of technological development different between 'small' and 'large' corporations.

The second finding concerns the identification of a 'target' degree of technological diversification, at which both smaller and larger firms aim. The econometric analysis allows one to identify a cross-industry convergence in diversification over time. As in other studies (Cantwell and Bachmann, 1998; Bachmann, 1998; Piscitello, 1998), the results confirm the firms' attempt to reach an 'optimal' balance of technological diversification. The opportunities opened up by the current more integrated technological systems enable firms to converge towards the target level of diversification in order to take advantage of the increased related technological development. Therefore over time firms still seem to attach great significance to technological diversification. This has been explained by the corporate need for technological portfolios broader than product portfolios amidst a general background of increasing technological interrelatedness and fusion. These phenomena push firms toward more related diversification strategies. A firm engaging in random diversification is likely to experience difficulties due to the lack of competencies in the newly acquired fields. For this reason, the changes in the nature of technological diversification are linked to the changes in the nature of organisational capabilities (Pavitt, 1998). The new technological and competitive environment has altered the organisational form by promoting the organisational shift from the divisionalised M-from to the heterarchical N-form (Hedlund and Rolander, 1990; Hedlund, 1992; Ridderstråle, 1992, 1996; Hedlund and Ridderstråle, 1995; Argyres, 1996). However, firms can no longer rely fully on their internal organisation. The development of inter-firm relationships is an important factor in order to cope with the speed of learning required to assimilate a diverse range of complementary but different capabilities usefully. Networks and other inter-firm arrangements can provide better access to other firms' capabilities, otherwise hardly sustainable by a single firm by itself (Loasby, 1994, 1998).

The industrial trends revealed by the econometric results of the present chapter in terms of corporate technological specialisation seem to call for a better understanding of the relationships between spatial and sectoral development of corporate technology in the information age. This issue is analysed in the next chapter.

NOTES

1. The relation is given by $H = (CV2 + 1)/n$, where 'n' is the number of sectors in the distribution. Thus, the use of the CV here for a fixed 'n' is in practice equivalent to the Herfindahl Index (see Hart, 1971). CV has been adopted as a measure of technological concentration/dispersion in other empirical studies at firm level (Cantwell and Fai, 1999a, 1999b; Cantwell and Piscitello, 1997, 1999, 2000), at industry level (Cantwell and Andersen, 1996) and at country level (Vertova, 1998b).
2. The 'Motor vehicles' industry shows intensive links with science-based industries (e.g. 'Electrical equipment n.e.s. and Office equipment') in terms of application of innovations and technological development.
3. The term is used by the author in reference to corporate decisions to reduce the scope of the firm's activities in order to concentrate on the 'core' business (Markides, 1995a).

4. Globalisation and innovation management

4.1 INTRODUCTION

This chapter concludes Part One by examining the relationships between the phenomena of corporate technological internationalisation and specialisation analysed in Chapters 2 and 3 respectively. The aim of the present chapter is to test whether an increased specialisation in ICT as a new core pervasive technology may have promoted an extension of the firm's international network. Following Archibugi and Michie (1995), it is investigated whether the increasing worldwide phenomenon of generation, transmission and diffusion of technology is influenced by fast-rising technological opportunities in microelectronics and computerised systems, which the current techno–socio–economic conditions have opened up.

The increase in international integration of the affiliates networks of MNCs can be historically located in the era of declining American world leadership contemporary with the rise of new technological leaders such as Japan and the Newly Industrialising Countries (NICs) (Dunning, 1994; Amin and Thrift, 1995). In the current age of capitalism, globalisation is taking place through 'globe-standing networks of transnational corporations and high levels of foreign direct investment between and among nations' (Florida, 1995, 529). Although globalisation has led to more open technological systems, the local dimension still plays an important role, when looking at the technological and geographical diversification of multinational R&D facilities (Papanastassiou and Pearce, 1997). The geographical dispersion of R&D activity has been adopted as a strategy to tap into alternative sources of knowledge.

Besides the flexibility provided by ICT specialisation (in general) and computerisation (in particular) in promoting the development of just-in-time distribution skills and consequent geographical dispersion (Bordeau et al., 1998), an analysis focusing on ICT should consider at least two interrelated ways in which ICT specialisation can influence corporate internationalisation.

A first way can be identified in the fact that the shift into ICT has played a great role in strengthening the globalisation of economic activity by providing a new mode of diversification. Since innovations tend to cluster together, in each major cluster, it is possible to identify a core technology underpinning the innovation processes (Rosenberg, 1976; Freeman and Perez, 1988). In the current technological era, ICT can be identified as the leading pervasive technology playing this role. ICT specialisation leads to an ability to fuse together different kinds of technology across national boundaries in an intra-firm network.

The increasing process of technological interrelatedness may be understood as a second consequent avenue influencing the geographical dispersion of R&D facilities. The growing pace of technological change in ICT has doubtless provoked the rise of 'techno-globalism' (Archibugi and Michie, 1995) at a cross-firm level as a result of technological interrelatedness. Andersen (1998) suggests a historical shift towards more integrated technological systems through the fusion of diverse and formerly separated branches of technology. Thus the specialisation in a core pervasive technology (such as ICT nowadays) allows the firm to develop tacit capabilities, which, in turn, facilitates its corporate activity in different kinds of technology across national boundaries through an intra-firm network organisation. In this context, following on the grounds of a previous study (Santangelo, 2001) two hypotheses are tested:

Hypothesis 1: An increase in corporate specialisation in ICT (broadly defined – computing + communications) leads to a growing internationalisation of R&D activity over time by facilitating technological diversification.

Furthermore given the distinctive features of computing and communications, the analysis goes further by testing the association between increasing specialisation in ICT and growing internationalisation at more detailed levels of sectoral aggregation. Within the ICT field a distinction is made between computing and communications technology in order to assess the weight of each of these two components on internationalisation over time. In fact, within the broad ICT realm computing and communications specialisation may have a different impact on corporate international diversification due to the wider applicability of computing over communications in both product and production processes. Similarly, computing and communication specialisation may impact differently on the firm's ability to explore new related technological combinations across geographically distant centres of excellence due to the fact that the former (rather than the later) specialisation may allow for a more effective exploitation of new technological opportunities.

Hypothesis 2: Within the broad field of ICT, by distinguishing between greater specialisation in computing and in communications, the former (rather than the latter) technology leads to greater internationalisation of research activity.

This argument is consistent with the resource-based view of the firm, which understands the firm as an institution developing capabilities through an internal learning process that needs to extend them into new related activities and new geographical locations (Penrose, 1959). The competitive argument leads to diversification strategies in both industrial and geographical terms (Zander, 1996). Industrial diversification involves multi-products and multi-technology operations based upon technological inter-relatedness. Geographical diversification concerns gradual internationalisation of advanced technological capabilities and increasing entropy within the international innovation network. Cantwell and Piscitello (1997, 2000) demonstrate that the two dimensions are complementary one to another. For the sake of competition, multinational firms have to gain access to paths of technological development complementary to their core competencies. Therefore they establish global affiliate networks, which are strategically located in host countries characterised by high-quality competencies in special technological fields (among the other location advantage factors). In fact the entrepreneurial subsidiary, defined as world (or regional) product mandate (Papanastassiou and Pearce, 1994), adopts operations which enable the whole multinational company to tap into a much wider range of resources as an integrated part of their global activity. In these terms multinationals maintain and increase their competitive advantage by geographically dispersing research facilities according to nations' and regions' specific streams of knowledge (Cantwell, 1995).

The chapter is organised into five sections. Section 4.2 illustrates the econometric methodology. The section explains the measures used and sheds some light on the model adopted. Section 4.3 reports and discusses the empirical results of the regression analysis. Section 4.4 investigates the role of technological diversification and interrelatedness. Section 4.5 summarises the main findings and conclusions.

4.2   METHODOLOGICAL NOTES

In this chapter the relationship between corporate ICT specialisation and internationalisation is investigated with a cross-sectional regression model at firm level. Yet, before venturing into the exploration of the model, the measures adopted must be presented.

The RTA index (previously described in section 1.4) is used as a proxy for technological specialisation. The index is calculated as a weighted average at two different levels of sectoral aggregation (i.e. 'k' and 'm') as summarised in Table 4.1.

Table 4.1 – Levels of aggregations

k level of aggregation	m level of aggregation
Communications sectors	* telecommunications * other electrical communication systems * special radio systems * image and sound equipment
Computing sectors	* semiconductors * office equipment and data processing systems

Source: Santangelo (2001).

At the first level of aggregation:

$$RTA_{ik} = (P_{ik}/\Sigma_i P_{ik}) / (\Sigma_k P_{ik}/\Sigma_{ik} P_{ik}) \qquad (4.1)$$

where (*i*) indicates the firm and (*k*) is equal to either communications technological sectors ('telecommunications', 'other electrical communications systems', 'special radio systems', 'image and sound equipment') or computing sectors ('semiconductors' and 'office equipment and data processing systems'). In the former case

$$RTACM_i = RTA_{ik} \qquad (4.2)$$

whilst, in the latter,

$$RTACP_i = RTA_{ik} \qquad (4.3)$$

At the broadest level of aggregation:

$$RTA_{im} = (P_{im}/\Sigma_i P_{im}) / (\Sigma_m P_{im}/\Sigma_{im} P_{im}) \qquad (4.4)$$

where *m* is equal to all the ICT technological sectors (i.e. communications + computing as specified above). Thus

$$RTAICT_i = RTA_{im} \qquad (4.5)$$

Instead the foreign patent share (FS), which is fully explained in Chapter 3, is adopted as a proxy for internationalisation of technological activity. This measure of internationalisation here is defined as the share of total patenting of firm (i) that is attributable to research or other technological activity located outside the home country relative to its portfolio. Thus

$$FS_i = \Sigma_j FP_{ij} / \Sigma_j P_{ij} \qquad (4.6)$$

where FP_{ij} indicates the number of US patents granted for research conducted outside the home country of the parent firm to firm (i) in one of the usual 56 technological sectors (j), whilst P_{ij} denotes the number of US patents granted in the same sectoral activity (j) to the same firm (i).

The entire period considered (1969–95) is divided into the usual three sub-periods:

- 1969–77 (sub-period 1),
- 1978–86 (sub-period 2) and
- 1987–95 (sub-period 3).

The data are classified by the world's largest firms holding at least 60 patents in each of the three sub-periods. Firms with null values in their FS in the sub-periods 1979–86 and 1987–95 are excluded from the analysis in order to consider only internationally dispersed firms. Accordingly firms with a growth patenting rate of less than –100 between the first sub-period and the second and between the second and the third are eliminated as declining firms. Similarly in 1969–77 and 1978–86, GKN and Asahi Glass are dropped from the sample of analysis as special cases of R&D geographical dispersion. The geographical dispersion of research activity of the former is due to a strategy of international acquisition rather than to an increase in corporate ICT specialisation. The British company restructured its specialisation profile in automotive components and non-manufacturing business by acquiring Parts Industries Corporation of Memphis, Tennessee, Unigep Group of France, Amstrong Autoparts and Sheepbridge Engineering (Hast, 1991). If this strategy promotes further specialisation in the automotive sectors, it also enhanced corporate internationalisation. Conversely in the overseas expansion of Asahi Glass, the increase in ICT corporate competencies played a major role. The introduction of a process innovation in the glass industry eroded the competitive advantage of the Japanese firm which, so far, had been an international exporter of this product. The new conditions in the glass industry pushed Asahi to diversify internationally outside the glass market by expanding its chemical and electronics business (ibid.). This goal was met through an increased specialisation in ICT technology.

Thus the sample of analysis counts 195 and 231 companies respectively in the periods 1969–77/1978–86 and 1978–86/1987–95, as listed in Table A.1. After having identified the variables, the ICT specialisation–internationalisation relationship is investigated with a cross-firm regression model in the periods 1969–77/1978–86 and 1978–86/1987–95. In the first instance the association between the specialisation in all ICT technological sectors and the geographical dispersion of R&D activities is taken into account. Then the ICT technological field is broken into communications and computing in order to assess the weight of each of these two components on the changes in FS_i. Thus in the first period (1969–77/1978–86) the model takes the following form:

$$\Delta FS_i = \alpha + \beta_1 \Delta RTAICT_i + \beta_2 D_{(CA)} \Delta RTAICT_i + \varepsilon_i \qquad (4.7)$$

where

(i)	=	1, 2,..., 195;
ΔFS_i	=	absolute changes in FS of each firm (i) in the sample between 1969–77 and 1978–86;
$\Delta RTAICT_i$	=	absolute changes in the RTA index calculated across the ICT sectors for each firm (i) in the sample between 1969–77 and 1978–86;
$D_{(CA)} \Delta RTAICT_i$	=	Canadian firms slope dummy;

$$\Delta FS_i = \alpha + \beta_1 \Delta RTACM_i + \beta_2 \Delta RTACP_i + \beta_3 D_{(CA)} \Delta RTACM_i + \varepsilon_i \quad (4.8)$$

where

(i)	=	1, 2, ..., 195;
$\Delta RTACM_i$	=	absolute changes in the RTA index calculated across the communications sectors for each firm (i) in the sample between 1969–77 and 1978–86;
$\Delta RTACP_i$	=	absolute changes in the RTA index calculated across the computing sectors for each firm (i) in the sample between 1969–77 and 1978–86.

In the second period (1978–86/1987–95), the regression model is specified as:

$$\Delta FS_i = \alpha + \beta_1 \Delta RTAICT_i + \beta_2 D_{(FRCPI)} \Delta RTAICT_i +$$

$$+ \beta_3 D_{(UKCPI)} \Delta RTAICT_i + \beta_4 D_{(SEMI)} \Delta RTAICT_i + \varepsilon_i \qquad (4.9)$$

where

(i)	$= 1, 2, \ldots, 231$
ΔFS_i	= absolute changes in FS of each firm (i) in the sample between 1978–86 and 1987–95;
$\Delta RTAICT_i$	= absolute changes in the RTA index calculated across the ICT sectors for each firm (i) in the sample between 1978–86 and 1987–95;
$D_{(FRCPI)} \Delta RTAICT_i$	= French computing industry slope dummy;
$D_{(UKCPI)} \Delta RTAICT_i$	= British computing industry slope dummy;
$D_{(SEMI)} \Delta RTAICT_i$	= Swedish mechanical industry slope dummy.

$$\Delta FS_i = \alpha + \beta_1 \Delta RTACM_i + \beta_2 \Delta RTACP_i + \beta_3 D_{(FRCPI)} \Delta RTACP_i + \varepsilon_i \quad (4.10)$$

where $(i) = 1, 2, \ldots, 231$ and all other variables have the same meaning as specified above.

In each of the periods 1969–77/1977–86 and 1978–86/1987–95 at each of the two levels of sectoral aggregation (i.e. 'k' and 'm') dummy variables are introduced to account for qualitative phenomena. In the first period considered at both levels of sectoral aggregation, a country's significance of domestic resources and the consequent firms' resource-based advantage (rather than ICT specialisation) can explain the increasing geographical dispersion of Canadian corporate research activity (Rugman, 1987). Canadian companies have based their corporate advantage on national resources rather than high technological competencies. Their approach to global competition is mainly linked to corporate development of exclusive marketing and managerial skills as well as distribution networks. The absence of such a control variable in the latter period considered may be explained by the mid-1980s domestic crisis in Canada as well as by the conclusions of the NAFTA agreement. Both events forced to Canadian companies to move up the value chain and proceed to the restructuring of the composition of the country's export by strengthening their technological base (Leyton-Brown, 1994; Molot, 1994).

Turning to the period 1978–86/1987–95, at both levels of sectoral aggregation the internationalisation of the French computing industry appears to be better explained by French domestic policy. In the 1960s and 1970s French firms were the least internationalised in comparison with their European competitors (Cantwell and Kotecha, 1994, Caron, 1995). The implementation of high-technology based national projects (e.g. Minitel, Telecom1 and TDF1), supported by a new kind of public policy approach (i.e. 'colbertisme high-tech'), met the goal and later the national champions became powerful multinational enterprises (e.g. Thomson, GCE and CII-Honeywell Bull) (Cohen, 1992, Caron, 1995). However whilst in the case of the French communications companies (e.g. Thomson and GCE) R&D internationalisation went hand in hand with an increased in ICT specialisation, still in the 1980s and in the early 1990s the internationalisation of research conducted within the computing industry (e.g. CII-Honeywell Bull) depends on political factors (Hast, 1991). This result suggests that the French 'colbertisme high-tech' was more successful in boosting communications rather than computing national companies. The case of the British computing industry is somehow different. Unlike the French state-driven approach, UK public policy was inspired to liberalisation and privatisation. Although this environment pushed British companies to develop a competitive R&D activity without any public incentive, corporate internationalisation seems to be mainly due to foreign acquisitions – as shown by the take-over of ICL by Fujitsu in 1990 – rather than by an increased in ICT technological competencies. Yet, the late 1980s increase in the internationalisation of R&D activity by Swedish mechanical firms can be read in the context of a massive acquisition strategy dictated by structural changes in the economy of the country (Fors, 1998) rather than in the context of an enhancement of the industry comparative technological advantage in ICT. In fact in Sweden recent decades have witnessed the progressive establishment of a more service-oriented and knowledge-based society, which has gone hand in hand with the fading importance of more traditional sectors. In the late 1980s the shifting away from manufacturing based on raw materials (e.g. steel production, dairy and agricultural equipment, etc.) to production based on highly skilled workers corresponded with a high-cost and labour shortage situation, and consequent high inflation (de Vylder, 1996). This particular situation, together with the dimension of the local market (Ivarsson, 1996), affected the mechanical industrial sectors rather than others, which were either riding the technological wave (e.g. telecommunications) or being the target of regulatory reforms (e.g. the services sector). Therefore Swedish mechanical companies internationalised their activity as a consequence of difficulty in expanding in the domestic market – due to the current techno–economic situation – as well as of the recognised importance of being represented in foreign markets – dictated by the need of this industry to carry out development work close to its customers. This goal was accomplished through merger and acquisition strategies (Granstrand et al., 1992, Zander, 1994, 1998) rather than through an increase in technological competencies in ICT and related fields.

4.3   MNCs AND THE NEW AVENUES TO TECHNOLOGICAL GLOBALISATION

Cross-firm regressions are run in order to test whether an association between the increased specialisation in the new leading technology in the microelectronic era and the process of technological globalisation exists. In the first instance, all selected ICT technological sectors are taken into account ('m' level of aggregation), then, a distinction is made between communications and computing technology ('k' level of aggregation) in order to evaluate the association between each of the latter and the dependent variable. As reported in Tables 4.4 and 4.5, at both levels of aggregation, it is found that changes in internationalisation (ΔFS_i) are correlated with changes in technological specialisation in the ICT sectors considered as a whole ($\Delta RTAICT_i$) in the period 1978–86/1987–95, but not in the previous period (Tables 4.2 and 4.3). Therefore Hypotheses 1 and 2 are confirmed in the later period considered, but not in the previous (Tables 4.4 and 4.5, and 4.2 and 4.3 respectively).

Table 4.2 – Results of the regression in equation 4.7

	Coefficient	Standard Error	t-Ratio	
$\Delta RTAICT_i$	0.580	0.423	1.370	
$D_{(CA)}\Delta RTAICT_i$	−20.389	4.186	−4.871	***
Intercept	1.334	0.499	2.671	***
R^2	0.113			
Adjusted R^2	0.104			
No. of observations	195			

Note:
*** significant at 1% level.

Source: Santangelo (2001).

Table 4.3 – Results of the regression in equation 4.8

	Coefficient	Standard Error	t-Ratio	
$\Delta RTACM_i$	0.291	0.311	0.935	
$\Delta RTACP_i$	0.161	0.345	0.466	
$D_{(CA)}\Delta RTACM_i$	−17.920	3.441	−5.208	***
Intercept	1.248	0.498	2.505	**
R^2	0.127			
Adjusted R^2	0.113			
No. of observations	195			

Notes:
*** significant at 1% level.
** significant at 5% level.

Source: Santangelo (2001).

Table 4.4 – Results of the regression in equation 4.9

	Coefficient	Standard Error	t-Ratio	
$\Delta RTAICT_i$	1.635	0.773	2.116	**
$D_{(FRCPI)}\Delta RTAICT_i$	−231.189	43.073	−5.367	***
$D_{(UKCPI)}\Delta RTAICT_i$	−61.976	25.612	−2.420	**
$D_{(SEMI)}\Delta RTAICT_i$	−93.257	33.966	−2.7456	***
Intercept	2.619	0.682	3.839	***
R^2	0.170			
Adjusted R^2	0.155			
No. of observations	231			

Notes:
*** significant at 1% level.
** significant at 5% level.

Source: Santangelo (2001).

Table 4.5 – Results of the regression in equation 4.10

	Coefficient	Standard Error	t-Ratio	
$\Delta RTACM_i$	−1.121	0.880	−1.274	
$\Delta RTACP_i$	1.601	0.451	3.554	***
$D_{(FRCPI)}\Delta RTACP_i$	−67.741	12.835	−5.4264	***
Intercept	2.582	0.681	3.793	***
R^2	0.153			
Adjusted R^2	0.142			
No. of observations	231			

Note:
*** significant at 1% level.

Source: Santangelo (2001).

The results seem to suggest that the two phenomena occurred independently of each other in the 1970s, whilst they appear to be linked only in the mid-1980s. Radical new technologies such as ICT have long gestation periods before their characteristics and opportunities are understood and exploited (Rosenberg, 1996). In this sense the period 1969–77/1978–86 may be identified as a gestation period during which potential developments of the new ICT technology were explored. In the ICT era, this 'exploratory' stage seems to have led to an increase in technology fusion between formerly unrelated technological fields over time (Kodama, 1992a, 1992b). In her analysis of a century of technological development Andersen (1998) remarks that the shift from a technological epoch of intragroup divergence in the three biggest broad technological groups – chemicals, electrical/electronic and mechanical – to an epoch of inter-group convergence can be chronologically located in the 1960s. Andersen (ibid.) demonstrates empirically that new paradigms governing the evolutionary paths of technological trajectories build to a greater extent on inter-group complementary and interrelatedness rather than more isolated individual channels of development. In the period 1969–77/1978–86 the absence of a relationship between a growth in the corporate share of foreign R&D and firms' increased specialisation in ICT may be due to the early development of an inter-group model of technological development. Increasingly science–technology linkages run across a wide range of formerly separate disciplines. In this context ICT can be viewed as a 'transmission belt' for innovation between formerly separate economic activities in the way in which the capital good sector was in the mechanisation era of the past (Rosenberg, 1976). In the later period considered ICT seems to play a major role in establishing new areas of interconnectedness (Cantwell and Santangelo, 2000). Due to the cumulative character of technology, the inter-group model of technological change appears to be fully established in the mid-1980s. This promoted the increase in specialisation in ICT and the consequent impact on corporate internationalisation of R&D activity. If increasingly higher technological expertise in ICT may provide manufacturing companies with a greater incentive to source technologies internationally, it strengthens the technological core of electrical corporations and in particular their ability to source diverse technologies across national boundaries. Given the complex nature of contemporary technological interdependence, technological specialisation in ICT opens new windows on new kinds of technology close to the firm's core fields and, likewise, enables it to exploit technological skills or promising market applications. The opportunities created for the fusion of formerly unrelated types of technology through ICT have made feasible new combinations of activities, the best centres of expertise for which may be geographically distant from one another. Therefore a growing firm needs to specialise in ICT in order to improve technological development in its own fields of interest or in related fields.

Firm-specific technological competencies in ICT led to corporate internationalisation by facilitating technological diversification. Technological diversification arose as corporate imperative as a consequence of the more intensive local linkages between science and technology in the most recent period. Large firms are increasingly more broadly diversified in their technological competencies in comparison with their range of products (Granstrand and Sjölander, 1990; Granstrand and Oskarsson, 1994; Granstrand, 1996; Granstrand et al., 1997; Patel and Pavitt, 1997). The development of competencies distributed across a large number of technical fields and geographical locations (Granstrand et al., 1997) enables multi-technology corporations to explore new technological opportunities. The full establishment of the inter-group model of technological development enables corporations to increase their capabilities in core technologies (e.g. ICT) in order to enhance their business performance. ICT specialisation seems to amplify the firm's technological flexibility by enabling it to fuse together a wider range of formerly separate technologies. However, since knowledge diffusion is spatially bounded, MNCs gain an important source of competitive advantage by dispersing their R&D geographically. It follows that geographical dispersion of research activity provides access to new lines of innovation. Therefore an international technological strategy enables the firm to benefit from dynamic economies of scale arising from technological complementarities between related activities, and complementarities between corporate learning in different institutional environments. In this sense technological internationalisation effects can be captured through corporate diversification. A mainstream chemical company, for instance, needs to develop knowledge skills in many diverse areas (such as electronics and biotechnology) in order to succeed in its own production systems, even if it does not intend to enter markets which are most directly connected with the principal products of these fields (see Chapter 3).

This is all the more true in the case of increased specialisation in computing technology. As suggested by the results of the regression analysis, in the later period considered, the internationalisation of research activity is linked with increased specialisation in computing technology, but not in communications. This may be due to the rising pervasiveness of the former technology within the information age. Although little evidence is provided on the convergence between communications and computing in a unique technological sector (Duysters and Hagedoorn, 1995a, 1998), different industries come to share similar technological bases through a process of 'creative combination' that builds on complementary kinds of technology (Yoffie, 1997). The enhanced expertise in computing technology seems to provide a company with greater flexibility in the management of its geographically dispersed network, and an enhanced ability to combine distant learning processes in formerly separate activities. If this is the case for manufacturing companies in general, it is all the more true for electronic equipment and ICT specialist companies. Accordingly the current managerial problem is to combine the pervasiveness of digital technology with the increasing multi-technology base required in the production process. As more and more technologies are incorporated into each particular product, companies need to reshape in the face of these external changes by adjusting what they do and how they do it internally (von Tunzelmann, 1999). The establishment of these new technological conditions has pushed multinational corporations to revise both their internal organisation and also their technological strategy by dispersing their R&D divisions geographically (see Chapter 2).

4.4 THE TWO AVENUES: TECHNOLOGICAL DIVERSIFICATION AND INTERRELATEDNESS

The results of the regression analysis seem to suggest that the effects of the geographical dispersion of research activity may be captured through diversification in the period 1978–86/1987–95. As in Chapter 3, for each firm $1/CV_i$ calculated across the usual 56 technological sectors is adopted as a proxy for corporate technological diversification. Time is accounted for by considering the absolute changes in $1/CV_i$ ($\Delta 1/CV_i$) between the sub-periods 1978–86 and 1987–95. To introduce diversification into the story, for each of the broadly defined industrial groups (CEMTind classification), a Pearson's correlation coefficient is calculated between $\Delta 1/CV_i$, $\Delta RTAICT_i$, $\Delta RTACM_i$ and $\Delta RTACP_i$. By focusing the correlation analysis on the period in which statistically significant results are obtained from the regression analysis (i.e. 1978–86/1987–95), four correlation matrices are built, as reported in Table 4.6.

Table 4.6 – Correlation matrix, 1978–86/1987–95

Broadly defined chemical industrial group		
	$\Delta RTACM_i$	$\Delta RTACP_i$	$\Delta RTAICT_i$
$\Delta 1/CV_i$	–0.0175	–0.1228	–0.1012
obs.	*61*	*61*	*61*
Broadly defined electronic industrial group		
	$\Delta RTACM_i$	$\Delta RTACP_i$	$\Delta RTAICT_i$
$\Delta 1/CV_i$	0.0066	0.2428*	0.2654*
obs.	*48*	*48*	*48*
Broadly defined mechanical industrial group		
	$\Delta RTACM_i$	$\Delta RTACP_i$	$\Delta RTAICT_i$
$\Delta 1/CV_i$	–0.0012	0.0134	0.0111
obs.	*86*	*86*	*86*
Broadly defined transport industrial group		
	$\Delta RTACM_i$	$\Delta RTACP_i$	$\Delta RTAICT_i$
$\Delta 1/CV_i$	0.1168	–0.2608	–0.0347
obs.	*36*	*36*	*36*

Note:
* significant at 10 % level.

Source: Santangelo (2001).

A statistically significant correlation between diversification and specialisation in ICT (in general) and in computing (especially) – but not in communications – over time is found for the broad electronic industrial group. This seems to suggest that an increase in ICT (particularly in computing) technological competencies enable MNCs to internationalise their R&D activities by providing a new model of diversification.

Technological diversification strategies are dictated by the imperative of broadening corporate portfolios of technological capabilities which enable the firm to explore new opportunities and to avoid failures in product development, production, marketing and organisational adaptation (Granstrand et al., 1997).

However, as suggested by Cantwell and Fai (1999b) and Cantwell and Santangelo (2000), technological interrelatedness should be considered as well because this phenomenon has influenced the changes in the nature of technological diversification. In line with Teece's argument (1988) that technological change leads to corporate diversification, Cantwell and Fai (1999b) show empirically that firms have moved from a Chandlerian growth-related diversification to one that is associated with an increasing degree of technological interrelatedness. Besides the identification of a diversification target over time, Cantwell and Santangelo (2000) found that relatively small companies move into new related areas by diversifying their technological portfolio, whilst relatively large companies show greater 'coherence' of technological combinations (see Chapter 3). The fact that firms do not diversify randomly, but rather enhance their portfolios of competencies in related fields, is widely acknowledged by the literature (Scott and Pascoe, 1987; Dosi et al., 1992; McDonald, 1995). Firms seem to follow 'coherent' technological paths of diversification by entering areas related to their core fields (Montgomery and Hariharan, 1991; Teece et al., 1994; Piscitello, 1998; Silverman, 1999).

Following this empirical line of research, the analysis selects electronic firms on the grounds of their degree of diversification over time. Table 4.7 ranks the electronic firms in the sample showing an increase in both internationalisation (ΔFS_i) and computing specialisation ($\Delta RTACP_i$) by the largest $\Delta 1/CV_i$ in 1978–86/1987–95.

In the table, firms are distinguished between decreasing and increasing technological diversifiers. To investigate into which technological areas the former are moving and which degree of 'coherence' of technological combinations the latter show, the analysis narrows down to the corporate specialisation profile of four electronic companies: Thomson–Brandt and Hitachi, and Mitsubishi Electric and Control Data.

These companies are selected on the grounds of their internationalisation (ΔFS_i), diversification ($\Delta 1/CV_i$) and computing specialisation ($\Delta RTACP_i$) profiles over time. Thomson–Brandt and Hitachi show a decrease in diversification but the highest combination of internationalisation and specialisation in computing. Mitsubishi Electric and Control Data seem to associate increase in geographical dispersion of research activity with greater specialisation in computing and diversification. For each of these firms, the corporate profiles of technological specialisation are investigated by adopting

Table 4.7 – Electronic firms showing both an increase in ΔFS_i and $\Delta RTACP_i$ ranked by the largest $\Delta 1/CV_i$, by nationality of the parent company, 1978–86/1987–95

Parent Company	$\Delta 1/CV_i$	ΔFS_i	$\Delta RTACP_i$
Decreasing diversifiers			
Siemens (G)	−0.0022	12.0565	0.0623
CGE (FR)	−0.0010	46.7227	0.0817
TRW (US)	−0.0006	11.5102	0.0004
Hitachi (JP)	−0.0006	0.3619	0.3016
General Electric (US)	−0.0004	1.8757	0.0228
Thomson-Brandt (FR)	−0.0002	44.5838	0.1636
Racal Elelctronics (UK)	−0.0001	45.2119	0.0143
Increasing diversfiers			
Mitsubishi Electric (JP)	0.0002	0.2008	0.5533
Control Data (US)	0.0004	2.0025	0.3036

Source: Author's elaboration on University of Reading database.

the RTA distribution across the 56 technological sectors for the sub-periods 1978–86 and 1987–95. Here the 56 technological sectors are grouped into four categories. Considering the computer sectors as a category on its own (category 1), the firms' RTA values in the other technological sectors are compared with the total average of the RTA distribution of the electronic firms in sub-period 1978–86 (sub-period 2), which is equal to 1.3. For all the four companies, categories 1, 2 and 4 are created on the basis of the same criterion, whilst category 3 is identified differently for increasing and decreasing diversifiers. As reported in Tables 4.8 and 4.9, the categories are:

1. computing sectors;
2. sectors showing RTA values above average in both sub-periods 2 and 3, which identify 'existing technological fields of specialisation continuing';
3. for the decreasing diversifiers (Thomson-Brandt and Hitachi):
   - sectors showing RTA values above average in sub-period 2 and below average in sub-period 3, which identify 'exited previous fields of specialisation';

   for the increasing diversifiers (Control Data and Mitsubishi Electric):
   - sectors showing RTA values below average in sub-period 2 an above average in sub-period 3, identifying 'entered new fields of specialisation';

4. all other sectors that do not fall in the previous categories (which have been dropped from the tables).

Table 4.8 illustrates the changes in technological profiles of Thomson-Brandt and Hitachi. By increasing its specialisation in computing, the French company shows a great degree of 'coherence' by consolidating its existing specialisation (Category 2) in general electronic fields (e.g. 'illumination devices') and in more specific ICT areas ('image and sound equipment' and 'special radio systems').

Table 4.8 – A selection of sectoral technological profiles of specialisation of electronic firms showing a decrease in diversification, grouped in three categories, by parent company, 1978–95

Thomson-Brandt (FR)				Hitachi (JP)			
1. Computing sectors				**1. Computing sectors**			
	RTA_2	RTA_3	ΔRTA		RTA_2	RTA_3	ΔRTA
Semiconductors	1.2	1.5	0.4	Semiconductors	1.0	1.0	0.0
Office equipment and data processing systems	0.6	0.7	0.1	Office equipment and data processing systems	1.0	1.4	0.4

2. Existing fields of specialisation continuing				**2. Existing fields of specialisation continuing**			
	RTA_2	RTA_3	ΔRTA		RTA_2	RTA_3	ΔRTA
Illumination devices	1.6	2.3	0.7	Pharmaceuticals and biotechnology	1.6	4.8	3.2
Image and sound equipment	1.7	2.0	0.3	Coal and petroleum products	3.0	4.5	1.5
Ships and marine propulsion	3.8	3.8	–0.1	Power plants	2.3	2.5	0.2
Special radio systems	5.6	5.3	–0.3	Chemical and allied equipment	1.4	1.4	0.0
Aircraft	6.1	5.8	–0.3	Other general industrial equipment	2.3	2.1	–0.3
				Metal working equipment	1.9	1.6	–0.3
				Motor vehicles	2.4	2.0	–0.4

Table 4.8 – continued

Thomson-Brandt (FR)	Hitachi (JP)			
	Cleaning agents and other compositions	2.0	1.5	–0.5
	Internal combustion engines	6.3	3.4	–2.9

3. Exited previous fields of specialisation	**3. Exited previous fields of specialisation**			

	RTA$_2$	RTA$_3$	ΔRTA		RTA$_2$	RTA$_3$	ΔRTA
Bleaching and dyeing	1.6	0.0	–1.6	Other transport equipment	3.7	1.1	–2.6
Cleaning agents and other compositions	1.9	0.6	–1.3	Distillation processes	1.7	0.0	–1.7
Rubber and plastic products	1.5	0.3	–1.2	Nuclear reactors	2.3	1.3	–1.0
Telecommunications	1.8	0.8	–1.0	Inorganic chemicals	1.5	0.8	–0.7
Other instruments and controls	1.7	0.9	–0.8				

Notes:
RTA$_2$: RTA distribution across 56 technological sectors in 1978–86.
RTA$_3$: RTA distribution across 56 technological sectors in 1987–95.
ΔRTA: absolute changes between RTA$_2$ and RTA$_3$.

Source: Author's elaboration on University of Reading database.

Table 4.9 – A selection of sectoral technological profiles of specialisation of electronic firms showing an increase in diversification, grouped in three categories, by parent company, 1978–95

Control Data (US)	Mitsubishi Electric (JP)			
1. Computing sectors	**1. Computing sectors**			

	RTA$_2$	RTA$_3$	ΔRTA		RTA$_2$	RTA$_3$	ΔRTA
Semiconductors	0.1	0.4	0.3	Semiconductors	0.9	1.7	0.8
Office equipment and data processing systems	2.3	2.5	0.2	Office equipment and data processing systems	0.7	1.1	0.4

Control Data (US)			Mitsubishi Electric (JP)		

2. Existing fields of specialisation continuing   **2. Existing fields of specialisation continuing**

	RTA_2	RTA_3	ΔRTA		RTA_2	RTA_3	ΔRTA
Printing and publishing machinery	5.1	2.6	−2.5	Textile and clothing machinery	1.7	3.8	2.1
				Motor vehicles	3.7	7.0	3.3
				Ships and marine propulsion	1.7	1.4	−0.4
				Other general electrical equipment	2.5	1.8	−0.7
				Internal combustion engines	10.1	9.4	−0.7
				Assembly and material handling equipment	4.0	1.7	−2.3

3. Exited previous fields of specialisation   **3. Exited previous fields of specialisation**

	RTA_2	RTA_3	ΔRTA		RTA_2	RTA_3	ΔRTA
Non-metallic mineral products	0.0	3.0	3.0	Food and tobacco products	0.0	3.4	3.4
Chemical and allied equipment	1.1	2.4	1.2				
Metallurgical processes	1.3	2.3	1.0				

Notes:
RTA_2: RTA distribution across 56 technological sectors in 1978–86.
RTA_3: RTA distribution across 56 technological sectors in 1987–95.
ΔRTA: absolute changes between RTA_2 and RTA_3.

Source: Author's elaboration on University of Reading database.

Accordingly, Thomson seems to exit previous unrelated fields of specialisation concerning chemical technologies ('bleaching and dyeing' and 'cleaning agents and other composition'). The decline of corporate specialisation in 'telecommunications' may be attributed to a domestic restructuring of the ICT French industry. As a result of the French high-technology policy, each of the largest ICT companies specialises in specific ICT fields, while dropping others. The case of 'telecommunications' is even more policy driven. In the context of the 1983 nationalisation Thomson exited this field in favour of CGE (Fridenson, 1997). None the less the general increasing ICT specialisation seems to have encouraged the geographical dispersion of innovative activities of the French companies (in general) and Thomson (in particular) which, in the past, were amongst the technologically least internationalised (Cantwell and Kotecha, 1994; Caron, 1995). The case of Hitachi is somehow different. The Japanese company consolidates its specialisation in some chemical technologies ('Pharmaceuticals and biotechnology', 'Coal and petroleum products'). Accordingly, some other chemicals and transport fields, where the firm showed a comparative technological advantage, are exited. This trend may suggest a restructuring of the firm's corporate profile. The increased corporate specialisation in some of the computing sectors enables the company to expand its research facilities overseas. In turn this strategy allows Hitachi to explore new interrelated technological capabilities, thus confirming that, as technological interrelatedness is firm-specific, firms select their own path of diversification (Winter, 1987).

Turning to the analysis of the corporate profile of technological specialisation of Control Data and Mistubishi Electric, different trends are found. The US company appears to enter new mechanical technological fields whilst maintaining its competitive advantage in others, as a result of its increasing computing specialisation and internationalisation. The new technological fields entered by Control Data ('non-metallic mineral products', 'chemical and allied equipment' and 'metallurgic processes') may be explained by its corporate internationalisation strategy. In 1985 the US electronic firm concluded a joint venture with Kobel Steel, which is a large producer of new materials, semifinished and nonferrous metal products (Stafford and Purkins, 1989; Hast, 1991). This may have promoted technological learning between the two partners and consequently influenced the direction of technological diversification of Control Data (Cantwell and Barrera, 1998). The case of Mitsubishi Electric can be explained on the grounds of country and firm specificities. The Japanese company maintains its specialisation in electronic and transport technologies, which is a common technological pattern in the Japanese model of specialisation. Vertova (1999) provides empirical evidence of the country comparative advantage in electronic and transport technologies since the mid-1960s. The author argues the importance of the Japanese Ministry of International Trade and Industry and of the leading electronic companies in fostering Japanese specialisation in areas related to computer technologies. In this context the selection of the transport ('motor vehicles', 'ships and marine propulsion', 'internal combustion engine') and electronic ('other general electric equipment') technologies as corporate fields of specialisation is firm-specific.[1] The specialisation of Mitsubishi in 'food and tobacco products' is due to the way the RTA index is built (see section 1.4). This technological sector is not a core field in the electronic industry, thus implying a low patenting in the sector by electronic companies. Therefore, if a company (e.g. Mitsubishi Electric) counts a few patents, the RTA index takes high values, as the industry average (the denominator of the RTA index) is quite low.

These results on the direction of technological diversification are consistent with the ex-post approach to technological interrelatedness and 'coherence', which considers both these processes as firm-specific. By exploring new combinations of capabilities, the firm selects capabilities related to its core field of activity by trial and error through an incremental and cumulative process (Cantwell, 1998b). In this sense technological relatedness is an ex-post concept, embodying firm specificites and based on the idea that 'one does not know what is related until one tries' (Teece et al., 1994). However if the dynamics in the technological profiles of Hitachi, Control Data and Mitsubishi confirm the specificity of the firms' technological 'coherence', the case of Thomson-Brandt is to some extent different. In understanding the profile of the French company, industry specificities should be taken into account as well as the political environment discussed above. This seems to be consistent with the empirical evidence provided by Lemelin (1982) on the fact that industry characteristics are relevant to, although not the principal determinant of, corporate diversification.

4.5   CONCLUSIONS

This chapter investigates whether the increased specialisation in ICT has influenced the geographical diversification or internationalisation of firms, by considering the globalisation process with which corporate technological development and innovative activity are experimenting. Empirical evidence of an association between the rising specialisation in microelectronic and the increased geographical dispersion of R&D activity in the period 1978–86/1987–95 are found. In these years the likelihood of an increase in the corporate internationalisation of research activity seems to be positively associated with a higher corporate technological specialisation in ICT (Santangelo, 2001). Following Andersen (1998), the shift to a model of inter-group convergence of technological development is identified as a possible explanation of these results. Whilst the past technological accumulation was characterised by intragroup technological diversification and by a structure of specialised engineering and science-based fields, more integrated technological systems seem to emerge in the recent period. If the historical shift towards more integrated technological systems occurred in the 1960s, it may well be that this inter-group model of technological development fully established itself only later because of the 'gestation' period of the new core technology (e.g. ICT). Therefore the increased specialisation in the ICT field as a whole can be identified as a major motive for geographical dispersion of corporate R&D from the late 1970s. Increasing technological interrelatedness and technology fusion seem to be the core characteristics of the current technological environment. In this context ICT can be viewed as a connector between previously separate technologies. As technological evolution has become increasingly interrelated and complex (ibid.), ICT specialisation enables the firm to fuse together different kinds of technology across national boundaries in an intra-firm network. The incremental learning of firm-specific competencies in ICT seems to have facilitated diversification in related sectors. These findings seem to be consistent with Cantwell and Piscitello's argument (1999), according to which related diversification is achieved through an increasing geographical dispersion of firms' technological activity. MNCs developing technology in more than one location hold potential opportunities for cross-border learning, enhanced by an increased take-up of ICT technologies. ICT specialisation appears to amplify the firm's flexibility in combining different kinds of technology. As these technologies are usually located in geographically dispersed centres of expertise, firms need to adopt an international R&D strategy. This enables the firm to benefit from technological complementarities between related activities and between corporate learning in different institutional environments. The analysis of the specialisation profiles of the four selected electronic firms has also confirmed the firm-specific character of the direction of the diversification process.

The results of the regression analysis at a more disagreggated level seem to indicate computing technology (rather then communications) as the ICT component driving the relationship between internationalisation and ICT specialisation. A possible explanation for this may be found in the increasing technological interrelatedness as well in the increasing multi-technology expertise required in producing specific products. As argued by von Tunzelmann (1999), a wider range of technologies is needed in the production of specific products. However, to combine different technologies, companies should develop capabilities in core technologies (e.g. ICT). In the current ICT-based era, although computing and communications do not seem to converge in a unique technological sector (Duysters and Hagedoorn, 1995a, 1998), the pervasive character of digitalisation as well as its wide applicability may explain the key role of computing technology in the corporate development of technological capabilities in different related fields. In the process of generation of new technologies, these technologies allow an increasing reduction in the cost of trial and error search. New instruments based on ICT have improved simulation on speed or supercomputers of complex physical, chemical and biotechnological interactions, as well as routine technological operations such as quality testing (Dalum et al., 1999). The matching of both technological and product capabilities represents a key issue in corporate management. Specialisation in a product without breath of technological expertise erodes the firm's ability to remain in the market when technological needs advance rapidly. Conversely, firms attempting to retain a presence in a full range of products which could be developed from electronics technology may face serious problems and eventually be forced to make choices, if they do not fulfil the requirement of broader technological specialisation.

If an international R&D strategy enables manufacturing companies to source knowledge internally in many diverse areas, it enhances the core competencies of ICT specialists. The analysis of the technological profiles of the four selected electronic firms reveals in which areas these companies develop their technological expertise. The companies under analysis have geographically dispersed their research activity as well as increased their specialisation in computing and their technological diversification. As suggested by the literature (Scott and Pascoe, 1987; Montgomery and Hariharan, 1991; Dosi et al., 1992; McDonald, 1995; Teece et al., 1994; Piscitello, 1998; Silverman, 1999), these companies appear to have diversified in firm-specific areas. In all four cases, the selected companies seem to follow their own corporate paths in the choice of continuing/exiting sectors of specialisation. Therefore the findings confirm the argument that firms follow 'coherent' rather than 'random' technological avenues of diversification.

By discussing the relationships between spatial and sectoral patterns of corporate technological development in the period under analysis, this chapter concludes Part One. The statistical and econometric results of this part of the thesis provide a general overview of the management of corporate technological portfolios as well as on the location of corporate research activity. The analysis moves further by framing these issues in the context of the European ICT industry in Part Two.

NOTE

1. Although Mitsubishi Electric's technological specialisation in 'ships and marine propulsion', 'internal combustion engines' and 'other general electric equipment' drops between 1978–86 and 1987–95, in the last sub-period the Japanese company still shows an above-average index of technological specialisation.

PART TWO

The Experience of the European ICT Industry

5. The evolution of European corporate competencies in ICT

5.1   INTRODUCTION

This chapter opens Part Two, which frames the issues of sectoral composition of corporate technological portfolios and spatial location of innovative activity in the context of the European ICT industry. The analysis is developed throughout Chapters 5, 6 and 7. The present chapter aims to test whether technological characteristics specific to a European ICT industry emerged over time in terms of firms' profiles of specialisation. In the context of a European integration process, the analysis takes into account the role played by country-specific factors. The level of integration of the European ICT industry is investigated in terms of specialisation similarities among the leading European MNCs in order to test if (and which) firms come closer together, while others move further apart. On the grounds of a previous study (Santangelo, 2001), the argument is based upon the fact that technological interrelatedness and to some extent the on-going European integration process promote the overlap of technological profiles of ICT European firms.

The fast-growing process of technological interrelatedness has provoked the reduction in the firms' degree of (concentration of) technological specialisation as a result of the broadening-out of firms' technological activities (Cantwell, 1993). The interrelatedness process increases the corporation's competitive advantage in its main technological activity as well as its product range. Bearing in mind that discretionary firm differences exist and do matter within an industry (Nelson, 1991), a crucial outcome of the growing technological interrelatedness can be identified in the interaction and overlapping of technological competencies among firms operating in the same industrial output sector because of inter-industry differences (Cantwell, 1991a). Following an evolutionary approach to industry dynamics (Cantwell, 1993; Bresnahan and Malerba, 1997), as innovations do not occur in isolation (Nelson and Winter, 1982), firms do not search in isolation. They are, instead, 'the members of a population of simultaneous searching organisations' (Stuart and Podolny, 1996, 36). Indeed each industry can be identified as an 'evolving technological network' (ibid., 35), tied together by technological commonalties among inventions belonging mainly to corporate innovators. In this sense technological change and, therefore, technological specialisation are industry-specific (Malerba and Orsenigo, 1996, 1997). Accordingly, technological change and specialisation are country-specific, as pointed out by the studies on national systems of innovations (Archibugi and Pianta, 1992a; Patel and Pavitt, 1994; Vertova, 1998a, 1999). Thus national groups of firms are likely to be technologically more similar to one another in comparison with any international rivals, when considering the importance of country-specific factors in the development of specialisation profiles.

Evidence of the theory is found in the European ICT industry, which has been characterised by nation- and firm-specific features. The technological gap in ICT between Europe on the one hand, and the US and Japan on the other, was clearly illustrated by the dominance of foreign companies in Europe as well as by the development in the Japanese and American markets since the mid-1960s. This situation pushed the European governments to pursue national procurement policies aimed at supporting national champions. At the time the reasons for the European 'backwardness' were, indeed, identified in the small size of companies and markets. Historically, European multinationals were rather small compared with their American competitors. As a solution to this problem, most of them chose a different strategy from the Americans by diversifying in a broad range of activities (Van Tulder and Junne, 1988). However this strategy did not lead to an increase in competitiveness when considering two main factors. First, European corporations were mainly active in home markets, where national policy guaranteed them a semi-monopolistic position. Second, as a consequence of the diversification strategy in relation to size constraints, the R&D expenditures of the European companies were spread over a large variety of fields, the result being that they spent less on R&D in any field than their specialised competitors.

This 'followers strategy' (ibid., 127) was detrimental for the European multinationals since it accompanied the development of firm institutionalised routines, which have been identified as key factors in mastering technology by the evolutionary literature (Nelson and Winter, 1982). The lack of these routines made European companies unable to apply core technologies in a wide range of products and processes. None the less if this was the case in the beginning of the microelectronics revolution, later the European firms switched to a 'niche survival strategy' (Bresnahan and Malerba, 1997), which allowed them to explore technological niches not already occupied by American producers. This new approach to the competitiveness problem was promoted by the adoption of EU co-operative policies (e.g. ESPRIT).

Thus in the European case the overlapping of firms' technological specialisation profiles over time may have also been emphasised by the on-going integration process, which has increased the extent of market-based and technology-based interaction between firms. Caracostas and Soete (1997) put forward the argument of what has been labelled a European System of Innovation, based on the building of cross-border institutions and emerging from the fragmented national systems of innovation represented by the member states.

The chapter is divided into five sections. In section 5.2, some light is thrown on the statistical methodology adopted. Section 5.3 discusses the general trends of European ICT competence both within Europe and in the global scenario. Section 5.4 focuses on the evolution of European corporate technological specialisation in ICT by analysing the dynamic development of companies' clusters in terms of size and composition. The last section presents some concluding remarks.

5.2   METHODOLOGICAL NOTES

The empirical analysis of this chapter focuses on two main issues. First, the breadth of competence of European corporations in ICT is investigated. The analysis is carried out at both country and firm levels by adopting the patent share (PS) of ICT technologies. PS is used as a measure of technological size (see Chapter 3) relative to Europe as a whole and to the world.

The second issue concerns the convergence/divergence in technological specialisation profiles and is analysed with a correlation analysis. In each of the three usual sub-periods (see section 1.5), for each of the 21 European electronic companies (Table A.1), the pattern of corporate technological specialisation in ICT is measured by the RTA index (see section 1.4) which is calculated across the original ICT patent classes corresponding to the ICT technological sectors (see Appendix A). As explained in Appendix B, some companies are dropped from the analysis on the ground of the absence of total patenting activity in the ICT patent classes. The outcome is the variation in the number of firms in the sample from one sub-period to another. Therefore 20 firms are examined in the sub-period 1969–77, whilst 21 and 19 are taken into account in the two later sub-periods respectively (see Table A.1).

The degree of similarity between the firms' sectoral specialisation profiles is investigated with the use of the Pearson's correlation coefficient (r_{12} between the RTA distributions of any pairwise combination of firms 1 and 2) across the considered ICT patent classes in the sub-periods 1969–77, 1978–86 and 1987–1995. This allowed the building of three correlation matrices for each of the sub-periods considered and, accordingly, the distinction between negative and positive correlations between the profiles of European corporate technological specialisation. It is worth noting that a statistically significant positive correlation is the result of firms showing similar profiles of technological specialisation in some advantaged (RTA > 1) and disadvantaged (RTA < 1) patent classes. Thus it was assumed that a statistically significant positive correlation is evidence of overlapping in the technological structure of corporate R&D.

The analysis moves further by focusing on these pairwise combinations of firms in each of the three sub-periods in order to group them on the grounds of the technological patent class(es) of specialisation. The criterion adopted in grouping these companies requires a firm to be significantly positively correlated with 50 per cent or more of the other firms in the group and, at the same time, positively correlated with all of them. The criterion allows the formation of clusters of technologically similar specialised (i.e. co-specialised) firms. This means that firms showing similar RTA profiles of specialisation – thus specialised in the same patent classes – fall into the same cluster. Therefore in each cluster similarity between corporate profiles is driven by particular technology/ies. Then each cluster is labelled according to the technological patent class(es) driving the correlation among the firms within it. In addition to these labels, a letter was allocated to each cluster for ease of exposition. For the same purpose, each letter is numbered to follow the evolution of the cluster over time. No letters are allocated to clusters appearing in only one of the three sub-periods. This enables one to investigate the evolution of technological clusters over time in both size and composition.

5.3   GENERAL TRENDS OF EUROPEAN ICT COMPETENCIES

Before going into the analysis of the dynamics of European corporate specialisation, European ICT corporate competencies over time are discussed. To assess the European technological competence position in ICT, the relative technological size of the European firms in ICT is taken into account.

For each of the European electronic multinationals aggregated by nationality of the parent company, Table 5.1 reports the share of US patents granted in the ICT patent classes relative to the European electronic industry as a whole.

It appears clearly from the figures that the absolute level of technological activity of the German and French companies in ICT increased relative to the other European national groups of firms in the same industry. The German corporate trend confirms the traditional industrial strength of the national economy. As argued by Cantwell and Harding (1998), electronics is one of the key German industries in terms of concentration of patenting activity, despite the fears of technological decline. A strong tradition of education and scientific research has been suggested as being the reason for German corporate success in ICT (Stubbs and Saviotti, 1997). This tradition has been enhanced by federal and state government support for research. Whilst the state contribution targeted mainly university research, federal research funding was directed at business and private non-profit research institutions. The performance of the French electronic corporations in ICT might be explained, instead, by a 'dirigiste' public policy. As pointed out in the literature (Cohen, 1992; Cantwell and Kotecha, 1994; Caron, 1995; Stubbs and Saviotti, 1997), French electronic companies were a main target of French industrial and technology policy. The emphasis was on the need for the continuation of funding and developing co-operation between public laboratories and industry (Stubbs and Saviotti, 1997).

Table 5.1 – Share of the patenting activity attributable to European electronic industry-owned research in ICT classes relative to the European electronic industry as a whole, by nationality of the parent firm, 1969–95

Nationality of the Parent Firm	1969–77 %	1978–86 %	1987–95 %
France	14	19	24
Germany	23	29	30
Italy	3	1	0
The Netherlands	35	35	32
Sweden	4	3	5
Switzerland	1	2	0
UK	20	11	8
Total	**100**	**100**	**100**

Source: Author's elaboration on University of Reading patent data.

Although the relative technological competence position of the Dutch, Swiss and Swedish electronic firms appears to be almost stable over time from the figures shown in Table 5.1, Philips leads the European ICT industry. *De facto* whilst the situation of the Dutch and Swiss companies worsens slightly from the first to the last sub-period, in the Swedish case, the companies' technological competence in ICT improved slightly. In each case, the technological performance is fully linked to a single company (i.e. Philips, LM Ericsson and Brown Boveri respectively). In all three countries, national governments have helped enterprises by creating conditions for technological dynamism.

The size of British technological activity in the ICT technologies considered dropped dramatically from the first to the last sub-period, decreasing from 20 per cent to 8 per cent of the total European patenting activity. A reason for this pattern may be identified in a less incisive (relative to other European companies) technology policy. The overriding importance of the role of defence policy made the UK-owned companies over-dependent on secure government defence contracts rather than competitive in international markets for consumer electronics. The British approach to improving industrial and technological performance was, indeed, more concerned with establishing a more competitive managerial environment rather than increasing government R&D expenditures, which was, instead, left to firms (Stubbs and Saviotti, 1997).

Similarly, the Italian corporate competence position deteriorated over time, thus showing a decrease in the size of patenting activity in these types of technology from 3 per cent to 0 per cent of the total European patents. The Italian corporate performance is fully led by Olivetti. During the years 1969–77 Olivetti arose from a corporate crisis after the transition from its mechanical to its electronic age. Completed under the De Benedettis' leadership, the entry into the computing market was accomplished through company-specific commitment to design. Olivetti's successful conversion to computing was then characterised by an increasing in ICT specialisation industry as well as by an acquisition strategy of 'infant companies' operating in particular key technologies. However, in the latest years, the Italian company went through major difficulties in the stock market and risked closure as a result of lack of capital. These events slowed down Olivetti's R&D activity in ICT.

In Table 5.2, the breadth of European competence in ICT technology relative to the world electronic industry as a whole is investigated in order to establish a comparison with the previous analysis.

As a result of incisive state intervention in science-based sectors, only the French companies seem to maintain their position of technological competence over time at world level, showing a slight increase in the ICT technological size. However, it should be pointed out that the French policy had some effect in communications, in which the role of the state is more significant than in computing. This latter sector is not a similar state-run sector, as illustrated by the fact that the world's most successful companies depend little on government. This argument seems to be confirmed by the findings of the firm-level analysis that is discussed below. Unlike the French, the German corporate competence position assumes a different dimension when related to the world's technological activity in ICT. Whilst the German electronic corporations emerged strongly within Europe, their technological size was stable around 4 per cent of the world patenting in the selected technologies over time.

Table 5.2 – Share of patenting activity attributable to European electronic industry-owned research in ICT classes relative to the world electronic industry, by nationality of the parent firm, 1969–95

Nationality of the Parent Firm	1969–77 %	1978–86 %	1987–95 &
France	2	3	3
Germany	4	5	4
Italy	0	0	0
The Netherlands	6	6	4
Sweden	1	0	1
Switzerland	0	0	0
UK	3	2	1
Europe	17	17	13
Japan	14	29	48
US	69	53	37
Others	0	1	2
Total	**100**	**100**	**100**

Source: Author's elaboration on University of Reading patent data.

The Italian and Swiss technological activity in ICT becomes irrelevant in the world context from 1969 to 1995. This confirms the technological decline of both Italian and Swiss corporations in ICT within Europe. The ICT competence of the Swedish electronic industry is found to be quite stable relative to the world. This compares with its slight increase relative to the European electronic industry. The Dutch corporate competence position in ICT relative to the world confirms the downward trend shown in the European scenario, although Philips shows still the highest figures among the other European electronic national corporate groups. Similarly, the deterioration of the UK corporate competence position in ICT is also confirmed in the context of the world electronic industry.

In Table 5.2, the ICT competence of the European electronic industry as a whole relative to the world electronic industry is also taken into account. The European backwardness in ICT is shown clearly in comparison with Japan. Europe's technological competence position decreased from 17 per cent to 13 per cent relative to the world, whilst the Japanese moved in the opposite direction, increasing from 14 per cent to 48 per cent between 1969 and 1995. Indeed the Japanese electronic industry shows the fastest growth rate in the size of its patenting activity in ICT. Instead the decline in the technological size of the US electronic companies in electronics and electronics-based technologies should be interpreted carefully. It should be kept in mind that the US patenting system has become more internationalised (Patel and Pavitt, 1987). The technological importance of the American market has attracted an increasing patenting activity from foreign companies (such as European), aiming to protect their R&D outcomes by using the propriety right in the world's largest technological market. However, the choice of the US as a recipient country raises the problem of correctly estimating US innovative activity. As discussed in section 1.4, the international comparison is between foreign firms patenting in the US versus US firms patenting in their own domestic market. Therefore US corporate patenting activity may be underestimated. None the less the growth in patent share of foreign companies (ibid.) together with attempts to improve the quality and availability of US patents statistics (Soete, 1987; Pavitt, 1988), also confirm US patent data as a relevant indicator of international innovative capacity also in the case of European companies.

The relative competitive position of each single European electronic corporation is investigated in Table 5.3 where, for each of them, the share of patenting activity in ICT patent classes is calculated relative to all other European electronic companies. Table 5.3 provides a rather detailed picture of European technological competence at firm level.

The strong French position seems to be due to the performance of Thomson-Brandt and CII-Honeywell-Bull rather than Compagnie Générale d'Electricité (CGE). The former doubled their technological activity in ICT between 1969 and 1995. In the early 1980s Thomson-Brandt switched from a diversified specialisation in electronics to telecommunications, with the support of the French government. Thomson-Brandt adopted a policy of spreading of risk by using its diversified technological profile to move from one market to another according to demand shifts (Cantwell and Kotecha, 1994). Due to its presence in numerous markets, the French company had to face high R&D costs, which could have hardly been afforded without public support. High-tech industrial sectors were, indeed, the target of a new French public policy (i.e. the 'colbertisme high-tech'), under which the so-called 'grand projects' (Minitel, Telecom 1 and TDF) were launched (Cohen, 1992). Accordingly, CII-Honeywell Bull was involved in French public

Table 5.3 – Share of patenting activity attributable to European electronic industry-owned research in the ICT classes relative to the European electronic industry as a whole, by home country and parent firm, 1969–95

Firms	1969–77 %	1978–86 %	1987–95 %
Germany			
AEG-Telefunken (G)	3	1	1
Bosch-Siemens Hausgerate (G)	1	1	1
Nixdorf Computer (G)	0	1	0
Siemens (G)	19	27	29
UK			
BICC (UK)	0	0	0
General Electric Co. (UK)	7	3	3
ICL (UK)	1	1	1
Plessey (UK)	8	3	1
Racal Electronics (UK)	2	1	1
Standard Telephones and Cables (UK)	0	1	1
Thorn EMI (UK)	2	1	1
Italy			
Olivetti (IT)	2	1	0
Zanussi Group (IT)	0	0	0
France			
CII-Honeywell Bull (FR)	2	3	4
Compagnie Générale d'Electricité (FR)	4	2	3
Sagem (FR)	0	0	0
Thomson-Brandt (FR)	8	13	17
Switzerland			
Philips (NL)	35	35	32
ABB (SZ)*	n.a.	n.a.	2
Brown Boveri (SZ)	1	2	n.a.
Sweden			
Asea AB (SE)	0	0	n.a.
Electrolux (SE)	0	0	0
LM Ericsson (SE)	4	3	3
Total (all the above parent firms)	**100**	**100**	**100**

Note:
* The company is the result of the 1988 merger between Brown Boveri (SZ) and ASEA AB (SE).

Source: Author's elaboration on University of Reading patent data.

policy. In this case the competitive strategy was rather different from the one pursued by Thomson-Brandt. CII-Honeywell Bull has attempted to develop a greater specialisation in technological niches by adopting a so-called open-system approach, whereby all computers and software will eventually be compatible with one another. However, as argued elsewhere (Santangelo, 2001), the success of the French computing company in ICT was still linked to the public policy during President Mitterand's time. CGE shows a slight decrease in its technological size in ICT. As Thomson-Brandt, CGE was one of the major targets of the French 'colbertisme high-tech'. Its decline in patent size between the first sub-period and the last might be explained by the shift from government to private-sector control and by the consequent problems in adapting to the new situation.

As already emphasised, the Italian pattern seems to be attributable to the decrease in Olivetti's ICT patenting. As pointed out above, Olivetti is not a technological high-flier since its R&D expenditures are rather limited in comparison with its competitors. If the De Benedetti chairmanship promoted a new entrepreneurial management, the recent events highlighted above might be identified as the cause of a drawback in the company's competence in ICT.

The impressive performance of German industry relative to Europe as a whole can be linked to the increase in the ICT competence of Siemens, which appears to be one of the strongest European corporations in electronics. Besides the national facilities supporting ICT research, the success of Siemens was achieved through a diversification strategy into computer technologies and electronics, pursued through internal growth and acquisition.[1] Moreover, this strategy went hand in hand with a vertical market approach such as banks and retailing. In contrast, the decline of AEG-Telefunken, which might be due to the tough Japanese competition in video home system (VHS), does not seem to have affected the European performance of the German electronic industry.

The UK pattern is fully led by the steep decrease in ICT competence of General Electric Co. and Plessey. The pattern of Plessey's technological competence might find an explanation in the company's orientation as a supplier of military equipment as well as in its lack of overseas manufacturing or assembly plants. This led, in turn, to a weakness in production and marketing sectors, which provoked the take-over of the company by General Electric Co. and Siemens on an equal basis in 1989 (Morris, 1990). The fall in the ICT technological size of General Electric Co. reflects a loss of competence in comparison with its French and German competitors, despite the technological leadership that the company maintained in the domestic market. The reduction in technological size of Racal Electronics and Thorn EMI was less drastic and, in the latter case, attributable to a lack of evaluation of consumer preferences when developing products. With this background, only Standard Telephones and Cables (STC) show a slightly growing technological size in the types of technology under consideration. This was a result of the early 1980s switch from capital-intensive to more consumer electronic products.

The Swiss competence position follows the Brown Boveri history of technological development in electronic engineering and its successful merger with ASEA AB in 1988. The almost stable Swedish pattern in ICT over time is explained by LM Ericsson. State support in science-based technology played a major role in the company development of its technological niche in cellular phones.

As confirmed by the figures in Table 5.3, Philips' ICT technological size is the largest among the European electronic companies in each of the three sub-periods considered. The performance of the Dutch company can been explained by continuous innovative efforts throughout its history. Philips concentrated its resources on its most profitable and fast-growing product lines (i.e. consumer electronics) by implementing a policy of acquisitions and joint ventures. Since the late 1980s, the Dutch company has indeed focused resources more closely on electronics and dropped unrelated activities. This allowed the firm to differentiate its range of products widely and at the same time to maintain a large share in each market.

5.4   COMPETENCIES DYNAMICS IN THE EUROPEAN ICT INDUSTRY

As stated above, the aim is to test whether technological characteristics specific to a European Information and Communications Technology industry emerged over time in terms of firms' profiles of specialisation amidst the on-going European integration process. Within this analytical framework, it is of major interest to distinguish firms that came closer together from others that moved further apart.

Before going into the analysis of the results of these procedures, it must be mentioned that the number of significantly positively correlated pairs of firms relative to all possible pairwise combinations grew over time, thus confirming the hypothesis of an increasing overlap in specialisation. The results of an analysis of the firms' clustering are shown in Figure 5.1, where the sub-periods are taken into account by the columns, whilst the historical evolution of each single group is highlighted by arrows.

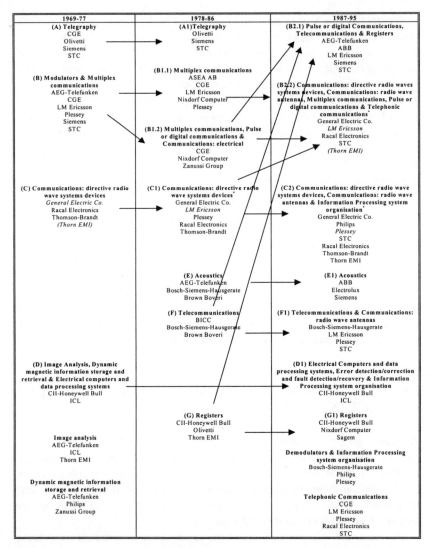

1969-77	1978-86	1987-95
(A) Telegraphy CGE Olivetti Siemens STC	**(A1)Telegraphy** Olivetti Siemens STC	**(B2.1) Pulse or digital Communications, Telecommunications & Registers** AEG-Telefunken ABB LM Ericsson Siemens STC
(B) Modulators & Multiplex communications AEG-Telefunken CGE LM Ericsson Plessey Siemens STC	**(B1.1) Multiplex communications** ASEA AB CGE LM Ericsson Nixdorf Computer Plessey	**(B2.2) Communications: directive radio waves systems devices, Communications: radio wave antennas, Multiplex communications, Pulse or digital communications & Telephonic communications**[*] General Electric Co. *LM Ericsson* Racal Electronics STC *(Thorn EMI)*
	(B1.2) Multiplex communications, Pulse or digital communications & Communications: electrical CGE Nixdorf Computer Zanussi Group	
(C) Communications: directive radio wave systems devices *General Electric Co.* Racal Electronics Thomson-Brandt *(Thorn EMI)*	**(C1) Communications: directive radio wave systems devices**[*] General Electric Co. *LM Ericsson* Plessey Racal Electronics Thomson-Brandt	**(C2) Communications: directive radio wave systems devices, Communications: radio wave antennas & Information Processing system organisation**[*] General Electric Co. Philips *Plessey* STC Racal Electronics Thomson-Brandt Thorn EMI
	(E) Acoustics AEG-Telefunken Bosch-Siemens-Hausgerate Brown Boveri	**(E1) Acoustics** ABB Electrolux Siemens
	(F) Telecommunications BICC Bosch-Siemens-Hausgerate Brown Boveri	**(F1) Telecommunications & Communications: radio wave antennas** Bosch-Siemens-Hausgerate LM Ericsson Plessey STC
(D) Image Analysis, Dynamic magnetic information storage and retrieval & Electrical computers and data processing systems CII-Honeywell Bull ICL		**(D1) Electrical Computers and data processing systems, Error detection/correction and fault detection/recovery & Information Processing system organisation** CII-Honeywell Bull ICL
Image analysis AEG-Telefunken ICL Thorn EMI	**(G) Registers** CII-Honeywell Bull Olivetti Thorn EMI	**(G1) Registers** CII-Honeywell Bull Nixdorf Computer Sagem
		Demodulators & Information Processing system organisation Bosch-Siemens-Hausgerate Philips Plessey
Dynamic magnetic information storage and retrieval AEG-Telefunken Philips Zanussi Group		**Telephonic Communications** CGE LM Ericsson Plessey Racal Electronics STC

Note:
[*] *Italics* denote consideration of sector-specific factors, which create correlation problems between each of the companies, whose name is in italic, and all the others and between each other in the case of the 1969–77 cluster.

Source: Santangelo (1998).

Figure 5.1 – Firms clustered on the ground of the technological patent class of specialisation by sub-period, 1969–95

For each of the three sub-periods considered, it is possible to cluster six, seven and seven groups of firms respectively on grounds of the above-specified criterion. For four out of the six clusters identified in the years 1969–77, it is possible to follow a dynamic evolution in the following sub-periods. The remaining two clusters (i.e. 'Image' and 'Dynamic magnetic information storage and retrieval') do not seem to have evolved over time. In the years 1978–86, six out of seven clusters had a historical persistence in the later sub-period. The correlation between the firms in group A, which fell apart in the third sub-period, was driven by the 'Telegraphy' technology. In the years 1987–95 two out of seven clusters (i.e. 'Demodulators & Information Processing system organisation' and 'Telephonic communications') seem to be completely new, thus not showing any link with the technological groups of firms in the previous sub-periods. The average number of entrances made by each firm into the clusters increased from one period to another, such that it doubled between the first sub-period and the third. The average number of firms getting into clusters is calculated by dividing the number of firms in the clusters (i.e. 21, 25 and 37 respectively) by the total number of firms in each period (i.e. 20, 21 and 19 respectively). The result is a total average equal to 1.05 in the years 1969–77, 1.19 in the years 1978–86 and 1.94 in the years 1987–95. This confirms that the ICT specialisation profiles of the European electronic companies considered overlapped increasingly. Accordingly this result also confirms the process of corporate technological diversification over time, which had the effect of widening the average size of clusters over and above the 'European integration effect'.

The 'Telegraphy' cluster shows an evolution between 1969 and 1986 in terms of chronological persistence, size and composition. The technological group is present in the second sub-period with a smaller size due to the absence of CGE. The reason for this might be explained by the 1981 nationalisation of the French company and its consequent restructuring. The composition of the group might provide some explanatory elements for the disappearance of this cluster in the years 1987–95. As argued in the previous section, all the companies in it moved to a more computing-based specialisation. This argument is consistent with the presence of these firms in other clusters in the last sub-periods.[2]

The development of the 'Modulators & Multiplex communications' cluster (B) is historically rather more complicated in size as well as in composition. The technological group developed two clusters in the second sub-period (i.e. 'Multiplex communications' (B1.1), and 'Multiplex communications, Pulse or digital communications: electronic & Communications: electrical' (B1.2)), which evolved, in turn, in another (B2.2) and two other technological groups (B2.1 and B2.2) respectively in the years 1987–95. In the 'Multiplex communications' cluster (B1.1), Siemens, AEG-Telefunken and STC are missing in comparison with the 1969–77 'mother technological group' (B). In the second sub-period Siemens and STC seemed to focus mainly on consumer-electronic manufacturing for retail and banking use, whilst AEG-Telefunken moved into other technologies (such as 'Acoustics'). The latter technological group (B1.2) identified has, in contrast, a relatively new composition since CGE is the only common company with the 1969–77 'mother cluster' (i.e. B). In both of them Nixdorf Computer is found to be a newcomer. In the later sub-period both these two clusters (B1.1 and B1.2) came together into a single group (B2.2) as shown in Figure 5.1. The outcome cluster shows a broad technological specialisation and a rather different size. Besides LM Ericsson and STC, the other two multinationals can be identified as late-comers. The fact that all of them are British may be understood as a national pattern of the industry, which broadened its technological specialisation in order to provide a better response to the market in line with the argument of Granstrand et al. (1997) on technological diversification (see Chapters 3 and 4). However a further development of the 'Multiplex communications, Pulse or digital communications & Communications: electrical' cluster (B1.2) is also found in another 1987–95 technological group (B2.1), as illustrated in Figure 5.1. In this case, it seems to be persistence in terms of technological development rather than composition between the middle and the later sub-period. The firms in the cluster B2.1 can be found in the 1969–77 'mother technological group' B, but not in the middle sub-period cluster B1.2.

The 'Communications: directive radio waves system devices' cluster (C) presents a consistent evolution pattern over time (i.e. C evolved in C1 and C2). First, it is possible to follow its history from 1969 to 1995. Second, its size grew incrementally from one sub-period to another. Third, this growth in size seems to occur through a broadening process of the original group of firms to latecomers. None the less, it must be mentioned that the composition of the cluster is highly affected by sector-specific factors in all the three sub-periods. In each of the three sub-periods, the companies in the cluster are highly specialised in the patent classes 'Communications: directive radio waves system devices'. However, the high specialisation in this patent class seems to drive companies to develop their overall specialisation profiles in different directions in the sub-period 1969–77. This is true of General Electric Co. and Thorn EMI, which show high RTA value in the class in question but overall different profiles of technological expertise. The sector-specific factors seem to have a smoother impact on the companies' specialisation profiles over time. In 1978–86 and in 1987–95 high RTA values in 'Communications: directive radio waves system devices' are associated with closer paths of corporate technological development within clusters C1 and C2. None the less, some correlation problems still exist between LM Ericsson and all other firms in C1, and between Plessey and all others in C2. For this reason, the criterion adopted in the composition of all other clusters has been relaxed in the case of C, C1 and C2. Sector-specific factors and their impact on the technological groups over time are taken into consideration in Figure 5.1 by the use of italics.

The last 1969–77 cluster (D), which appeared to have a further development only in the later sub-period considered (i.e. D evolved in D1), maintained the same size and composition, but broadened its technological specialisation by targeting more merely computing technologies. It is worth comparing the cluster D with the 'Registers' technological group (G), which appears only in the sub-period 1978–86. CII-Honeywell Bull seems to be the common element, thus confirming its role as one of the major computing companies in the European electronic industry. The French company shows a distributed technological specialisation in computing technologies, which might be identified as the key to its success in the adoption of the open-system approach discussed above. It is also worth noting the presence of Olivetti in the middle sub-period (in cluster G), but not in the latter (in cluster G1). This pattern is consistent with both the 1970s company's conversion to computing and its more recent technological decline. The presence of Nixdorf Computer in the cluster G1 confirms the new entry of the company in the European microcomputer sector. As shown in Figure 5.1, the 'Registers' technology group (G) developed also in another technological group (B2.1), confirming once again the theory of 'distributed' technological competencies in order to perform successfully in the market.

The 'Acoustics' cluster (E) appeared from the middle sub-period onwards by showing a slightly different composition, but no changes in size. The 'Telecommunications' cluster (F) is, instead, different in both size and composition over time, although developing from 1978 onwards as well. The cluster F evolved in two technological groups (i.e. F1 and B2.1) in the sub-period 1987–95. It is worth noting the move of AEG-Telefunken from an 'Acoustic' (E) to a 'Telecommunications' (B2.1) pattern of specialisation in comparison with the persistence of the Brown Boveri (then ABB) specialisation in both technologies. The company was, indeed, in the 'mother technological groups' E and F as well as in the clusters developed from them (i.e. E1 and B2.1).

5.5 CONCLUSIONS

This chapter provides empirical evidence of an increasing overlap between the ICT technological specialisation profiles of European multinationals.

This pattern is consistent with the argument on technological diversification according to which a growing company should develop 'distributed' as well as 'core' competencies. In the European electronic industry, firms seem to have widened their specialisation profiles in ICT by diversifying within the ICT fields, the result being the increasing overlapping in their technological profiles. European multinationals have, indeed, become active in a broader range of technologies, as illustrated by the growing average of firms entering into clusters between 1987 and 1995. This diversified specialisation allowed them to adopt successful niche strategies. In a study focusing on the US and largest European electronic companies, Gambardella and Torrisi (1998) arrive at the conclusion that long-run related diversification is a profitable strategy. Technological diversification provides MNCs with different technology, which can be used to enter into different markets, but also to improve the existing products of the companies. The latter point is illustrated by Granstrand and Oskarsson (1994). The two authors show that the technology of cellular phones evolved from the use of technologies in five classes and one engineering competence to 14 technologies and 4 engineering competencies.[3]

These findings support Caracostas and Soete's (1997) arguments on the emergence of a European System of Innovation from the European research institutions' fragments. Within the European context, Dutch, German and French firms seem to lead the European electronic industry, whilst the British companies appear rather weak. German and French firms are more clearly from nationally identifiable backgrounds than the Dutch, although even this is beginning to change. French and German companies appear to be increasing their levels of R&D abroad (Cantwell and Kotecha, 1994; Cantwell and Harding, 1998). This pattern is also confirmed at the global level, where Europe is still lagging behind within the Triad. Thus, despite the emergence of common features within the European electronic industry, national components still play a major role in defining company specialisation and R&D orientation. Therefore the establishment of technological standards as well as an active policy aiming at homogenising the market may be efficient remedies for the lack of European competitiveness in the field of ICT (Dalum et al., 1999).

In evaluating this trend, the fact that European integration has increased the extent of market-based and technology-based interaction between firms should be taken into account. Furthermore, it is worth mentioning that convergence in the profiles of technological specialisation of European electronic multinationals occurred in the years that the EU technological policy began to be developed. In this sense, it may be suggested that the launch and development of a European technology policy may have played its role in providing the grounds for a more harmonised ICT industry within the Union. However, it is undoubtedly beyond the scope of this chapter to evaluate the impact of institutional initiative and economic integration processes on European corporate activities.

The statistical results of the chapter provide an understanding of the evolution and direction followed by European ICT multinationals in the management of their technological portfolios. On the basis of these findings the analysis carried out in the next chapter evaluates the role of corporate technological specialisation factors in the inter-firm development of technology.

NOTES

1. Siemens acquired Nixdorf Computer in 1990.
2. The absence of Olivetti in any of the 1987–95 clusters is due to the lack of statistically significant correlation between the Italian company and all others.
3. Technologies and engineering competencies are defined on the basis of a classification developed by the authors.

6. The dynamics of corporate competencies and STPs

6.1 INTRODUCTION

On the basis of the statistical results of the previous chapter, the empirical analysis of the present chapter focuses on the inter-firm strategy of technology development within the European ICT industry. The chapter aims to evaluate the role of corporate technological specialisation factors in the completion of strategic technological partnerships (STPs) in the European ICT industry. Strategic technological agreements are understood as inter-firm co-operative relationships concerning one or more areas of activity, where combined innovative activity or an interchange of technology is at least part of the agreement and the contractual mechanisms can be more or less formally specified. The 'strategic' character is given by the fact that the agreement improves the future value of the firm rather than simply minimising the net costs.

Over the last decade systemic technological and political changes have promoted a new trajectory of market-based capitalism amidst the process of increasing globalisation. Unlike in the previous phases based on markets and firms as alternative organisational modes of production and transactions ('hierarchical capitalism'), in the new trajectory of the capitalist system co-operation between both economic and political agents has been identified as a new organisational mode. In this sense, corporate alliances are understood as a means of furthering capability creation, which requires non-market co-ordination of necessity, rather than as a response to market failure. Therefore alliances represent more a flexible means of co-ordination. The adoption of collaborative agreements as organisational forms of economic activity characterised the early 1980s and increased sharply over the mid-1980s (Chesnais, 1988; Contractor and Lorange, 1988; Hagedoorn and Schakenraad, 1992; Hagedoorn, 1993a, 1995a, 1995b; Narula and Hagedoorn, 1997). This phenomenon has mainly involved the companies from the Triad – US, Japan and Europe – (Hagedoorn and Schakenraad, 1993a; Freeman and Hagedoorn, 1995). This trend seems to suggest that inter-firm alliances are a first option rather than an alternative to hierarchical organisational forms (Ciborra, 1991). In this case, a shift away from hierarchical capitalism towards 'alliance capitalism' (Gerlach, 1992; Dunning, 1995, 1997) refers to the growing adoption of co-operative and collaborative organisational forms of corporate activity in order to increment partners' competitive advantage.

The reasons for concluding alliances have been differently identified by the literature.[1] The transaction cost approach (Williamson, 1990) suggests that alliances may eventually be preferred to pure hierarchies because of higher financial risks and barriers to entry in the latter case (Buckley and Casson, 1976, 1988; Mariti and Smiley, 1983; Kogut, 1988; Casson, 1990). Thus, according to these authors, the advantage in adopting alliances relies on the minimisation of the sum of production and transaction costs due to the failure-prone characteristic of technological knowledge (Caves, 1982). However, as argued by the eclectic paradigm (Dunning, 1993), STPs may be a better strategy than subsidiaries if the location advantage cannot be completely captured by the foreign investor because it is specific to domestic firms. One of Chesnais' criticisms (1996) to the transaction cost approach as a framework for analysis of co-operative alliances is the fact that it ignores the firm as the central institution in capitalist economies for the transformation and creation of resources. In this context it is worth distinguishing between a cost-economising agreement and a strategic alliance. As mentioned above, in the latter case the strategic element implies the improvement of the future value of the firm, not simply the minimisation of the net cost. Thus the strategic element implies somehow the transfer of some knowledge as part of the agreement. In this sense the agreement may take place in a location where traditional locational advantages are absent if the primary objective is to acquire firm-specific ownership advantage through partnering. This is all the more true in the case of technology development, where these advantages are often non-codificable and specific to intra-firm learning processes. None the less international strategic technology partnering may enable firms to spread their innovative capabilities over many countries, where local scientific and technological advantage may be eventually used as outsourcing (Duysters and Hagedoorn, 1996; Hagedoorn, 1996, 1998; Narula and Dunning, 1998).

Recently the goal of most strategic alliances has been identified in gaining access to new complementary types of technology in order to enrich the firms' innovatory and learning process rather than to enhance the overall prosperity of the partners (Hagedoorn, 1993a; Chesnais, 1988; Cantwell, 1998c; Coombs and Metcalfe, 1998; Dyer and Singh, 1998; Inkpen, 1998). This may be interpreted as a result of the increasing technological interrelatedness (Pavitt et al., 1989), which has underlined the need for both corporate technological diversification (Granstrand and Sjölander, 1990; Granstrand et al., 1997) and strategic alliances with other companies in order to access capabilities closely related to their own profile of competencies. Access to competencies in fields unrelated to the firms' own capabilities is extremely costly and difficult since firms are able to learn to use and adapt effectively the knowledge they have access to only if they possess potential absorptive capacity (Cohen and Levinthal, 1989, 1990). These authors understand absorptive capacity as the accumulation of knowledge, skills and organisational routines necessary to identify and utilise externally generated knowledge (ibid.). For these reasons firms sharing some complementary capabilities are more likely to enter technological alliances, in which the interaction between partners' paths of innovative learning enhances their own respective internal development. However, the degree of interaction depends largely on the organisational form of the alliance and, furthermore, on the technological similarity (or dissimilarity) between the partners' profiles of technological capabilities. As shown empirically by Cantwell and Colombo (2000), different technological profiles between allied firms require a greater effort to match partners' competencies, thus promoting more equity forms of agreement (i.e. joint ventures). Conversely, technologically similar alliances will find it easier to co-ordinate their competencies, thus preferring more arm's length forms of co-operation (e.g. licensing, non-equity agreements, etc.). Similarly, Narula and Hagedoorn (1999) demonstrate that the use of non-equity agreements grew in high-technology and fast-evolving sectors between the early 1980s and the mid-1990s. Accordingly, forms of co-operation based on co-ordinated learning tend to encourage convergence in the patterns of corporate technological competencies, whilst forms of co-operation organised in terms of exchange of knowledge tend to create divergent trajectories of corporate learning, which can eventually move further apart (Cantwell and Barrera, 1998).

In the overall explosion of STPs the evidence of a steep increase in technological alliances in core technologies (such as ICT, biotechnology and new materials) since the early 1980s has been widely observed (Hagedoorn and Schakenraad, 1992; Hagedoorn, 1993b; Duysters and Hagedoorn, 1995b; Powell, 1998; Narula, 2001). Among core technologies, ICT has been the largest field of co-operation, especially during the first half of the 1980s. The development of the new socio–economic conditions has been identified as a major explanation of this trend since it requires a wide application of a range of technological capabilities which may not be implemented on the grounds of the firm's individual competencies. As a result of the greater role of basic science in technology, firms need to have some mastery of a wider range of disciplines. Therefore the new role of technological systems together with the rise in technological internationalisation and greater costs of R&D budgets marked a new avenue in technological development, which goes beyond the boundaries of a particular firm. As highlighted by Porter and Fuller (1986), the rate of technological change is a main determinant of the growth of STPs in the sense that corporate competitive advantage is mainly related to the rate of increase in knowledge rather than the absolute increment of the stock of knowledge. Due to the complexity of cutting-edge technologies (such as ICT), uncertainty, risks and R&D costs are consequently larger and product life cycles shorter. For these reasons technology partnering in high-tech sectors is highly characterised by contractual agreements in comparison with medium- and low-tech sectors where the adoption of joint ventures is rather large (Harrigan, 1988; Hagedoorn and Narula, 1996). In this light, co-operation becomes a crucial factor in strengthening corporate competitiveness.

The 1980s increase in STPs in ICT fields characterised also Europe, where, besides private technology alliances, the growth in the so-called cost-sharing technology partnerships was registered (Sharp and Shearman, 1987; Mytelka and Delapierre, 1988). Cost-sharing technology partnerships refer to international R&D collaborations stimulated by international organisations' and/or governments' subsidies to companies. In Europe, international collaborative private research was subsidised by the European Commission with the launch of an increasing number of technology programmes since the mid-1980s (Santangelo, 1996, 1997). As confirmed by the simultaneous start-up of joint R&D private and cost-sharing European projects (Hagedoorn and Schakenraad, 1993b), in this period both types of strategic technology collaborations expanded. None the less the subsidised European R&D networks for ICT companies appeared to resemble the privately established networks (ibid.). These results seem to suggest that these subsidised R&D networks reproduced the structure of the European large firm co-operations by adding to existing or emerging privately networks. In this sense EU technology programmes are likely to have played a crucial role in promoting an oligopolistic structure in the European ICT industry, characterised by a small number of large European companies (ibid.). In this light, it has been argued that strategic alliances appear to represent a process of 'flexible integration' between major oligopolies in the 1980s (Amin, 1993). However, in the 1990s, intra-European alliances have run out of steam, and US–European alliances have been more buoyant (Narula, 1999). The decrease in intra-European alliances in the 1990s has been interpreted as due to the oligopolistic structure of the industry. This means that intra-European alliances are no longer as necessary as in the previous decade. According to the author, these results seem to show that the SEM failed to achieve the aim of closer competition among European firms in undertaking co-operative R&D.

As discussed above, firms are willing to enter alliances in order to acquire partners' capabilities related to their fields of competencies. Therefore firms with overlapping portfolios of technological specialisation are likely to become partners. On the basis of a previous study (Santangelo, 2000b) the following hypothesis is tested over the period 1978–95 in the context of the European ICT industry by combining the patent data drawn from the Reading database with the Advanced Research Programme on Agreements (ARPA) data on strategic technological partnerships (see Appendix C).

Hypothesis: partners' technological specialisation over time is likely to further converge in the case of alliances between firms that were co-specialised in the previous period, while already dissimilar partners are likely to further diverge if they have concluded alliances previously. Further technological convergence/divergence may be linked as well to the extent of technological diversification of firms over time.

The organisation of this chapter is as follows. The econometric methodology and the measures adopted are exposed in section 6.2. Section 6.3 discusses the general trends in STPs in the European ICT industry during the 1980s. Section 6.4 focuses on the specialisation dynamics in the European ICT corporate STPs by presenting evidence from the econometric analysis. Section 6.5 draws some conclusions.

6.2   METHODOLOGICAL NOTES

In order to analyse the relationship between STPs and corporate technological specialisation in the European ICT industry, two datasets are jointly considered – the University of Reading and the ARPA databases (see Appendix C). The data concerning technological specialisation relate to the corporate patenting in the US of the world's European largest ICT firms over the period 1978–95 as recorded in the Reading database. The dataset concerning strategic technological partnerships is drawn from the ARPA database. The sample of analysis refers to 14 of the European largest ICT companies, which lie at the intersection of the two databases mentioned above (see Table A.1).

The RTA index, calculated across the original ICT patent classes corresponding to the six ICT technological sectors (see section 5.2), is used as a proxy for corporate technological specialisation. In order to test the hypothesis, the technological similarity between allied firms' sectoral specialisation profiles is investigated with the use of the Pearson's correlation coefficient calculated between the RTA index distributions of all 91 possible pairwise combinations of firms across the considered ICT patent classes in the period 1978–86 (i.e. $r_{(78-86)}$).

Using the ARPA data, a dummy variable (ALLIES), equal to 1 for allied pairs of firms and to 0 otherwise, is built. In order to test the robustness of the econometric results, the hypothesis stated in Section 6.1 is investigated empirically by classifying these agreements in alliances between technologically similar and dissimilar partners at a detailed level (Classification 1), and between technologically co-specialised and non-co-specialised partners at a broader level (Classification 2). Classification 1 is based on the technological clusters identified in the period 1978–86 in Chapter 5 (see Figure 5.1). Firms are classified as technologically similar if they are in the same cluster (see Figure 5.1) and if their RTA distributions across the ICT patent classes (see section 5.2) are positively correlated in the same period. If these two criteria are not met at the same time, the partners are classified as technologically similar/dissimilar on the basis of the value of the Pearson's correlation coefficient. Similarly, if one of the partners (or both of them) is not in the clusters, the technological similarity (dissimilarity) between them is established on the basis of the correlation coefficient. Therefore two dummy variables are set equal to 1 for technologically similar allied pairs of companies and 0 otherwise (SIMI and DIS respectively). Classification 2 is based on the RTA distribution of the 14 companies not across the detailed ICT patent classes (see section 5.2), but across the six ICT sectors (Table A.3). In this case allied pairs are classified as co-specialised if they show RTA value > 1.5 in the same ICT sector. To take into account the profile of technological generalist of Philips, the Dutch company is defined as co-specialised with its partners if both of them show the three highest RTA values in the same ICT sectors. Therefore two dummy variables are set equal to 1 for co-specialised allied pairs of companies and to 0 otherwise (COSP and NON-COSP respectively). The reason for classifying the firms in the sample as similar (dissimilar) and co-specialised (non-co-specialised) partners lies in the fact that co-operation may well occur through joint equity ventures between companies which, although active in the same broad technological area and with some similarity in their products, are quite different in their detailed individual fields of technological specialisation.

In order to investigate whether similar (SIMI) partners converge over time as a result of an alliance in the previous period, while technological divergence is likely to increase further in the case of already dissimilar (DIS) or firms which enter an alliance in the previous period, an OLS regression analysis is adopted. The hypothesis is also tested by distinguishing between co-specialised (COSP) and non-co-specialised (NON-COSP) allies – Classification 2.

Moreover the Hypothesis is tested empirically by using the absolute changes in the coefficient of correlation between 1978–86 and 1987–95 ($\Delta r_{(78-86/87-95)}$) as a proxy for technological convergence (divergence). In this process the role of technological diversification is also taken into account since most of the leading diversified companies play a prominent role in strategic partnerships in ICT (Hagedoorn and Schakenraad, 1992). Corporate technological diversification is proxied as

$$DIVE = 1/CV \tag{6.1}$$

where CV is the coefficient of variation of the RTA index calculated across the USPTO original ICT patent classes (see section 2.2). For each pairwise combination of European electronic companies, whichever company had the largest absolute changes in technological diversification between 1978–86 and 1987–95 ($\Delta DIVE_{(78-86/87-95)}$) is the change taken into account. Thus, using Classification 1 the regression function is specified as follows:

$$\Delta r_{(78-86/87-95)} = f(SIMI, DIS, D_{comp}, D_{tele}, \Delta DIVE) \tag{6.2}$$

while, adopting Classification 2:

$$\Delta r_{(78-86/87-95)} = f(COSP, NON-COSP, D_{comp}, D_{tele}, \Delta DIVE) \tag{6.3}$$

where D_{comp}, D_{tele} are two dummy variables introduced to control for industry divergence of alliances between similar/co-specialised partners. The variable D_{comp} takes into consideration allied pairs of European electronic companies where one of the two partners moves towards a computing specialisation. In equation 6.2, D_{comp} refers to the partnerships between GCE and CII-Honeywell Bull, Olivetti and CII-Honeywell Bull, and STC and Siemens, whilst in equation 6.3 the variable D_{comp} concerns the last two partnerships only. If in the early 1980s all three (two in the case of equation 6.3) pairs of allied companies show similar/co-specialised profiles of technological specialisation, in the later 1980s their technological profiles diverged. The divergence between GCE and CII-Honeywell Bull may be attributed to the French 'colbertisme high-tech' which pushed the latter to consolidate its specialisation in computing and drop its communications-related activities. Accordingly, the consolidation of CII-Honeywell Bull's computing specialisation seems to be the reason for the divergence with Olivetti. As a result of the major difficulties the Italian company went through in the later period considered, Olivetti experimented a despecialisation in computing after transition from its mechanical to its electronic age. Instead the case of STC and Siemens is driven by the 1990 acquisition of Nixdorf Computer by Siemens and the consequent move to a specialisation in computing technologies by the latter. The variable D_{tele} is introduced in both equation 6.2 and 6.3 in order to take into consideration allied pairs of European electronic companies where one or both partners moved towards non-defence telecommunications. In both equations this is the case of General Electric Co. and Plessey, General Electric Co. and Racal Electronics, and LM

Ericsson and Plessey. In the late 1980s and early 1990s all three British corporations show a technological profile less focused on defence electronics and more oriented to telecommunications fields, which were, however, different from one another.

6.3 GENERAL TRENDS IN STPs IN THE EUROPEAN ICT INDUSTRY

Before going into the details of the results of the econometric analysis, this section provides an overview of the phenomenon of STPs in the European ICT industry in the 1980s. Despite the technological convergence among the companies from the Triad countries (Freeman and Hagedoorn, 1995), the increase in STPs during the 1980s seems to correspond to a rise in intra-bloc partnering (i.e. intra-US, intra-Japanese and intra-European technological alliances) (Hagedoorn, 1993a, 1996). It has been argued that the strong regional nature of inter-firm R&D collaboration may be attributed to the additional complexity that the internationalisation of R&D activity creates in STPs' organisation (Duysters and Hagedoorn, 1996). This trend also seems to have characterised the European ICT industry (Hagedoorn, 1996). Figure 6.1 shows the distribution of European ICT partnerships over the period 1980–86. STPs between European electronic companies appear to be far larger than STPs between these companies and US and Japanese electronic firms.

It is worth noting that these data drawn from the ARPA database do not include alliances made in the context of European technology programmes such as ESPRIT and Eureka. Therefore the higher percentage of intra-European technology co-operation in ICT may be explained by the attempt of the European electronic companies to fill the gap with US and Japanese competitors. However, as suggested by Cainarca et al. (1989), the role played by the overall economic integration process should not be understated when considering the launch of the SEM with the 1986 Single European Act (SEA). By creating an imperative for competitiveness within Europe, the SEM initiative required a restructuring of the various individual European firms. As far as innovative activities are concerned, Cantwell (1992b) shows that the degree of interdependence among the MNC's distinct units is relatively higher in Europe than in other areas of the world. This may explain the adoption of a more 'regionally' rather than 'globally' oriented strategy by European corporations (Hagedoorn, 1993a; Duysters and Hagedoorn, 1996). None the less within the European context there are substantial cross-country differences. For instance, UK- and German-owned firms are more US-oriented than Dutch- or Swedish-owned firms (Cantwell and Janne,

1999). Despite the cross-country differences, the integration process has created an imperative for intra-area rationalisation of innovative activity. This argument is confirmed in Figure 6.2, where 86 per cent of the European electronic companies appears to be involved in intra-block partnering within the European ICT industry.

The empirical evidence proposed in Figures 6.1 and 6.2 seems to be consistent with Narula's study (1999) on intra- and inter-European alliances over the decade 1980s–1990s. The author confirms a sharp increase in intra-European alliances in the 1980s, which reinforced the oligopolistic industrial structure within Europe. According to Narula, in the 1990s this meant that agreements were now in place informally to an extent that intra-European alliances have fallen off.

As the establishment of STPs seems to have characterised the European ICT industry since the 1980s, it is worth investigating the distribution of alliances in the industry by nationality of both parent and partner company. The aim is to trace the main networks of intra-European partnerships in the ICT industry by distinguishing between European and home partners and, in the former case, going into details of nationality of the partner company.

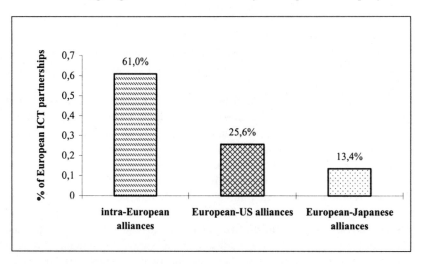

Source: Author's elaboration on University of Reading patent data.

Figure 6.1 – Distribution of European ICT partnerships by European company and regional block (%), 1980–86

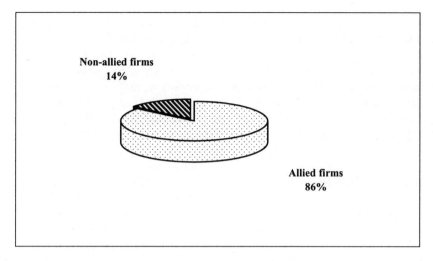

Source: Author's elaboration on University of Reading patent data.

Figure 6.2 – Share of European ICT companies involved in intra-EU alliances relative to the sample of analysis (%), 1980–86

For each European national group of electronic companies, Table 6.1 records the distribution of alliances within ICT partners from other European member states and from the same home country relative to the European electronic industry as a whole over the period 1980–86.

Table 6.1 – Distribution of alliances within the European ICT industry relative to the total number of alliances concluded in the industry, by nationality of the parent and partner company, 1980–86 (%)

Nationality of the Parent Company	Other European Partner %	Home Partner %	Total %
France	28,0	8,0	36,0
Germany	14,0	0,0	14,0
Italy	4,0	0,0	4,0
The Netherlands	8,0	0,0	8,0
Sweden	2,0	0,0	2,0
UK	24,0	12,0	36,0
Total	80,0	20,0	100,0

Source: Author's elaboration on University of Reading patent data.

In Table 6.1 the overall total depicts a clear preference for partners from other European member states. Of the alliances concluded within the European electronic industry 80 per cent seem to involve parent companies located in different European countries. The launch of the SEM may have speeded up the movement towards co-operation in order to compete in a global environment characterised by globalisation of competition and increased rate of innovation (Urban and Vendemini, 1992). This pattern is led mainly by German ICT companies and to a lesser extent by Dutch, Italian and Swedish corporations. For all these national groups of firms the figures show a clear preference for other European partners rather than for partners from the same home country. In the case of the German companies (i.e. AEG-Telefunken, Siemens and Nixdorf Computer) this trend might be explained by a corporate approach to international competitiveness based on globalisation of R&D activity (Cantwell and Harding, 1998). Moreover, as in all other European countries, the largest national electronic corporations have historically dominated the national ICT market by operating in different markets and technological segments. Thus for each of them it was easier to found technological capabilities complementary to their technological specialisation profile in foreign companies active in the same types of technology than in other German companies.

Partnerships by French and British electronic corporations appear to follow a different pattern. As reported in Table 6.1, both these ICT national groups of firms are the most active in entering STPs relative to all others accounting for 36.0 per cent each of the total alliances concluded in the European ICT industry as a whole. However, even if French and British corporations seem to prefer European partners, they still enter alliances with home firms. This trend is more marked for the British than for the French electronic corporations. For the former, alliances with a home partner count for 12.0 per cent of the total STPs entered into by electronic companies within the European ICT industry. In the latter case, home partnership accounts for slightly less (8.0 per cent) of the total STPs entered by electronic companies within the European ICT industry. National champions' policies and a 'fortress Europe' approach to the competitiveness issue in ICT foreign markets may provide an explanation for the fact that intra-French partnerships still play an important role. As a result of the national champions' policies, the largest French electronic corporations (i.e. Thomson-Brandt, CGE and CII-Honeywell Bull) have grown accustomed to working primarily for the domestic market. In this sense the European arena represents an extension of this national logic to the regional market (Delapierre and Zimmerman, 1991). Therefore strategic partnerships are aimed at defining the existing market base in a context of globalising industries. None the less the high percentage of European partnerships concluded by French electronic companies may be read as an indirect effect of the early European technology policy, which promoted the adoption of a 'springboard Europe' strategy (ibid.). This strategy is characterised mainly by the preference for partnerships with European firms which could then be expected to evolve into or be supplemented by commercial and global agreements in order to structure the complementarity of the two partners. In this context a rather widespread technological specialisation is likely to explain the overall greater degree of technological collaboration with European ICT companies by French multinationals.

The British situation is somewhat different when considering the high percentage of intra-UK ICT alliances in comparison with all other national groups of firms. Following the finding of a previous empirical study on similarities between corporate technological specialisation profiles in the European ICT industry (Santangelo, 1998), the reason for this may be identified as closer technological complementarity among British ICT companies in the period considered. Similarly, in the UK ICT industry there is a long history of co-operation, in which academic and industrial communities interact closely (Oakley, 1984). However, it is worth noting that STPs concluded by UK electronic companies with European partners account for a relevant percentage of the total alliances in the ICT industry, thus confirming somehow an active role of UK corporations in the European electronic industry.

For each national group of European ICT companies Table 6.2 reports the cross-country distribution of alliances with partners from other European countries.

A glance at the figures reveals that French and British electronic firms are the favoured allies of German-owned corporations. Following the findings of the empirical study referred to above (Santangelo, 1998), the establishment of alliances between these national groups of companies may be due to the fact that these partners moved along similar technological trajectories in the period in question (Santangelo, 1998). In this context STPs may have been viewed as a forum to combine different corporate partners' competencies. From Table 6.2 it is also possible to depict the existence of alliances between German ICT companies (namely Siemens) and Philips.

Like the German ICT corporations, Philips shows a strategic alliance profile oriented to European rather than to home partners. In evaluating the figures in Table 6.2, the company's corporate strategy should be taken into consideration as well as its position in the European ICT industry. Philips focused its resources on its most profitable and fast-growing product lines by implementing a policy of acquisitions and joint ventures. This strategy promoted the Dutch corporation as a technological leader in the European ICT industry in terms of technological size and specialisation (ibid.) as well as market share. The high degree of internationalisation of Philips' R&D activity (Cantwell and Janne, 1998) may also provide a further explanation for the company's preference for European partners. The range of nationalities of Philips' allies confirms the profile of technological generalist of the Dutch company. If product and technological diversification are key factors in explaining the leading position of Philips in the European ICT industry, they also provide a major explanation for the company partnering strategy, since Philips' product and technological corporate competencies complement a large number of European competitors' capabilities.

In contrast, French partners seem to absorb completely Olivetti's alliance profile. This pattern is fully driven by the specialisation in computing technology between CII-Honeywell-Bull and Olivetti. The Italian pattern is fully led by Olivetti's partnering strategy defined by its chief executive, Carlo De Benedetti. STPs have played a major role in Olivetti's history since it was believed that links with high technology companies were vital in allowing a relatively modest-sized firm such as Olivetti to keep updated with advanced development, while concentrating its own R&D in specialist areas (Jowett and Rothwell, 1986). European collaborations appeared to be appealing also when considering the structure of the Italian electronic industry mainly dominated by Olivetti and characterised by small and medium-sized enterprises.

Table 6.2 – Distribution of alliances between European ICT partners* relative to the total number of alliances concluded in the European ICT industry, by nationality of the parent and partner company, 1980–86 (%)

Nationality of the Parent Company		%
France	Germany	21,4
	Italy	14,3
	The Netherlands	14,3
	Sweden	0,0
	UK	50,0
Total		**100,0**
Germany	France	42,9
	Italy	0,0
	The Netherlands	14,3
	Sweden	0,0
	UK	42,9
Total		**100,0**
Italy	France	100,0
	Germany	0,0
	The Netherlands	0,0
	Sweden	0,0
	UK	0,0
Total		**100,0**

Nationality of the Parent Company			%
The Netherlands		France	50,0
		Germany	25,0
		Italy	0,0
		Sweden	0,0
		UK	25,0
	Total		**100,0**
Sweden		France	0,0
		Germany	0,0
		Italy	0,0
		The Netherlands	0,0
		UK	100,0
	Total		**100,0**
UK		France	58,3
		Germany	25,0
		Italy	0,0
		The Netherlands	8,3
		Sweden	8,3
	Total		**100,0**

Note:
* Alliances between European ICT companies from the same home country are excluded.

Source: Author's elaboration on ARPA database, Politecnico di Milano

Accordingly, the figures in Table 6.2 illustrate that the UK electronic companies enter into alliances with French companies and to a lesser extent with German, Dutch and Swedish. In the case of LM Ericsson the preference for British partners may be due to the complementary expertise in communications technology as well as to the Swedish corporation strategy. LM Ericsson seems to choose its partners according to its market targets (Jenkins, 1991).

6.4 COMPETENCIES DYNAMICS IN CORPORATE STPs IN THE EUROPEAN ICT INDUSTRY

To test the hypothesis an OLS model is used. The econometric analysis is carried out by adopting the two classifications of the 91 pairs of allied companies illustrated in section 6.2 in order to guarantee the robustness of the results.

As far as the econometric results are concerned, as shown in Tables 6.3 and 6.4, the results of the regression analysis confirm the findings of previous empirical studies (e.g. Mowery et al., 1997; Santangelo, 2000b), according to which partners' technological similarities are reinforced over time through strategic alliances. Similar technological profiles seem to converge as a result of the acquisition of partners' capabilities. Following Cantwell and Barrera's (1998) argument, inter-firm co-operations between technologically similar/co-specialised partners are likely to promote technological learning since mutual research efforts in the shared field of specialisation may create a detailed division of labour. In contrast, inter-firm co-operation between dissimilar/non-co-specialised partners cannot go beyond exchange of knowledge since there are no common capabilities promoting coordination of research and learning processes. In the latter case inter-firm co-operation is likely to lead to a much broader division of labour, which may move the allies' specialisation profiles further apart. However, as suggested by Nakamura et al. (1996), in the case of divergent technological portfolios, partners' competitive capabilities are complementary even if becoming more dissimilar. In this sense alliances represent a mean of corporate specialisation since companies focus more on some areas. In the case of convergent alliances the leading capabilities of the European electronic partners are mutually enhanced, thus enabling them to deal with the increasing level of technological complexity. In turn this should push them to improve their productivity and competitiveness, thus expanding their share of non-European markets. In this sense co-operative management of knowledge has been identified by the European Commission as a key tool in promoting the European ICT industry.

However inter-firm co-operation can only partially explain the process of technological convergence (divergence) since the specialisation profiles of the European electronic companies seem to have became more similar or have moved further apart also as a result of corporate technological diversification strategies.

The results seem to suggest that technological diversification has played a crucial role in the process of technological convergence (divergence) (Tables 6.3 and 6.4).

In the development of technology, alliances and in-house investments in new technological competencies should be understood as complements, rather than substitutes. Both strategies enable large multi-technology companies to develop (besides their 'core') technological competencies that are distributed across an increasing number of technical fields in order to avoid failures in product development, production, marketing and organisational adaptation (Granstrand et al., 1997). The importance of technological diversification as a crucial determinant of corporate co-specialisation within the European ICT industry is also confirmed in Figure 6.3, where the changes in technological co-specialisation between European ICT partners relative to the total number of alliances are shown.

Table 6.3 – Results of the OLS regression analysis based on the clusters classification

Regressor	Coefficient	Standard Error	T-Ratio	
Intercept	–0,038	0,048	–0,796	
SIMI	0,260	0,150	1,735	*
DIS	0,016	0,100	0,156	
Dcomp	–0,941	0,241	–3,901	***
Dtele	–0,466	0,215	–2,168	***
ΔDIVE	0,005	0,003	2,001	**
R-Squared	0,188			
R-Bar-Squared	0,141			
No. obs.	91			

Notes:
*** significant at 1% level.
** significant at 5% level.
* significant at 10% level.

Source: Author's elaboration on University of Reading patent data.

Table 6.4 – Results of the OLS regression analysis based on the RTA values classification

Regressor	Coefficient	Standard Error	T-Ratio	
Intercept	–0,038	0,047	–0,817	
COSP	0,211	0,113	1,864	*
NON-COSP	–0,071	0,106	–0,668	
Dcomp	–1,045	0,253	–4,134	***
Dtele	–0,483	0,212	–2,278	**
ΔDIVE	0,005	0,003	2,068	**
R-Squared	0,203			
R-Bar-Squared	0,156			
No. obs.	91			

Notes:
*** significant at 1% level.
** significant at 5% level.
* significant at 10% level.

Source: Author's elaboration on University of Reading patent data.

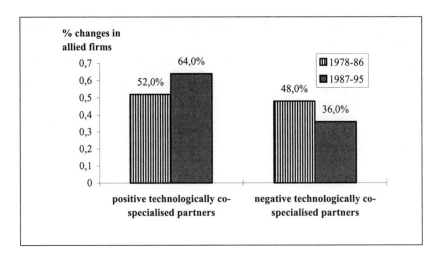

Source: Santangelo (2000b).

Figure 6.3 – Changes in technological co-specialisation between European ICT partners (%) relative to the total number of alliances, 1978–95

It turns out that there was a 12 per cent increase in the number of technologically co-specialised partners between 1978–86 and 1987–95. This implies that previously negatively technologically co-specialised partners most likely came closer together over time as a result of corporate diversification strategies when combining the impression gained from Figure 6.3 with the results of the regression analysis (Tables 6.3 and 6.4). Thus, in the European ICT industry, partnering and technological diversification strategies appear to be major factors in promoting closer technological integration. None the less the role of European technology policy as well as the on-going integration process in orienting and directing corporate technological trajectories in the European ICT industry should not be understated.

6.5　CONCLUSIONS

Collaborative partnerships have been increasingly adopted as a form of business operation in the early 1980s. The 1980s increased adoption of strategic technological partnerships as a form of organisation of economic activity has been identified as a main feature of a new phase of the capitalist system (Gerlach, 1992, Dunning, 1995, 1997), where competitiveness is increasingly pursued through co-operation. This phenomenon has mainly characterised science-based fields of technological activity such as ICT as a result of the growing technological interrelatedness and complexity. In geographical terms, while the 1990s were characterised by an increase in inter-bloc STPs, the 1980s, trends in strategic technological partnership showed a clear intra-bloc specificity (Narula, 1999). During the 1980s the growth in the number of technological alliances was greater between partners from the same regional area. Thus even if the phenomenon involved mainly Triad countries and corporations, there appeared to be a strong regional connotation. In the European case in the 1980s this trend might have also been strengthened by the on-going economic and political integration process as well as by the European technology policy, which has became more structured over time.

Accordingly it is found that in the European ICT industry participation in STPs and corporate technological diversification are major determinants of technological convergence between already similar/co-specialised partners (Santangelo, 2000b). As far as technological collaboration is concerned, this is the case if corporate co-operation involved a transfer of knowledge rather than a simple exchange. In the former case a complementary division of labour is likely to develop between the partner companies, which come closer together in terms of specialisation profiles. The positive influence of technological diversification on partners' technological convergence is consistent with the view that large firms are required to master a wide range of technologies in order to be able to match radical changes in technology with equivalent changes in production. Thus technological specialisation profiles of European electronic partners are also found to be convergent as a result of the technological diversity developed within collaborative agreements.

From the overall findings it is possible to draw the conclusion that a collaborative approach to the issue of European competitiveness in ICT fields seems to have been rather successful in promoting common technological trajectories within the European electronic industry in the 1980s. This is likely to lead to a more structurally defined European ICT industry since collaborative agreements allow European electronic corporations to combine synergies and develop a division of labour between them. In addition, as in the 1980s privately established networks resembled subsidised European companies (Hagedoorn and Schakenraad, 1993b), the growth of STPs promoted an oligopolistic industry structure in the 1990s. That is agreements were now in place informally to an extent that intra-European alliances have fallen off in the early 1990s (Narula, 1999). In this sense European technology policy seems to have facilitated rather than imposing this process which has already taken place at corporate level.

After having examined the dynamic strategies of European ICT multinationals in the management of their intangible assets both in terms of similarity of technological portfolios in Chapter 5 and inter-firm development of technology in the present chapter, the analysis moves further by focusing on the locational aspects of corporate research activity in the European ICT industry.

NOTE

1. For a brief review of the different approaches explaining the reasons for concluding alliances see Coombs et al. (1996).

Appendix C: The ARPA database

The data on STPs are drawn from the ARPA database developed at Politecnico di Milano. The database surveyed agreements in the ICT industrial system for the entire world. The ICT industrial system comprises more specifically microelectronics, data processing and office automation, and telecommunications over the period 1980–86. The term 'system' highlights the high range of interactions and innovative processes characterising the evolution of hardware, software and services within the ICT field (Cozzi et al., 1988). Strategic technological agreements refer to inter-firm long-term relationships, which allow the parties to regulate 'ex ante' their future conduct by means of more or less formally specified contractual mechanisms (Cainarca et al., 1992). The co-operative relationships concern one or more areas of activity, where combined innovative activity or an interchange of knowledge is at least part of the agreement. The agreement may determine a change in the firms' ownership structure (minority or parity shareholding) or promote a new company jointly owned by the partners (joint venture). In the ARPA database this distinction is made on the grounds of their organisational form (equity *versus* non-equity agreements) as well of partnerships' final aim (defined in financial terms) – see Table C.1 – (Cainarca et al., 1989).

As far as the organisational content is concerned, non-equity agreements (in all their sub-categories) include technology transfer (in the form of patents, licensing or know-how) and product distribution (e.g. original equipment manufacturer – OEM), whilst equity agreements (in all their sub-categories) refer mainly to joint ventures. If the distinction between equity and non-equity concerns the contractual form of the agreements, the ARPA database classifies the agreement also on the basis of the partnership's final aim or functional content (see Table C.1). This chapter focuses on research-based agreements. Therefore the data on STPs used in the econometric analysis refer to agreements classified in the ARPA databases as aiming at joint R&D development regardless of their contractual form. This means that, for instance, corporate venture capital can be taken into account (although classified among equity forms of agreements) if aiming at the joint development of R&D activity.

Table C.1 – Taxonomy of partnerships. Contractual forms and contents

	Contents Equity Forms					Non-equity Forms							
	PAR	MIN	CVC	JOV	SUB	FRN	LIC	OEM	VAR	TRS	SRC	CON	ACC
FIN	x	x	x	x								x	
RES	*x*	*x*		*x*						*x*	*x*	*x*	
KHE	x	x		x			x			x			x
PRD	x	x		x	x		x				x	x	x
PER								x					
COM	x	x		x		x	x	x	x		x	x	x
SER	x	x		x							x	x	x
ASS	x	x		x			x						x
ALT	x	x		x							x	x	x

Notes:

Contents		*Forms*	
FIN	financial resources	PAR	parity participation
RES	research and development	MIN	minority participation
KHE	know-how and engineering	CVC	corporate venture capital
PRD	production	JOV	joint venture
PER	customisation	SUB	sub-supply
COM	marketing and distribution	FRN	supply
SER	services	LIC	licence
ASS	post-selling assistance	OEM	original equipment manufacturing
ALT	others	VAR	value added retailing
		TRS	sources and know-how transfers
		SRC	implementation and joint development
		CON	consortia
		ACC	other agreements

Bold italics indicates the partnerships which this chapter focuses on.

Source: Cainarca et al., 1989.

In ARPA equity agreements, joint development agreements and consortia, and licences are the most prominent categories, accounting all together for 75.6 per cent of the total number of agreements surveyed. Among all these categories, equity agreements are by far the most numerous (589 in total). The 2,014 agreements involve 1,574 partners, which belong to 1,177 different autonomous economic units (including industrial groups, independent firms, public bodies and institutions). Agreements in semiconductors represent 20.9

per cent of the total number of surveyed agreements, whilst agreements in data processing count for 42.6 per cent and 37.8 per cent in telecommunications (Cainarca et al., 1992). As far as the information technology industry is concerned, Carbonin and Maglione (1987) hold that the number of agreements in the ARPA database is clearly higher than in other databases. In this database subsidiaries' nationality was established on the grounds of the geographical location of the parent company. For instance, IBM Italy has been considered as a US company.

This information was gathered through what may be called a 'literature-based alliances counting' method, based upon the consultation of international press, technical magazines and specialist studies. Possible biases and distortions were reduced by adopting meticulous survey and cross-checking procedures. In this process of collection of inter-firm alliances the coverage of local sources of information for all three most developed areas (US, Europe and Japan) allows a more balanced role for the Japanese firms, which seems to have been overlooked in most previous databases (Cainarca et al., 1992). However, this method of information gathering has its drawbacks and limitations even if the authors further revised the sample.[1] First, ARPA data accounts for agreements that are made public. Second, newspaper and journal reports are likely to be incomplete. Another related problem is that the sources used do not publish systematically the dissolution of agreements. As in the databases assembled following these procedures (e.g. MERIT and LAREA-CEREM), one final problem relates to the fact that the sample is highly conditioned by an over-representation of European companies, for which information is also more complete. If the last point is not an issue in the analysis carried out in this book, for obvious reasons, the others should be taken into account when evaluating the econometric results reported.

NOTE

1. Carbonin and Maglione (1987) acknowledge the fact that in 1984–85 the original sample of agreements was updated and revised on the basis of a new gathering of information within a research project carried out by the consultancy agency Ruseau (Milan) and sponsored by the Olivetti Group.

7. Locational aspects of ICT corporate technological development: some evidence from German, Italian and UK regions

7.1 INTRODUCTION

This chapter concludes Part Two. After having investigated the sectoral composition of technological portfolios (Chapter 5) and its role in the process of inter-firm learning (Chapter 6), the analysis of the European ICT industry is here completed by focusing on the locational aspect of technology development. This chapter investigates the regional dispersion of European ICT research activity across Europe, placing major emphasis on German, Italian and UK regions. The reason for a spatial analysis at the regional level lies in the fact that nation-state investigations are likely to neglect intra-borders inequalities between regional economic units. If empirical studies at the country level have shown high levels of heterogeneity in the accumulation and diffusion of technology (Cantwell, 1987; Archibugi and Pianta, 1992b; Padoan, 1997; Vertova, 1998a, 1998b, 1999), the situation at the regional level is even more heterogeneous in terms of both GDP growth (Champion et al., 1996; Fagerberg, 1996; Iammarino et al., 1998; Iammarino and Santangelo, 2000; Magrini, 1998) and technology development (Cantwell and Dunning, 1991; Cowan and Foray, 1996; Cantwell and Iammarino, 1998, 2000), as a result of 'vicious' and 'virtuous' circles. None the less it should be borne in mind that, due to the lack of data availability (Clayton and Johnson, 1982; Iammarino et al., 1995), empirical analyses at regional level have been possible only recently.

The interest in regional analysis is due to the importance of economic geography in the information age. The importance of economic geography has been discovered by a relatively new stream of literature labelled as 'new economic geography' and developed mainly with the work of Krugman (1991a, 1991b, 1995, 1998), Arthur (1989) and Venables (1994).[1] The main argument concerns the view that increasing returns are essentially a regional and local phenomenon arising from regional economic agglomeration and specialisation. These basic models have been further elaborated by 'new endogenous growth theory' by focusing on inter-regional transfer of human capital or localised technological progress as the mechanisms underlying the locational concentration of economic activity (Thomas, 1986). Although space was a variable taken into account by economists, classical location theory (Lösch, 1954; Isard, 1956; Weber, 1984) explains agglomeration economies mainly in terms of reduction of transaction costs and cheap labour. Since the 1980s this model has expanded following three main lines: the neo-Marshallian model of industrial districts and local production systems (concerning mainly the studies on the 'Third Italy'); the development of the evolutionary theory and the notion of 'innovative milieu' (Aydalot, 1988; Aydalot and Keeble, 1988; Maillat, 1995; Camagni and Capello, 1997; Lawson, 1999) and 'technopole' (Castells and Hall, 1994); and the extension of work on the organisation of industrial production (Piore and Sabel, 1984).[2] Diverging about the starting-point (whether the 'global' – the MNC – or the 'local' – the territorial unit), all three lines of theoretical development underline the importance of the localised higher added value in explaining economic agglomeration and performance. Manufacturing, human, physical and communications, and industrial governance infrastructures (Florida, 1995, 1996; Guimarães et al., 1997; Sölvell and Bengtsson, 2000) are key factors defining the 'knowledge-based' or 'learning' region, able to maintain its sustainable advantage over time. The success of the 'learning' region relies on the capabilities to mobilise technical resources, knowledge and other inputs essential to innovation (Amin et al., 1994; Feldman and Florida, 1994). On these grounds Lawson (1999) proposes to extend the competence perspective from the study of the firm to the study of socio–economic systems. A strong path-dependent character is found in the local ability to develop an entrepreneurial environment through expertise accumulation (O'Farrell, 1986, Scott, 1988). As in the global arena host locations are competing in order to attract MNCs' quality investments, Howells (1999) remarks that regional systems of innovations do not undermine the globalisation process in terms of production and diffusion of technology but rather they reinforce it.

In the information age although time and space constraints have been reduced or (in some cases) completely eliminated by the pace of technological development, paradoxically geography seems to matter more than ever before. On the one hand, the shift towards a knowledge-based economy involves a shift in organisation away from top-down hierarchical infrastructures to flatter structures based on intra-firm networks of semi-autonomous corporate subsidiaries (Cooke and Wells, 1991; Dunning, 1994; Amin and Thirf, 1995; Archibugi and Michie, 1995; Cantwell, 1995; Zander, 1996, 1998; Stiglitz, 1999). On the other hand, the increasing globalisation of economic activity has emphasised the importance of clusters of innovative local centres over time accumulating new knowledge embodied in best practices (Amin and Goddard, 1986; Knox and Agnew, 1989; Sölvell and Birkinshaw, 2000). Therefore the higher the level of corporate internationalisation, the stronger the linkages the firm establishes with the local system (Loinger and Peyrache, 1988; Keeble et al., 1997). If this is a general trend across industries, it applies particularly to science-based industries (e.g. ICT), where links between corporate competitors, and firms–university and users–producers relationships are crucial in the development and adoption of new flexible technologies (Malecki, 1985; Oakey and Cooper, 1989; Gertler, 1995; Oakey, 1985; Audretsch and Stephan, 1994, 1996; Swann and Prevezer, 1996; Baptista, 2000; Baptista and Swann, 1998; Fedelman and Audretsch, 1999). In the case of science-based and related industries (e.g. ICT), local networks and infrastructures may promote potential for knowledge creation and learning. The point is illustrated in the case of the New Jersey telecommunications industry (Wymbs, 1998), Silicon Valley computer industry and Route 128 (Saxenian, 1994; McCann, 1995; Storper, 1997; Scott, 1988).

In the knowledge-driven economy regional territorial units have gained importance in the global development of technology (Oakey, 1985; Florida, 1995; Storper and Scott, 1995; Almeida, 1996; Storper, 1997). Although great emphasis has been placed on the role of geography in explaining local and corporate innovation, research has focused mainly on the US regions (Ullman, 1958; Burns, 1987; Jaffe et al., 1993; Audretsch and Feldman, 1994, 1996a, 1996b; Feldman, 1993, 1994; Feldman and Florida, 1994; Audretsch and Stephan, 1994, 1996; Angel and Engstrom, 1995; Feldman and Audretsch, 1999). Conversely, the focus on the European regional dimension in the development of innovation is rather recent (Caniëls, 1998; Cantwell and Iammarino, 1998, 2000; Verspagen, 1997a, 1997b). In an analysis of the spatial dimension of innovative activity across European regions the European integration process should be taken into account. Quévitt (1992, 1996) argues that the SEM completion together with global economic and technological changes impact on the performance of European regions. The first empirical results seem to point out that income disparities may owe their existence to the process of knowledge specialisation between 'knowledge creating' and 'knowledge applying' regions and that they have been exacerbated by EU integration (Magrini, 1998). The location of large MNCs seems to reinforce the top of the national urban hierarchies (Rozenblat and Pumain, 1993). A reason for this trend has been found in the European failure to take advantage of the opportunities offered by the information age (Begg et al., 1999). The pervasive character of ICT is provoking a transformation in urban and regional systems by generating a new network model involving core regions and neglecting the peripheral (Hepworth, 1986; Malecki, 1994; Antonelli, 1995, 1996; Castells, 1985). Therefore as technological change affects not only the long-term growth of economies, but also the spatial distribution of economic activity, a concentration phenomenon has emerged (Feller, 1975). The crucial role of innovation in boosting local economies has been recognised in the EU regional policy. In order to account for this new techno–socio–economic condition, the EU has implemented its own regional policy, which, articulated through the Structural Funds' action,[3] aims at economic and social cohesion across the Union (as officially stated in the Treaty on European Union).

In this context this chapter aims to analyse the dispersion/concentration of ICT innovative activity within the European ICT industry across European regions. The starting-point of the analysis is the results obtained in Chapter 5, where clusters of European electronic companies specialising in the same ICT technologies are identified over the period 1969–95 (see Figure 5.1). In what follows on the grounds of a previous study (Santangelo, 2000a), the following hypothesis is investigated.

Hypothesis: in each of the three sub-periods under analysis (1969–77, 1978–86 and 1987–95) technological clusters of companies grouped together as specialising in the same ICT technology (co-specialisation) also locate the relative R&D in the same region (co-location). In other words, what it is tested is whether co-specialised European electronic companies co-locate investment in the ICT field of technological co-specialisation in the same European region.

The chapter is organised into five main sections. The following section throws some light on the statistical methodology adopted as well as on the regional patent data currently available in the Reading database. Section 7.3 provides an overview of the geography of corporate development of ICT across Europe as well as focusing on the three national contexts under analysis by comparing the national and regional dimension. Section 7.4 discusses the results of the hypothesis testing. The conclusions are drawn in section 7.5.

7.2   METHODOLOGICAL NOTES

In this chapter, corporate geographical distribution of ICT technological development across Europe is investigated by adopting the patent share (PS) as a measure of corporate technological size (see section 3.2) in the ICT technological sectors (see Table A.3) in the locations under analysis, as specified in the next sections. The spatial analysis of the corporate research activity in the European ICT industry is carried out at both national and sub-national level in Germany, Italy and the UK, for which countries regionalised patent data are currently available in the Reading database. As exposed in Appendix A, for each of these three countries, the sub-national entities identified correspond to territorial units as classified by the NUTS nomenclature. In order to ensure as much comparability as possible, the NUTS 1 level is used to identify German and UK regions, while, as far as Italian regions are concerned, the NUTS 2 level is adopted. As pointed out by Eurostat (1995), despite the aim of ensuring that comparable regions appear at the same NUTS level, each level still contains great differences among the territorial units identified in terms of area, population, economic weight or administrative power. Therefore, the 16 German *Länder*, the 11 UK *standard regions* and the 20 Italian *regioni* seem to guarantee grounds of comparability as far as innovative activity is concerned (see Table 7.1).

Table 7.1– Regional location where European-owned research activity in ICT technological sectors in carried out, 1969–95

German Lander (NUTS 1)	Italian Regions (NUTS 2)	UK Standard Regions (NUTS 1)
Baden-Württemberg	Calabria	East Anglia
Bayern	Campania	East Midlands
Berlin	Emilia Romagna	North
Brandenburg	Friuli-Venezia Giulia	North West
Bremen	Lazio	Scotland
Hamburg	Liguria	South East
Hessen	Lombardy	South West
Mecklenburg-Vopormmern	Piedmont	Wales
Niedersachsen	Tuscany	West Midlands
Nordrhein-Westfalen	Sicily	Yorkshire & Humberside
Rheinland-Pfalz		
Sachsen		
Sachsen-Anhalt		
Schleswig-Holstein		
Thüringen		

Source: Santangelo (2000a).

In order to analyse whether the technological groups identified in Chapter 5 (see Figure 5.1) in each of the three sub-periods (1969–77, 1978–86 and 1987–95) are co-located in the regions under analysis, for each of the firms in the clusters an intra-firm cross-region RTA index is calculated at the level of the ICT patent classes (see Table A.3)[4] as a proxy for the geographical division of labour within the firm. For each European electronic firm (i), the index is defined as the share of US patents granted in region (r) in a patent class (c) relative to the firm's total number of US patents granted in the same patent class in all European regions divided by the share of patents granted to the same firm (i) in the same region (r) in all ICT patent classes considered relative to all patents granted to the same firm (i) in all European regions in all ICT classes considered. Thus the index can be mathematically formulated as:

$$RTA_{irc} = (P_{irc}/\Sigma_r P_{irc})/ (\Sigma_c P_{irc}/\Sigma_r\Sigma_c P_{irc}) \tag{7.1}$$

where P_{irc} is the total number of patents granted to firm (i) in region (r) in a patent class (c). It is worth emphasising that (r) is defined in terms of German, Italian and UK regions only at the numerators and in terms of all other European regions at the denominators. As the index is a comparative measure, high (low) values of RTA_{irc} indicate corporate advantage (disadvantage) in locating research activity in a specific patent class in the region in question. Therefore, the index enables one to evaluate for each European electronic firm the significance of the regional location in a patent class in Europe relatively to the significance of the same region in all ICT patent classes considered in Europe.

The analysis moves further by testing whether co-specialised firms co-locate their research activity in the technological fields of co-specialisation on the grounds of the intra-firm cross-region RTA index. The criterion adopted to identify eventual co-locations of corporate co-specialised research in ICT requires that, in each of the three sub-periods, at least 50 per cent of the firms in each technological cluster shows the highest RTA_{irc} value in the patent class, upon which the cluster is built (see section 5.2), in the same regional location and that this regional location is common to all other firms in the cluster.

7.3   THE NATIONAL AND REGIONAL DIMENSIONS IN GERMANY, ITALY AND THE UK

Before going into discussion of the statistical results, this section provides an overview on the geographical dispersion of European corporate research activity across Europe.

In order to analyse the host country dimension, the spatial analysis focuses on Germany, Italy and the UK for comparative purposes, as regional data are currently available in the Reading database for these three countries only. Therefore the dispersion of ICT activity in these locations is taken into consideration at two spatial levels – national and sub-national. Figure 7.1 shows the share of research activity carried out in each ICT sector by European-owned foreign electronic companies in Germany, Italy and the UK relative to Europe. Germany appears to be an appealing location for foreign European electronic companies in 'telecommunications', 'image and sound equipment' and 'office equipment and data processing systems'.

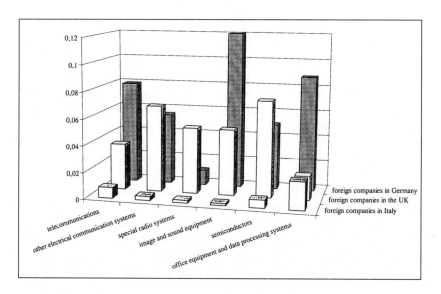

Source: Santangelo (2000a).

Figure 7.1 – Share of research activity carried out in the ICT sectors by European foreign electrical companies and located in the three countries under analysis relative to Europe as a whole, 1969–95

It is worth noting that these ICT sectors are the areas of expertise of Siemens and Nixdorf Computer. Italy, which is by far a less targeted location by European electronic companies across all ICT sectors, attracts some European foreign R&D in 'telecommunications' and 'office equipment and data processing systems'. As in the German case, this may be due to the technological competencies of Olivetti in the sectors in question. In contrast, the UK shows more distributed foreign research activity across all ICT sectors, appearing to be a more appealing location than the other two countries in 'other electronic communications systems', 'special radio systems' and 'semiconductors'. Historically these sectors have been crucial in the specialisation of UK electronic companies, which have developed their technological expertise around defence electronics (see Chapter 4). Therefore in all three local capabilities and consequent local competitive advantage in specific ICT sectors seem to attract foreign companies. By tapping into local expertise of home companies, foreign companies are able to source abroad knowledge complementary to their path of technological development. This pattern confirms that internationalisation of technological development enables the firm to enhance corporate capabilities by absorbing knowledge in local centres of expertise.

Before investigating whether the technological co-specialised groups of firms identified in Figure 5.1 are co-located in the regions under analysis, it is worth considering the significance of German, Italian and UK regions in the overall geographical distribution of European electronic research in ICT. Figure 7.2 reports the share of US patents attributed to European electronic companies in ICT technological sectors in the European regions over the period 1969–95.

In Europe almost half of the European R&D investments in ICT by European electronic companies are located in the regions under analysis. This confirms Caniël's (1998) findings of a high geographical concentration of innovative activity in few European regions as well as Verspagen's (1997b) argument of the existence of European 'regional clubs'. The heterogeneity characterising the European System of Innovation in terms of regional performance is defined as a major factor explaining high concentration of innovative activity in a few regional locations (Maurseth and Verspagen, 1998). As emphasised by Patel and Pavitt (1991a, 1996) international technology gaps (at both national and regional levels) are the results of historically different approaches to investments in technology. The authors distinguish between myopic and dynamic systems (either national or regional): the former treating investments in technological activities just like any conventional investment, the latter placing great emphasis on the development and accumulation of intangible assets. In this sense uneven technological development and consequent economic performance is due to the cumulative and localised character of technology (Cantwell, 1994b). Therefore the emergence of 'higher' and 'lower' order regions relies on the local ability to develop a regional system of innovation.

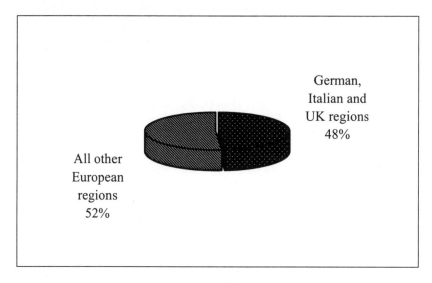

Source: Author's elaboration on University of Reading database.

Figure 7.2 – Share of US patents attributed to European electronic companies in all ICT technological sectors located in European regions, 1969–95

Although Figure 7.2 shows a high concentration of European ICT research carried out in German, Italian and UK regions, among those regions innovative activity appears to be even more polarised in fewer regional locations. Figure 7.3 illustrates that Bayern and South East account for 30 per cent of the total European-owned research in ICT sectors carried out in European regions between 1969 and 1995. This implies that, if almost 50 per cent of European-owned research in ICT is located in German, Italian and UK regions as a whole, Bayern and South East account for 30 per cent. Therefore in the European ICT scenario, the great polarisation in the development of innovative activity is also clear from these figures with these two regions confirmed as 'higher' order locations.

In order to explore further the terms under which this technological polarisation occurs, Table 7.2 ranks German, Italian and UK regions on the grounds of the percentage of European ICT technological activity located in each of them relative to Europe over the period 1969–95.

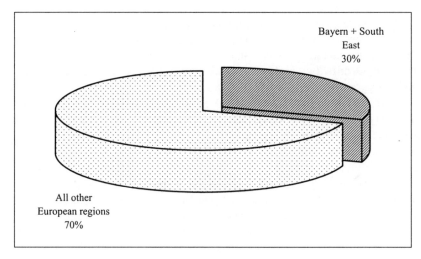

Source: Santangelo (2000a).

Figure 7.3 – Share of US patents attributed to European electronic companies in all ICT technological sectors relative to Europe, 1969–95

Table 7.2 – Distribtution of US patents attributed to European electronic companies in all ICT technological sectors relative to Europe (%), by region, 1969–95

Region	%	Region	%
Bayern	20,4	Yorkshire & Humberside	0,1
South East	9,9	Bremen	0,1
Baden-Württemberg	3,2	Wales	0,1
Niedersachsen	1,8	Sicily	0,1
Schleswig-Holstein	1,6	Emilia Romagna	0,1
Hamburg	1,4	Thüringen	0,1
Lombardy	1,2	Brandenburg	0,1
Nordrhein-Westfalen	1,2	North	0,1
Piedmont	1,2	Friuli-Venezia Giulia	0,1
Hessen	1,0	Lazio	0,1
North West	1,0	Mecklenburg-Vovpommern	0,0
East Midlands	0,8	Tuscany	0,0
West Midlands	0,7	Sachsen-Anhalt	0,0
East Anglia	0,7	Sachsen	0,0
South West	0,6	Calabria	0,0
Berlin	0,5	Liguria	0,0
Rheinland-Pfalz	0,3	Campania	0,0
Scotland	0,1	**Total**	**48,5**

Source: Authors's elaboration on University of Reading patent data.

As expected, Bayern and South East emerged as the centres of excellence in the technological development of ICT. German regions are on average at the top of the hierarchy. Baden-Württemberg, Niedersachsen and Schleswig-Holstein, identified as 'higher' order locations (although to different extents), are all top-ranked.

As far as UK regions are concerned, South East stands out from all others. Similarly, Lombardy is highly placed. In the Italian case two points should be made. First, Piedmont appears to host high percentages of R&D in ICT, although mainly indigenous, as shown in Figure 7.1. Second, Sicily is surprisingly the third Italian region to follow after Lombardy and Piedmont, although accounting for small percentages of the European total. This may suggest that regional policy has been more successful than in other southern Italian regions in attracting significant foreign investments in R&D.

A more detailed picture of the geographical distribution of ICT research across the European regions under analysis is drawn in Table 7.4. For each ICT technological sector, Table 7.3 ranks German, Italian and UK regions on the grounds of the European-owned research developed. Two main findings emerged clearly.

First, 'higher' order regions are confirmed across ICT sectors. This is the case for Bayern and South East, which are top ranked in any of the ICT technological sectors. Second, in each of these sectors, differences in ranking seem to follow the distinction between regional systems of innovation (e.g. Bayern, Baden-Württemberg, Niedersachsen and Schleswig-Holstein in Germany, Lombardy in Italy, and South East and East Anglia in the UK) and sector-specific systems (e.g. Nordrhein-Westfalen, Hessen and Rheinland-Pfalz in Germany, Piedmont in Italy, and North West, West Midlands and South West the UK). While the former always appear to host some percentage of R&D in any of the ICT fields, the latter may be well ranked in some fields and bottom ranked in others according to their sector-specific specialisation. To illustrate the case, European electronic corporations locate some R&D in Baden-Württemberg, Lombardy and East Anglia (although the percentages may vary) in any of the ICT sectors. Conversely, European electronic firms are not attracted at all, for instance, in South West in 'telecommunications' and in Rheinland-Pfalz and Piedmont in 'special radio systems'. Therefore, as far as the European ICT industry is concerned, the existence of 'knowledge creating' and 'knowledge applying' regions is confirmed over the period under analysis. In this sense it is crucial to distinguish between 'agglomeration economies', based on inter-industry co-location (e.g. Silicon Valley), and 'location economies', built upon intra-industry corporate co-location (McCann, 1995).

Table 7.3 – Distribution of US patents attributed to European electronic companies in each of the ICT technological sectors relative to Europe (%), by region and ICT sectors, 1969–95

Telecommunications	%	Other Electrical Communications Systems	%
Bayern	26,9	Bayern	22,1
South East	8,1	South East	14,8
Baden-Württemberg	3,1	Baden-Württemberg	2,8
Niedersachsen	2,1	Niedersachsen	2,6
Nordrhein-Westfalen	1,2	North West	2,1
East Anglia	1,1	Piedmont	1,9
West Midlands	1,0	Hamburg	1,4
East Midlands	0,9	Schleswig-Holstein	1,3
Hamburg	0,8	West Midlands	1,0
Piedmont	0,8	Nordrhein-Westfalen	0,9
Hessen	0,7	East Midlands	0,8
North West	0,7	South West	0,8
Lombardy	0,6	Hessen	0,7
Rheinland-Pfalz	0,5	Berlin	0,5
Schleswig-Holstein	0,5	East Anglia	0,5
Berlin	0,3	Scotland	0,5
Wales	0,2	Bremen	0,4
Yorkshire & Humberside	0,2	Yorkshire & Humberside	0,3
Bremen	0,1	Lombardy	0,3
North	0,1	Rheinland-Pfalz	0,3
Scotland	0,1	Thüringen	0,3
Lazio	0,1	Brandenburg	0,1
Sachsen-Anhalt	0,1	Wales	0,1
Brandenburg	0,0	Friuli-Venezia Giulia	0,1
Mecklenburg-Vorpommern	0,0	Emilia Romagna	0,1
Emilia Romagna	0,0	Calabria	0,1
Tuscany	0,0	Mecklenburg-Vorpommern	
Sachsen		Sachsen	
Thüringen		Sachsen-Anhalt	
South West		North	
Liguria		Liguria	
Friuli-Venezia Giulia		Tuscany	
Campania		Lazio	
Calabria		Campania	
Sicily		Sicily	
Total	**50,1**		**56,8**

Special Radio Systems	%	Image and Sound Equipment	%
South East	23,9	Bayern	12,3
Bayern	9,1	South East	9,7
Baden-Württemberg	1,8	Schleswig-Holstein	6,1
East Midlands	1,3	Hamburg	3,2
South West	1,3	Baden-Württemberg	3,0
Schleswig-Holstein	0,6	Niedersachsen	3,0
East Anglia	0,6	Nordrhein-Westfalen	1,3
Nordrhein-Westfalen	0,4	East Anglia	1,2
Niedersachsen	0,3	Hessen	1,0
North West	0,2	Piedmont	0,8
West Midlands	0,2	Rheinland-Pfalz	0,3
Wales	0,2	East Midlands	0,3
Scotland	0,2	South West	0,3
Brandenburg	0,1	Lombardy	0,3
Bremen	0,1	Mecklenburg-Vovpommern	0,2
Hessen	0,1	North West	0,2
Thüringen	0,1	Berlin	0,2
Yorkshire & Humberside	0,1	Brandenburg	0,2
Liguria	0,1	Bremen	0,2
Lombardy	0,1	West Midlands	0,2
Berlin		Wales	0,2
Hamburg		Friuli-Venezia Giulia	0,2
Mecklenburg-Vovpommern		Yorkshire & Humberside	0,1
Rheinland-Pfalz		Lazio	0,1
Sachsen		Sachsen	0,1
Sachsen-Anhalt		Thüringen	0,1
North		Scotland	0,1
Piedmont		Tuscany	0,1
Friuli-Venezia Giulia		Sachsen-Anhalt	
Emilia Romagna		North	
Tuscany		Liguria	
Lazio		Emilia Romagna	
Campania		Campania	
Calabria		Calabria	
Sicily		Sicily	
Total	**41,0**		**44,9**

Semiconductors	%	Office Equipment and Data Processing Systems	%
Bayern	27,1	Bayern	17,6
South East	8,7	South East	7,3
Baden-Württemberg	3,6	Baden-Württemberg	3,7
Lombardy	3,0	Piedmont	2,3
Hamburg	1,3	Lombardy	1,9
Nordrhein-Westfalen	1,2	Niedersachsen	1,7
East Midlands	1,1	Hessen	1,6
North West	1,0	Nordrhein-Westfalen	1,5
Schleswig-Holstein	0,9	Hamburg	1,3
Hessen	0,8	North West	1,3
West Midlands	0,7	Berlin	1,1
Sicily	0,6	Schleswig-Holstein	1,1
Rheinland-Pfalz	0,5	South West	0,9
East Anglia	0,5	East Midlands	0,7
South West	0,5	West Midlands	0,7
Niedersachsen	0,4	East Anglia	0,3
Berlin	0,3	Scotland	0,2
Friuli-Venezia Giulia	0,2	Emilia Romagna	0,1
Piedmont	0,1	Rheinland-Pfalz	0,1
Emilia Romagna	0,1	Thüringen	0,1
Brandenburg	0,1	Yorkshire & Humberside	0,1
Sachsen	0,1	Friuli-Venezia Giulia	0,1
North	0,1	Sachsen-Anhalt	0,1
Campania	0,1	North	0,1
Calabria	0,1	Calabria	0,1
Bremen		Bremen	0,0
Mecklenburg-Vorpommern		Sachsen	0,0
Sachsen-Anhalt		Campania	0,0
Thüringen		Brandenburg	
Yorkshire & Humberside		Mecklenburg-Vorpommern	
Wales		Wales	
Scotland		Liguria	
Liguria		Tuscany	
Tuscany		Lazio	
Lazio		Sicily	
Total	**52,7**		**45,9**

Source: Santangelo (2000a).

7.4   CO-LOCATION AND CO-SPECIALISATION IN THE EUROPEAN ICT INDUSTRY

As exposed in section 7.2, an intra-firm cross-region RTA index is built at the patent classes level as a proxy for the geographical dispersion of labour of each European electronic company in the sample. The aim is to investigate if corporate clusters in specific patent classes identified in Figure 5.1 are geographically co-located over time on the grounds of the criterion exposed in section 7.2. Figure 7.4 reproduces Figure 5.1 by reporting in a grey background the technological clusters of firms which are found co-located.

Before going on to discussion of the results, it is worth highlighting that in the sub-period 1969–77, 10 out of 15 firms in the clusters locate R&D in the ICT patent classes of co-specialisation in the regions under analysis; 14 out of 17 in the sub-period 1978–86; and 16 out of 18 in the sub-period 1987–95. In the first sub-period, 1 cluster out of 6 results to be co-located, 1 out of 7 in the second, and 2 out of 9 in the last. In all sub-periods, cluster C, C1 and C2 are located in South East. The reason may be found in the fact that the patent class/es upon which the clusters are built can be aggregated in the technological sector 'special radio systems', in which the UK attracts a greater percentage of foreign European companies in comparison with Germany and Italy (see Figure 7.1). The choice of the South East as regional host location of this corporate technological cluster may well be attributed to the agglomeration of economic activities much more based on general urbanisation economies. In the last sub-period (1987–95) South East seems also to host the cluster B2.2, built upon patent classes that can be aggregated in the technological sectors 'telecommunications' and 'special radio systems'. Although the co-location pattern appears to be driven by the UK's attractiveness for 'special radio systems', it may well be the case that South East emerged as an appealing location for R&D in 'telecommunications' in the late 1980s to early 1990s (as shown by the recent investments in the region).

Therefore the average trend is that electronic firms specialise in the same patent class/es, although their R&D in the class/es in question is carried out in different regional locations. However R&D activity in the ICT field as a whole as well as in each of the six ICT technological sectors (Tables 7.2 and 7.3 respectively) seems to be concentrated in a few regional centres of expertise (e.g. Bayern and South East), where regional institutions and culture, social division of labour and internal firm organisation are main competitive advantages (Saxenian, 1994; Justman and Teubal, 1996). Following Beeson (1987) and Malmberg (1996), the localised character of learning emphasises the importance of regional agglomeration economies.

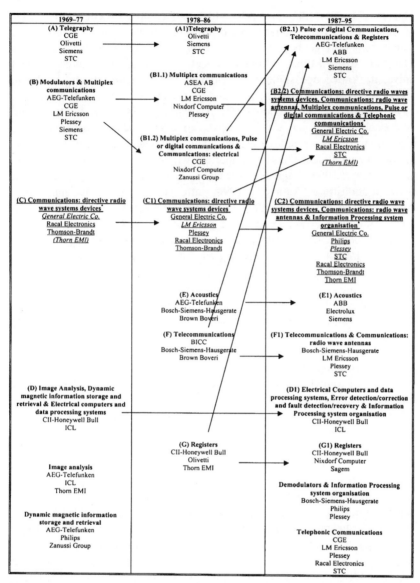

1969–77	1978–86	1987–95
(A) Telegraphy CGE Olivetti Siemens STC	**(A1)Telegraphy** Olivetti Siemens STC	**(B2.1) Pulse or digital Cemmunications, Telecommunications & Registers** AEG-Telefunken ABB LM Ericsson Siemens STC
(B) Modulators & Multiplex communications AEG-Telefunken CGE LM Ericsson Plessey Siemens STC	**(B1.1) Multiplex communications** ASEA AB CGE LM Ericsson Nixdorf Computer Plessey	**(B2.2) Communications: directive radio waves systems devices, Communications: radio wave antennas, Multiplex communications, Pulse or digital communications & Telephonic communications**[*] General Electric Co. *LM Ericsson* Racal Electronics STC *(Thorn EMI)*
	(B1.2) Multiplex communications, Pulse or digital communications & Communications: electrical CGE Nixdorf Computer Zanussi Group	
(C) Communications: directive radio wave systems devices[*] *General Electric Co.* Racal Electronics Thomson-Brandt *(Thorn EMI)*	**(C1) Communications: directive radio wave systems devices**[*] General Electric Co. *LM Ericsson* Plessey Racal Electronics Thomson-Brandt	**(C2) Communications: directive radio wave systems devices, Communications: radio wave antennas & Information Processing system organisation**[*] General Electric Co. Philips *Plessey* STC Racal Electronics Thomson-Brandt Thorn EMI
	(E) Acoustics AEG-Telefunken Bosch-Siemens-Hausgerate Brown Boveri	**(E1) Acoustics** ABB Electrolux Siemens
	(F) Telecommunications BICC Bosch-Siemens-Hausgerate Brown Boveri	**(F1) Telecommunications & Communications: radio wave antennas** Bosch-Siemens-Hausgerate LM Ericsson Plessey STC
(D) Image Analysis, Dynamic magnetic information storage and retrieval & Electrical computers and data processing systems CII-Honeywell Bull ICL		**(D1) Electrical Computers and data processing systems, Error detection/correction and fault detection/recovery & Information Processing system organisation** CII-Honeywell Bull ICL
	(G) Registers CII-Honeywell Bull Olivetti Thorn EMI	**(G1) Registers** CII-Honeywell Bull Nixdorf Computer Sagem
Image analysis AEG-Telefunken ICL Thorn EMI		**Demodulators & Information Processing system organisation** Bosch-Siemens-Hausgerate Philips Plessey
Dynamic magnetic information storage and retrieval AEG-Telefunken Philips Zanussi Group		**Telephonic Communications** CGE LM Ericsson Plessey Racal Electronics STC

Note:
Italics denote consideration of sector-specific factors, which create correlation problems between each of the companies, whose name is in italic, and all the others and between each others in the case of the 1969–77 cluster.

Source: Santangelo (2000a).

Figure 7.4 – European electrical firms specialised in the same patent class/es and located in the same region (underlined), by sub-period, 1969–95

This may suggest that European electronic companies concentrate their research in specific regional locations to benefit from untraded externalities, which may well go beyond intra-industry knowledge spillovers as in the Marshall–Arrow–Romer (MAR) model, involving inter-industry and university knowledge spillovers (Feldman, 1993; Audretsch and Feldman, 1994; Audretsch and Stephan, 1994; Liechtenberg, 1994; Anselin et al., 1997; Arufe and Diamond, 1998; Audretsch, 2000). As Feldman and Audretsch (1999) argue, diversity across complementary industries showing a common base is a source of greater innovation potential. Therefore if inter-sectoral geographical links are important within the same industry (Swann and Prevezer, 1996; Baptista and Swann, 1998), they appear to be crucial between industries (Antonelli, 1990; Jaffe et al., 1993, McCann, 1995; Audretsch and Feldman, 1996b; Blomström and Kokko, 1996; Malmberg, 1996; Malmberg et al., 1996; Bopp and Gordon, 1997; Guimarães et al., 1997; Storper, 1997; Baptista, 2000; Baptista and Swann, 1998; Dalum et al., 1999; Audretsch, 2000). According to Audretsch and Feldman (1996b), knowledge externalities in industries based on new economic knowledge are crucial. In this sense additional increases in concentration of production of innovative activity seem to lead to greater dispersion of innovative activity as new ideas need new space (Audretsch and Feldman, 1996a). Following Camagni (1988), this seems to be all the more true in the information age where the creation of spatial synergies is amplified by the new complex technologies adopted. In this context MNCs link together the localised processes of knowledge by ranking different centres when selecting their locations (Cantwell and Sanna-Randaccio, 1992; Malmberg et al., 1996).

However, if the impact of corporate activities is recognised, there is still room for policy in infrastructure and education in order to facilitate the process of local growth through FDI strategies (Young et al, 1994; Cappelen et al., 1999). On the host region perspective Vence-Deza (1996) places great emphasis on the importance of diversity and complementarity in boosting local expertise in lagging regions.[5] The magnitude of spillover effects largely depends on local capability and competition (Blomström and Kokko, 1996). The trend illustrated in this chapter reveals that agglomerations of high-technology firms are not based upon classical location theory advantages (e.g. cheap labour and lower transaction costs); rather they are rooted in higher added value (e.g. concentration of labour skills and linkage advantage) (Latham III, 1976; Scott and Storper, 1986; Oakey and Cooper, 1989; Scott, 1992). Paci and Usai (2000) show empirically that there is positive association between the regional distribution of innovative activity and labour productivity. This case is clearly illustrated in Silicon Valley and Route 128, where urban industrial clusters generate inter- and intra-industry externalities (Norton, 1992; Saxenian, 1994; Harrison et al., 1996), which are enhanced by proximity to early users (Baptista, 2000). However, according to Maurseth and Verspagen (1998), knowledge flows more smoothly within national borders as knowledge spillovers occur more easily between regions with similar or complementary specialisation. In this sense the European System of Innovation is characterised by several centres (which are not contiguous), where innovative activity is polarised especially in high-tech sectors (Caniëls, 1998).

7.5   CONCLUSIONS

The relevance of this chapter is twofold. First, it investigates whether the clusters of European electronic companies identified in Chapter 6 develop technological innovation in the patent classes of common specialisation in the same regional location. Second, it provides empirical evidence of the spatial development of ICT research activity in the European electronic industry at both national and regional levels (when permitted by data availability).

In analysing whether co-specialisation occurs simultaneously in the European corporate development of ICT technologies, it was found that European electronic companies do not locate research activity in the fields of co-specialisation in the same region. However they seem to concentrate geographically their R&D in ICT technologies. The discussion of the findings points out that companies co-locate their research activity in order to enjoy untraded externalities and complementary diversity. The location of R&D laboratories in a dynamic regional environment enables the whole MNC to source abroad knowledge complementary to its technological path. Therefore MAR spillovers do not seem to be a decisive factor influencing corporate location strategies. Conversely, European ICT companies enhance their competitive advantage in their core areas of technological expertise in heterogeneous dynamic environment through geographically dispersed intra-firm networks. Therefore diversity across complementary industries seems to drive corporate location strategy. Inter-industry co-location provides a source of greater innovation potential. In this sense the chapter argues that the increase concentration of production of innovative activity promotes a greater dispersion of R&D. In Audretsch and Feldman's (1996a) words, 'new ideas need new space'. The results also provide further support to the new role played by local laboratories within the whole corporate structure as outlined in the literature (Hedlund, 1986, 1992; Papanastassiou and Peace, 1994; Barlett and Ghoshal, 1995).

The findings of the chapter also confirm the importance of the regional dimension in the study of technological change. As expected, national systems, although still a useful tool, cannot provide a complete picture of intra-border phenomena. As far as German, Italian and UK regions are concerned, it is possible to identify two types of regional systems: regional systems of innovation based on agglomeration economies attracting foreign R&D in any of the ICT technological sectors; and sector-specific regional systems or 'locational economies' attracting R&D in particular ICT fields. This confirms previous findings on locations of innovative activity in Europe (Cantwell and Iammarino, 1998, 2000; Santangelo, 2000a). Agglomeration economies, characterised by co-located firms operating in different sectors (e.g. Silicon Valley), appear to provide multinationals with locational advantages that go well beyond the mere sectoral specialisation of the local centres. Electronic corporations seem to be mainly attracted by the overall economic structure of the regional system and by the consequent opportunities of successful corporate performance that this can offer them. Conversely, sectoral models of regional specialisation, characterised by co-located firms operating in the same sector (e.g. Route 128), are targeted for their narrow expertise only, as their local environments do not allow the corporation to exploit any additional complementary knowledge. If these two types of regional systems are clearly identifiable in the case of Italy and the UK, in Germany the situation appears to be more complicated. In the former cases Lombardy and South East qualify as regional systems of innovation confirming the findings of Cantwell and Iammarino (1998, 2000). In the latter cases Baden-Württemberg and Bayern show consolidated agglomeration economies, while Niedersachsen and Nordrhein-Westfalen are appealing locations on the grounds of the opportunities of cutting-edge technological combinations. None the less it is worth noting that German regions emerge on average as top-ranked locations in the development of ICT technology in comparison with Italy and the UK.

The chapter confirms that the success of innovative activity appears to be increasingly more embedded in local centres of expertise. This confirms Nelson's (1984) argument that, although national policies still impact on the development of high-tech industries, the globalisation process calls for a more integrated world. On the theoretical side, the evolutionary approach to technology location issues seems to shed some light on the factors driving corporate concentration of R&D in ICT technologies in the European regions under analysis (Schmenner, 1977). The existence of location hierarchies in ICT research in Europe confirms that local infrastructure, culture and business capabilities are key factors attracting foreign corporations. Therefore intra-European corporate development of ICT technology cannot be explained by the classical argument of corporate strategies aiming at the mere reduction of production costs. Rather, value added factors embedded in the social system determine European electronic MNCs' decisions in the choice of the regional location. As the building of local expertise is a path-dependent process, multinationals' investments widen the gap between core and peripheral regions as a result of 'vicious' and 'virtuous' cycles. This implies that the competition for attracting foreign R&D is highly uneven as established regional systems are more likely to host cutting-edge innovative activity (Cox, 1995). None the less the process is not irreversible as regions unable to adapt their institutions to cope with new opportunities may pass into relative decline and lagging regions may successfully open up to compensate with opportunities for development (Metcalfe, 1996).

This chapter concludes Part Two which provides a critical analysis of the sectoral and spatial aspects of corporate learning in the European ICT industry on the grounds of the more general background delineate in Part One. The main findings of Parts One and Two are brought together in the next chapter, where general conclusions are drawn and contributions to economic theory discussed by building some connecting threads throughout the whole book.

NOTES

1. For a critical review on the topic see Martin (1999).
2. For a critical review see Malecki (1991), and Courlet and Soulage (1995).
3. There are four Structural Funds: the European Regional Development Fund (ERDF), the European Social Fund (ESF), the European Agriculture Guidance and Guarantee Fund (EAGGF) and the Financial Instruments for Fisheries Guidance (FIFG).
4. A selection of ICT patent classes is considered in this chapter. The analysis focuses on the patent classes labelling the technological clusters in Figure 5.1 in each of the sub-periods (1969–77, 1978–86 and 1987–95).
5. The same point is made at country level by Verspagen (1997c).

PART THREE

Concluding Remarks and Implications

8. Conclusions: context-dependency, industrial models of innovation and corporate learning

8.1 INTRODUCTION

This book analysed corporate technological development in the information age in terms of both geographical dispersion and specialisation of innovative activity. The topic was theoretically approached in a neo-Schumpeterian perspective, while methodologically the statistical and econometric analysis was based mainly on patent statistics adopted as a measure of knowledge creation broadly understood. The first part of the book investigated the phenomena of corporate technological internationalisation and specialisation (Chapters 2 and 3 respectively), and their relationship in the new techno–socio–economic conditions in which firms operate (Chapter 4). The second part of the book focused on the European ICT industry by analysing the direction of corporate technological development in terms of overlap of firms' profiles of specialisation (Chapter 5), the role of technological specialisation factors in the conclusion of STPs (Chapter 6) and the location strategy of corporate R&D across European regional locations (Chapter 7). This concluding chapter attempts to bring together the findings exposed in the previous pages in order to highlight the main contributions of this research in analysing corporate technological development in the new information age. The specific empirical and qualitative analyses carried out in each chapter, based on a neo-Schumpeterian perspective and on a patent statistics methodology, are here linked by some connecting threads.

The contributions of this book to the study of innovation and innovation-related issues in general and to the evolutionary economic approach in particular seem to be of both a theoretical and a conceptual order. The book takes a position on some theoretical debates within the neo-Schumpeterian theory of technological change as well as providing further support to neo-Schumpeterian taxonomies of models of innovation. On the more conceptual side, the main contribution is identified in the changing nature of corporate learning in the new techno–socio–economic conditions. This chapter also suggests some perspectives for further research, which may follow on the lines of the contributions highlighted. However, in analysing the multi-national, multi-technology corporation over the ICT-based revolution, this book does not claim to have exhausted all issues which have arisen from the new techno–socio–economic conditions. Several studies from Schumpeterian as well as from other theoretical perspectives and disciplines can be found in the literature of recent years. Many of them focus on the impact of the new environment on corporate governance and learning, knowledge creation, diffusion and adaptation as well as on the rate and direction of technological development, the impact on growth of local economies and subsequent differences in local (national and/or regional) systems of innovations. The book has touched upon a few of the research areas of development. However, following a neo-Schumpeterian perspective, some contributions to the building of a comprehensive theory of technological change seem to have been provided, although much awaits to be done in future research.

The discussion is organised into five main sections. In the next two sections, the theoretical contributions of the book are exposed. Section 8.4 focuses on the issues raised by the book at a more conceptual level, while perspectives for future research are sketched in section 8.5.

8.2   CODIFICABILITY *VERSUS* TACITNESS IN THE INNOVATION PROCESS

The preceding chapters provide empirical evidence in favour of the significance of tacitness in knowledge creation and diffusion. Chapters 2 and 7 demonstrate the significance of face-to-face interaction and proximity in the development of ICT technology.

In Chapter 2, corporate development of science-based (e.g. ICT), and firm or industry core technologies are found to be still context-specific and highly reliant on face-to-face interaction. This illustrates the actual relevance of the tacit component of knowledge in an increasingly global techno–socio–economic environment. Although space and time constraints have been overcome and (to some extent) eliminated, technological development is locally embedded. The context-specificity of knowledge restricts the ability of firms to combine distant learning processes, and therefore constrains the international location of research activity within the firm. MNCs tend to disperse more their research activity related to mature and less context-dependent technologies, while increasingly dispersing R&D investments in mature or non-core technologies in centres of expertise, which may be distant from one another. Similarly, in providing empirical evidence of the high concentration of R&D in ICT technology within the European electronic industry across European regions, Chapter 7 confirms the significance of proximity in the production of science-based technologies. MNCs seem to benefit from inter-industry spillovers and added value stemming from the local environment. These findings seem to suggest that purely tacit knowledge has not become easily codifiable by the development and adoption of ICT technology as argued by Cowan and Foray (1997). Conversely the new techno–socio–economic environment confirms the path-dependency of the learning process and the geographically dispersed character of routinised processes. Therefore, it is still crucial to distinguish between an 'actual item of knowledge' and 'knowledge in process of development'. Arora and Gambardella (1994), and Arora et al. (1997) show that this distinction is confirmed when looking at the division of innovative labour. The production of basic knowledge is highly concentrated, while combinations and adaptation are more spread and closer to users. The still high costs of codification (Dasgupta and David, 1994) do not make it profitable for the firm to adopt a strategy of geographical dispersion. Therefore innovation, which depends mostly on tacit knowledge, tends to remain more agglomerated in the parent company as a source of competitive advantage (Leonard and Sensiper, 1998). In this context the main factors driving the occasional geographical dispersion of the creation of science-based and industry-specific core technologies (otherwise highly localised) are either locally embedded specialisation which cannot be accessed elsewhere, or company-specific global strategies that utilise the development of an organisationally complex international network for technological learning. In this sense these findings contribute to the theoretical debate by showing that, although ICT specialisation has promoted a growing geographical dispersion of intra-firm networks (Chapter 4), yet it does not seem that the pace of technological change has lowered the costs of the creation of more complex kinds of technological innovation, which remain largely concentrated in a few centres of excellence, and more highly dependent upon the localised contexts provided by these centres (Chapter 3 and 7).

8.3   INDUSTRIAL TYPOLOGIES OF MODELS OF INNOVATION

The analysis conducted appears to bring substantial support to the distinction between science-based and mature industries models of innovation.

Chapter 3, together with the second part of the book focusing on the European electronic industry (Chapters 5, 6 and 7), provides a specific contribution to the neo-Schumpeterian attempt to build up a coherent theory of technological change. Chapter 3 confirms a change from a Chandlerian-growth strategy to a more related-diversification growth strategy (Cantwell and Fai, 1999b). The past over-diversification of corporate activity in unrelated areas seems to call for a refocusing of the firm's technological portfolio in more coherent lines of technological development. However, if this is the case for 'giant' companies, which over-stretched their capabilities, relatively 'small' companies aim to reach a target level of diversification. The empirical evidence provided in Chapter 3 shows that this trend is highly industry-specific, as the distinction between 'smaller' diversifying firms and large rationalising corporations is found in science-based (e.g. Chemicals n.e.s. and Pharmaceuticals, Electronic equipment n.e.s. and Office equipment, Coal and petroleum products) and related industries (e.g. Motor vehicles), but lacking in mature industries (e.g. Metal and Mechanical engineering). These results seem to confirm the existence of industry-specific models of innovation (i.e. mature *versus* science-based industries) in terms of concentration of innovation among large firms as well as in terms of the extent of inter-firm mobility. 'Mature industry models of innovations' are identified with traditional sectors characterised by relative ease of entry and continuous erosion in competitive and technological advantage of established firms. Conversely, 'science-based industry models' are characterised by relevant entry barriers for new innovators and continuous innovative leadership of few firms based on their cumulative capabilities. Therefore high technological opportunities, high returns and rewards, and high appropriability seem to be the main features of the latter.

The findings of the second part of the book confirm the European ICT industry as a science-based industry model of innovation in terms of industrial structure and technological development. As shown in Chapter 5, the European electronic industry is characterised by an oligopolistic structure with a stable number of firms. Due to the inheritance of national champion policies, the barriers to entry are still high and the rate of technological concentration high. Chapter 6 demonstrates that intra-European alliances in the 1980s represent a process of 'flexible integration' between major oligopolies. The full establishment of an oligopolistic structure has been understood as a main explanation of the decrease in intra-European alliances in the 1990s by Narula (2001). Similarly, the industry reveals high degrees of sectoral and spatial concentration as well as high stability in the ranking of innovative regions across Europe (Chapter 7). As innovative activity takes place among a stable and very restricted number of locations, the tacit and complex nature of the knowledge base underpinning technological innovation in the industry affects the means of knowledge transmission.

In this sense, further support to neo-Schumpeterian models attempting to build theoretical tools to understand better the actual process of production and development of innovation seems to be provided.

8.4   THE EVOLUTION OF CORPORATE LEARNING

In a more conceptual dimension, the contribution of the book to the building of an evolutionary theory may be identified in Chapters 4, 5, 6 and 7. By tackling the issue from different perspectives, all four chapters put forward the argument that the increasing technological complexity – leading to more integrated technological systems (Andersen, 1998) – has promoted a major change in intra-firm corporate learning and a shift from a mere intra-firm to a more inter-firm corporate learning. As far as the management of knowledge is concerned, this change in the nature of corporate learning has impacted on intra- and inter-firm organisation. The relevance of this issue lies in the major role of the firm in generating innovation. This explains the importance of the theory of the firm being able to provide an understanding of the dynamics of knowledge creation, diffusion and utilisation.

In terms of intra-firm corporate learning and consequent organisation, Chapter 5 demonstrates empirically that the complex character of technology has created new opportunities for generating innovative profits through a more intensive cross-border interaction in corporate learning processes, and in the establishment of international intra-firm co-ordinated corporate networks. The increasing geographical dispersion of corporate R&D has been identified as a major feature of the current information age, in which many new technological combinations between formerly separate activities have been made feasible by the pervasive character of ICT. This implies that firm corporate organisation is following more heterarchical forms, within which the subsidiary has an active role in the overall corporate creation of innovation. Intra-firm networks call for a corporate division of labour and greater co-ordination, which occurs by means of communications and interaction. However, if it is possible to identify a general movement towards more decentralised organisational forms, the structure adopted is not absolute. Conversely, it is highly dependent on firm- and industry-specific dynamics. In different industries and within the same industry, different firms organise their assets in different ways. This last point is clearly illustrated in the adoption of a 'global matrix organisation' by ABB (Chapter 2). If this organisational form guarantees the success of the company, within the same industry Philips, for instance, has based its competitive advantage on a different form, although still highly geographically dispersed.

As far as the shift from a mere intra-firm to a more oriented inter-firm learning is concerned, Chapter 5 illustrates that European electronic companies are moving towards overlapping paths of technological development by clustering around specific technologies. It is found that the technological portfolios of European ICT companies have come closer together over time. Similarly, in Chapter 6 inter-firm alliances appear to be a major instrument in corporate learning as a result of the increase in technological complexity. STPs enable MNCs to follow the fast pace of innovation by acquiring new capabilities in related fields through closer co-operation. In the last two decades the growth in the number of technology-based inter-firm alliances has been so strong as to be defined as a major characteristic of the current stage of the world economic system labelled as 'alliance capitalism'. In this new era of capitalism the increasing number of STPs has been recorded mainly in the science-based fields, of which ICT is a leading sector. STPs provide the firm with a rather flexible tool as they enable them to outsource new knowledge into the company or just exchange routinised items of knowledge. Similarly, Chapter 7 demonstrates the significance of geographical proximity in the corporate production of technology. An average trend is shown by the co-location of European R&D laboratories in ICT technology. This phenomenon has led to the emergence of agglomeration economies across the European regions, which rooted their comparative advantage in local inter-industry externalities and technology spillovers. Therefore it seems to be the case that the complexity of technology has created a need for more co-operative forms of corporate learning. Although differently specified according to the companies' aims and technological portfolios, inter-firm interactions are a dominant global phenomenon.

This trend supports further the resource-based view of the firm according to which corporate learning is not merely automatic or procedural. Capabilities cannot be explained purely in terms of human capital (as in the classical production function approach) and the role of individual opportunism is more narrowed than in the standard contract-based models of the firm. Therefore, the understanding of the firm as a collection of capabilities implies that a higher level of knowledge flows between firms, increasing corporate intangible assets and, in the last instance, firms' corporate performance. In this context the success of inter-firm corporate learning lies not just in the generation of new knowledge from which new capabilities are created, but it is amplified by the increase in the firms' absorptive capacity of each others' relevant knowledge (Cohen and Levinthal, 1989, 1990).

8.5   PERSPECTIVES FOR FUTURE RESEARCH

The book has attempt to provide an insight-analysis of the impact of the ICT revolution on the multi-technology and multinational corporations, also taking into account the overall techno–socio–economic environment. This issue has been specifically analysed in the European ICT industry. The contributions of this research to the complete formalisation of a theory of technological change highlighted in the previous sections may suggest new perspectives for future research. Although since the 1980s the evolutionary approach has considerably increased its range of competencies in providing an alternative explanation of technological change, a comprehensive theoretical framework still seems to be missing. A complete formalisation of a theory of technological change will allow economists and social scientists to compile an effective public policy agenda addressing innovation and related issues (e.g. economic growth, and intra- and inter-borders uneven development) as well as guidelines for efficient corporate strategy.

By confirming the tacitness of knowledge in the process of development, the present research emphasises the significance of the complex and localised character of learning over the development of ICT technologies. However, further research is needed to understand fully the dynamics of knowledge creation and utilisation in a fast-changing techno–socio–economic environment. It appears to be crucial to frame this further research within a proper broader theory of the firm. As pointed out in the previous discussion, firms are key actors in the production, diffusion and adoption of technology. Dissatisfaction with the neoclassical explanation of firms as simply profit maximises pursuing a set number of other objectives (e.g. growth, market share, new products, new markets, etc.) calls for new theoretical tools able to explain the formation of corporate strategies. Given the significance of the 'tacit' element of knowledge, it may be the case that the creation process of corporate strategy is influenced by the external environment in which the firm operates and, somehow, by the firm-specific division of labour according to the distinction between tacit and routinised capabilities. Therefore future research may investigate the links (if any) between division of labour, and management strategy and performance within the firm and across industries. These lines of research (if explored) may well provide further insight into the management of technology and, broadly speaking, corporate activity.

Similarly, in order to build up a proper and comprehensive theory of the firm, taxonomies of models of innovation should be further encouraged. As the distinction between different models of industrial dynamics appears to be a valid theoretical attempt to formalise industrial dynamics, future research may move along these lines by specifying the boundaries of the identified models of innovation. Current theoretical development points out the historical shift towards more integrated technological systems. The impact of these changes in the nature of technology production within and between industries may be a starting-point for future investigations. On a more managerial aspect, it seems crucial to make these typologies as operational as possible in order to compile effective corporate strategies and public policy agenda.

A further perspective for future research stemming from the findings of this book concerns the changing nature of corporate learning. Besides the intra-firm move towards more heterarchical forms of corporate organisation, inter-firm interactions as a new way to produce and exchange new knowledge emerge as a dominant phenomenon. Firms seem to opt for a division of labour external to their boundaries and are increasingly based on co-ordination, although heterogeneously and often loosely shaped. However, the terms under which this mechanism is occurring as well as the organisational forms it is taking need to be investigated further. Due to the experimental stage of this phenomenon, a theoretical understanding and a subsequent formalisation are currently missing. It would be useful to have a better understanding of the overall phenomenon and its consequences for the production of successful management strategy.

9.   Management issues and policy implications

9.1   INTRODUCTION

In the information age, the increasingly complex nature of production of innovation impacts on MNCs and (national/regional) territorial units in terms of both corporate competitiveness, and local development and growth respectively. Therefore the conclusions drawn in the previous chapter arise management issues and policy implications as the contributions of the book to the current debate have immediate effect on the compilation of corporate strategies as well as on the policy-making process.

9.2   INNOVATION IN MNCs

The analysis conducted in this book and the results obtained seem to suggest that in the process of innovation production MNCs have to face new challenges due to the new techno–socio–economic conditions in which they are now operating. Following the lines of the previous chapter, three management issues can be identified.

The significance of tacitness in the innovation process over the ICT revolution generates strategic issues related to the identification of local territorial centres developing new knowledge complementary to the firm's learning path. In spite of the ease of global communications and data transmission, face-to-face interactions and proximity to corporate competitors still matter. The exploitation of localised knowledge spillovers and high added value appears to be context-dependent, implying that the creation of new, more complex kinds of technology is still highly costly. The inability of ICT to lower these costs (in spite of the fast pace of technological change) constrains multinationals to take into account territorial diversity in technological and economic terms in their corporate strategies. In this sense the new challenge to MNCs' competitiveness can be identified in establishing the value of 'local embeddedness' for the portfolio of corporate competencies. The novelty of these challenges lies in the fact that MNCs may be tempted to relax in a more global integrated world (in terms of both space and time) by relying completely on ICT as a solution to strategic competitiveness. However, MNCs neglecting territorial specificities in the idea that ICT codification can account for them are most likely to pass into relative decline and, in the medium period, exit the market because of their poor performance.

The significance of territorial diversity can be coupled with the renewed need for a successful firm to be more aware of corporate technological competencies. The possibility of combining formerly unrelated technologies made feasible by ICT may tempt the MNC to over-stretch its capabilities in an attempt to enrich its portfolios and enhance its competitiveness. However, the adoption of this management policy may lead to 'incoherent' lines of technological development due to the diversification of corporate activity in unrelated areas. Therefore corporate managers need to identify the 'optimal' balance between diversification and rationalisation of the corporate portfolio. The difficulty lies in the fact that the target level of diversification is firm-specific. This implies that competitors' strategies can provide only general indications of successful management lines for future corporate development. However, as suggested by the findings of this book, industry models of innovation may help in the definition of the fields of the future corporate expansion. Firms operating in mature and science-based industries seem to follow different patterns of corporate competitiveness due to the nature of industry structure. In a highly uncertain environment where the fast pace of technological change is increasing over time, industrial models of innovation may provide some guidelines for corporate management in order to avoid unsuccessful performance generated by 'incoherent' strategies of technological portfolio.

The complexity of technology due to the pervasive character of ICT raises also management issues related to the process of production of innovation by MNCs. The competencies of a single firm are increasingly unable to cope with this complexity, demanding technological profiles wider than the product profiles. As exposed in the preceding chapters, these new techno–socio–economic conditions have promoted an evolution of corporate learning from intra- to inter-firm development of new knowledge. The new learning trend impacts on corporate competitiveness for several reasons. First, the joint creation of new complex technologies calls for a flexible re-organisation 'within' the firm's borders in order for the company to have a fruitful interaction with different partners. This intra-firm reorganisation should aim at defining the directions of the development of the corporate technological path. Second, the firm should build its own tools to enable it successfully to identify potential partners following complementary avenues. However, as discussed above, the modes and terms under which this new emerging process is occurring are still vague. Therefore it is difficult to provide precise management guidelines going beyond the technological field and the industrial sectors in which the firms are interacting.

9.3   INNOVATION AND LOCAL SYSTEMS

If MNCs play a major role in the production of innovation, local systems are the spatial entities where the process occurs. The interplay between MNCs and local systems in the creation of innovation constitutes a crucial nexus in the generation of new knowledge. This implies that the contributions of the book also generate policy implication besides corporate management issues.

If the embedded character of technology in local environments calls for a major re-definition of corporate competitive strategies, it also impacts on local growth and development. The tacit character of knowledge makes some local (national/regional) systems more appealing to multinationals' FDI than others. As also confirmed by the analysis of the previous chapters, MNCs are extremely sensitive to the presence of local infrastructures, business culture, university research, etc. Therefore the presence of these and other factors defining a dynamic environment are elements discriminating between 'higher' and 'lower' order territorial units. However, the relationship between the R&D location of MNCs and local development follows a two-way direction: if the location of FDI impacts on local development, the latter forges corporate location. This implies that these forces are also self-feeding through 'virtuous' and 'vicious' cycles as demonstrated by the uneven competition (between national/territorial units) in attracting FDI in the European context. However, the possibility that these cycles can be broken generates a wide range of policy implications concerning local development and competitiveness. Local policies in 'higher' order centres should aim to sustain local competitiveness and boost the factors generating their attractiveness to FDI. The final aim should be the reproduction of the 'virtuous' cycle over time. Conversely, 'lower' order centres should identify potential local capabilities (if any) when compiling local development policies. The competitive advantage of the centre may be built on the amplification of this potential. Therefore, in this case the final aim should be to reverse the 'vicious' cycle.

As far as industrial typologies of new knowledge creation are concerned, industrial modes of innovation can provide significant elements in identifying/enhancing potential/actual capabilities according to the hierarchical position of the local centre. The different avenues followed in the process of innovation creation by MNCs operating in mature and science-based industries can provide useful guidelines to local policy makers. The awareness of 'specific' industrial models of innovation may allow one to identify 'specific' factors which are most likely to make the local centre more appealing to *specific* industries. On these grounds local policy makers may amplify targeted local embedded (potential or actual) capabilities according to the kinds of multinationals that are judged to boost/maintain the development/advantage of the local economy.

Similarly, the move from a mere intra-firm to a more inter-firm learning may generate new possibilities for maintaining local competitiveness in the case of 'higher' order centres and for boosting local development in the case of 'lower' order centres. The need for co-operation in the production of new knowledge may call for an interaction with the local environment which goes well beyond informal relationships with indigenous actors. More formal links may be necessary between multinationals and local actors in order to cope with the new complexity of innovation. Therefore more explicit forms of co-operation between foreign and indigenous firms may be encouraged. The co-operation between foreign and indigenous firms can be seen as a further avenue for reproducing/reversing 'virtuous'/'vicious' cycles. Thus on the grounds of local (potential or actual) capabilities, national/regional governments may target to attract MNCs operating in specific industrial sectors by showing the possibilities for direct interaction with local firms through more explicit forms of co-operation.

Bibliography

Almeida, P. (1996), 'Knowledge sourcing by foreign multinationals: patent citation analysis in the US semiconductor industry', *Strategic Management Journal*, **17**, 155–65.

Almeida, P. and B. Kogut (1997), 'The exploration of technological diversity and the geographic localisation of innovation', *Small Business Economics*, **9**, 21–31.

Amin, A. (1993), 'The globalisation of the economy', in G. Grabher (ed.), *The Embedded Firm*, London: Routledge.

Amin, A. and J.B. Goddard (1986), 'The internationalization of production, technological change, small firms and regional development an overview', in A. Amin and J. Goddard (eds), *Technological Change, Industrial Restructuring and Regional Development,* London: Unwin Hyman.

Amin, A., D. Bradley, J. Howells, J. Tomaney and C. Gentle (1994), 'Regional incentives and the quality of mobile investment in the less favoured regions of the EC', *Progress in Planning*, **41**, Part 1.

Amin, A. and N. Thrift (1995*), Globalisation, Institutions, and Regional Development in Europe*, Oxford: Oxford University Press.

Andersen, H.B. (1998), 'The evolution of technological trajectories 1890–1990', *Structural Change and Economic Dynamics*, **9**, 5–34.

Angel, D.P. and J. Engstrom (1995), 'Manufacturing systems and technological change: the US personal computer industry', *Economic Geography*, **71** (1), 79–102.

Anselin, L., A. Varga and Z. Acs (1997), 'Entrepreneurship, geographic spillovers and university research: a spatial econometric analysis', *ESRC Centre for Business Research, University of Cambridge Working Papers*, No. 59.

Antonelli, C. (1990), 'Induced adoption and externalities in the regional diffusion of information technology', *Regional Studies*, **24**, 31–40.

Antonelli, C. (1995), 'Localized technological change in the network of networks: the interaction between regulation and evolution of technology in telecommunications', *Industrial and Corporate Change*, **4** (4), 737–54.

Antonelli, C. (1996), 'Localized knowledge percolation processes and information networks', *Journal of Evolutionary Economics*, **6**, 281–95.

Archibugi, D. (1992), 'Patenting as an indicator of technological innovation: a review', *Science and Public Policy*, **19** (6), 357–68.

Archibugi, D. and S. Iammarino (1999), 'The policy implications of the globalisation of innovations', *Research Policy,* **28** (2–3), 317–36.

Archibugi, D. and S. Iammarino (2000), 'Innovation and globalisation: evidence and implications', in F. Chesnais, G. Ietto-Gilles and R. Simonetti (eds), *European Integration and Global Corporate Strategies*, London: Routledge.

Archibugi, D. and J. Michie (1995), 'The globalisation of technology: a new taxonomy', *Cambridge Journal of Economics*, **19**, 121.

Archibugi, D. and J. Michie (1997), 'Technological globalisation and national systems of innovation: an introduction', in D. Archibugi and J. Michie (eds), *Technology, Globalisation and Economic Performance*, Cambridge and New York: Cambridge University Press.

Archibugi, D. and M. Pianta (1992a), 'Specialisation and size of technological activities in industrial countries: the analysis of patent data', *Research Policy*, **21**, 79–93.

Archibugi, D. and M. Pianta (1992b), *The Technological Specialisation of Advanced Countries*, Dordrecht: Kluwer Academic Press.

Argyres, N. (1996), 'Capabilities, technological diversification and Divisionalisation', *Strategic Management Review*, **17** (5), 395–410.

Arora, A. and A. Gambardella (1994), 'The changing technology of technological change: general and abstract knowledge and the division of innovative labour', *Research Policy*, **23**, 523–32.

Arora, A., A. Gambardella and E. Rullani (1997), 'Division of labour and the locus of inventive activity', *The Journal of Management and Governance*, **1**, 123–40.

Arthur, W.B. (1989), 'Competing technologies, increasing returns, and lock-in by historical events', *The Economic Journal*, **99**, 116–31.

Arufe, J.F.F. and D. Diamond (1998), 'Spatial aspects of innovation policies: theory and applications', *Progress in Planning*, **49**, Part 3/4, 109–269.

Audretsch, D.B. (2000), 'Knowledge, globalisation and regions', in J.H. Dunning (ed.), *Regions, Globalization and the Knowledge Based Economy*, Oxford: Oxford University Press.

Audretsch, D. and M.P. Feldman (1994), 'Knowledge spillovers and the geography of innovation and production', *Centre for Economic Policy Research Discussion Papers*, No. 953, London.

Audretsch, D.B. and M. Feldman (1996a), 'Innovation clusters and industry life cycle', *Review of Industrial Organisation,* **11** (12), 253–73.

Audretsch, D.B. and M. Feldman (1996b), 'R&D spillovers and the geography of innovation and production', *The American Economic Review*, **86** (3), 630–40.

Audretsch, D.B. and P.E. Stephan (1994), 'How localized are networks in biotechnology', *Wissenschaftszentrum Berlin für Sozialforschung*, FS IV, 94–9.

Audretsch, D.B. and P.E. Stephan (1996), 'Company–scientist locational links: the case of biotechnology', *The American Economic Review*, **86** (3), 641–52.

Aydalot, P. (1988), 'Technological trajectories and regional innovation in Europe', in P. Aydalot and D. Keeble (eds), *High Technology Industry and Innovative Environments: the European Experience,* London: Routledge.

Aydalot, P. and D. Keeble (1988), 'High-Technology industry and innovative environments in Europe: an overview', in P. Aydalot and D. Keeble (eds), *High Technology Industry and Innovative Environments: the European Experience*, London: Routledge.

Bachmann, A. (1998), 'Profiles of corporate technological capabilities – a comparison of large British and German pharmaceutical companies', *Technovation*, **18** (10), 593–604.

Balassa, B. (1965), 'Trade liberalisation and "revealed" comparative advantage', *The Manchester School of Economic and Social Studies*, **33** (2), 99–124.

Baptista, R. (2000), 'Do Innovations Diffuse Faster within Geographical Clusters?', *International Journal of Industrial Organisation*, **18**, 515–35.

Baptista, R. and P. Swann (1998), 'Do firms in clusters innovate more?', *Research Policy*, **27** (5), 525–40.

Bartlett, C.A. and S. Ghoshal (1995), *Transnational Management. Text, Cases and Reading in Cross-Border Management,* Chicago: Irwin.

Basberg, B. (1987), 'Patents and the measurement of technological change: a survey of the literature', *Research Policy*, **16**, 131–41.

Beeson, P. (1987), 'Total factor productivity growth and agglomeration economies in manufacturing, 1958–73', *Journal of Regional Science*, **27** (2), 183–99.

Begg, I., J. Fagerberg and P. Guerrieri (1999), 'Conclusions and policy implication', in J. Fagerberg, P. Guerrieri and B. Verspagen (eds), *The Economic Challenge for Europe: Adapting to Innovation-Based Growth,* Cheltenham: Edward Elgar.

Blanc, H. and C. Sierra (1999), 'The internationalisation of R&D by multinationals: a trade-off between external and internal proximity', *Cambridge Journal of Economics*, **23**, 187–206.

Blomström, M. and A. Kokko (1996), 'Multinational corporations and spillovers', *Centre for Economic Policy and Research Discussion Papers*, No. 1365.

Bopp, R. and P. Gordon (1997), 'Agglomeration economies and industrial economic linkages: comment', *Journal of Regional Science*, **17** (1), 125–27.

Bordeau, M.C., K.D. Lock, D. Robly and D. Straud (1998), 'Going global: using information technology to advance the competitiveness of the virtual trasnational organisation', *Academy of Management Executive*, **12** (4), 120–28.

Bound, J., C. Cummins, Z. Griliches, B.H. Hall and A. Jaffe (1984), 'Who does R&D and who patents?', in Z. Griliches (ed.), *R&D, Patents, and Productivity*, Chicago: University of Chicago.

Brandes, O. and S. Brege (1993), 'Strategic turnaround and top management involvement', in P. Lorange, B. Chakavarthy, J. Roos and A. Van de Ven (eds), *Implementing Strategic Processes,* Oxford: Blackwell.

Breschi, S., (2000), 'The geography of innovation: a cross-sector analysis', *Regional Studies*, **34**, 213–29.

Bresnahan, T. and F. Malerba (1997), 'Industrial dynamics and the evolution of firms' and nations' competitive capabilities in the world computer industry', *CESPRI Working Papers*, No. 94, Univerità Bocconi.

Buckley, P.J. and M.C. Casson (1976), *The Future of Multinational Enterprise*, London: Macmillan.

Buckley, P.J. and M.C. Casson (1988), 'A theory of co-operation in international business', in F.J. Contractor and P. Lorange (eds), *Cooperative Strategies in International Business,* Massachusetts: Lexington Books.

Burns, L.S. (1987), 'Regional economic integration and national economic growth', *Regional Studies*, **21** (4), 327–39.

Cainarca, G.C., M.G. Colombo and S. Mariotti (1992), 'Agreements between firms and the methodological life cycle model: Evidence from information technologies', *Research Policy*, **21**, 45–62.

Cainarca, G.C., M.G. Colombo, S. Mariotti, C. Ciborra, G. De Michelis and M.G. Losano (1989), *Tecnologie dell'Informazione e Accordi tra Imprese,* Milano: Edizioni di Comunità.

Camagni, R. (1988), 'Functional integration and locational shifts in new technology industry', in P. Aydalot and D. Keeble (eds), *High Technology Industry and Innovative Environments: the European Experience,* London: Routledge.

Camagni, R. and R. Capello (1997), 'Innovation performance of SMEs in Italy: the relevance of spatial aspects', *ESRC Centre for Business Research, University of Cambridge Working Paper*, No. 60.

Canïels, M. (2000), *Knowledge Spillovers and Economic Growth: Regional Growth Differentials Across Europe*, Cheltenham: Edward Elgar.

Cantwell, J.A. (1987), 'The reorganisation of European industries after integration: selected evidence on the role of multinational enterprise activities', *Journal of Common Market Studies*, **26** (2), 127–51.

Cantwell, J.A. (1989), 'Introduction', in J.A. Cantwell (ed.), *Technological Innovation and Multinational Corporations*, Oxford: Basil Blackwell.

Cantwell, J.A. (1991a), 'The theory of technological competence and its applications to international production', in D. McFetridge (ed.), *Foreign Investment, Technology and Economic Growth*, Calgary: The University of Calgary Press.

Cantwell, J.A. (1991b), 'Historical trends in international patterns of technological innovation', in J. Foreman-Peck (ed.), *New Perspective on the Late Victorian Economy: Essays in Quantitative Economic History, 1860–1914*, Cambridge: Cambridge University Press.

Cantwell, J.A. (1991c), 'The international agglomeration of R&D', in M. Casson (ed.), *Global Research a Strategy and International Competitiveness*, Oxford: Basil Blackwell.

Cantwell, J.A. (1992), 'The effects of integration on the structure of multinational corporation activity in the EC', in M. Klein and P.J.J. Welfens (eds), *Multinationals in the New Europe and Global trade*, Berlin: Springer-Verlag.

Cantwell, J.A. (1993), 'Corporate technological specialisation in international industries', in M.C. Casson and J. Creedy (eds), *Industrial Concentration and Economic Inequality: Essays in Honour of Peter Hart,* Aldershot: Edward Elgar.

Cantwell, J.A. (1994a), 'Introduction', in J.A. Cantwell (ed.), *Transnational Corporations and Innovatory Activities,* London and New York: Routledge.

Cantwell, J.A. (1994b), 'Introduction: transnational corporations and innovatory activities', in J.H. Dunning (ed.), *Transnational Corporations and Innovatory Activities*, Vol. 17, London and New York: Routledge.

Cantwell, J.A. (1995), 'The globalisation of technology: what remains of the product cycle model?', *Cambridge Journal of Economics*, **19**, 155–74.

Cantwell, J.A. (1998a), 'Innovation in the global economy', in D. Archibugi, J. Howells and J. Michie (eds), *National Systems of Innovation or the Globalisation of Technology?*, Cambridge: Cambridge University Press.

Cantwell, J.A. (1998b), 'Technology and the firm: introduction', *Research Policy*, **27**, III–IV.

Cantwell, J.A. (1998c), 'Innovation as the principal source of growth in the global economy' in D. Archibugi, J. Howells and J. Michie (eds), *Innovation Policy in a Global Economy,* Cambridge: Cambridge University Press.

Cantwell, J.A. and H.B. Andersen (1996), 'A statistical analysis of corporate technological leadership', *Economics of Innovation and New Technology*, **4**, 221–34.

Cantwell, J.A. and H.B. Andersen (1999), 'How firms differ in their types of technological competencies and why it matters', *CRIC Discussion Papers*, No. 25.

Cantwell, J.A. and A. Bachmann (1998), 'Changing patterns of technological leadership: evidence from the pharmaceutical industry', *International Journal of Innovation Management*, **2** (1), 45–77.

Cantwell, J.A. and M.P. Barrera (1998), 'The localisation of corporate technological trajectories in the interwar cartels; co-operative learning *versus* an exchange of knowledge', *Economics of Innovation and New Technology*, **6** (2), pp. 257–90.

Cantwell, J.A. and M. Colombo (2000), 'Technological and output complementarities, and inter-firm co-operation in information technology ventures', *Journal of Management and Governance*, **4**, forthcoming.

Cantwell, J.A. and J.H. Dunning (1991), 'MNEs, technology and competitiveness of European industries', *Aussenwirtschaft*, **46**, 45–65.

Cantwell, J.A. and F. Fai (1999a), 'Firms as the source of innovation and growth: the evolution of technological competence', *Journal of Evolutionary Economics*, **9** (3), 331–66.

Cantwell, J.A. and F. Fai (1999b), 'The changing nature of corporate technological diversification and the importance of organisational capability', in S. Dow and P. Earl (eds), *Economic Knowledge and Economic Coordination: Essay in Honour of Brian J. Loasby*, Aldershot: Edward Elgar.

Cantwell, J.A. and R. Harding (1998), 'The internationalisation of German companies' R&D', *National Institute Economic Review*, (163), 99–115.

Cantwell, J.A. and O.E.M. Janne (1998), 'The internationalisation of technological activity: the Dutch case', in R. van Hoesel and R. Narula (eds), *Multinational Enterprises from the Netherlands*, London: Routledge.

Cantwell, J.A. and O.E.M. Janne (1999), 'Technological globalisation and innovative centres: the role of corporate technological leadership and locational hierarchy', *Research Policy*, **28**, 119–44.

Cantwell, J.A. and O.E.M. Janne (2000), 'Globalisation of innovatory capacity: the structure of competence accumulation in European home and host countries', in F. Chesnais, G. Ietto-Gilles and R. Simonetti (eds), *European Integration and the Global Corportate Strategies,* London: Routledge.

Cantwell, J.A. and U. Kotecha (1994), 'L'internationalisation des Activités Technologiques: le Cas Français en Perspective', in F. Sochwald (ed.), *Les Defis de la Mondialisation,* Paris: Masson.

Cantwell, J.A. and S. Iammarino (1998), 'MNCs, technological innovation and regional systems in the EU; some evidence in the Italian case', *International Journal of the Economics of Business*, **5** (3), 383–407.

Cantwell, J.A. and S. Iammarino (2000), 'Multinational corporations and the location of technological innovation in the UK regions', *Regional Science*, **34** (4), 317–32.

Cantwell, J.A. and L. Piscitello (1997), 'A note on the causality between technological diversification and internationalisation', *University of Reading Discussion Papers in Quantitative Economics & Computing*, No. 52.

Cantwell, J.A. and L. Piscitello (1999), 'The emergence of corporate international networks for the accumulation of dispersed technological competences', *Management International Review*, **39**, Special Issue, 123–47.

Cantwell, J.A. and L. Piscitello (2000), 'Accumulating technological competence – its changing impact on corporate diversification and internationalisation', *Industrial and Corporate Change*, **9** (1), 21–51.

Cantwell, J.A. and F. Sanna-Randaccio (1992), 'Intra-industry direct investment in the European Community: oligopolistic rivalry and technological competition', in J.A. Cantwell (ed.), *Multinational Investment in Modern Europe,* Hants: Edward Elgar Publishing.

Cantwell, J.A. and G.D. Santangelo (1999), 'The frontiers of international technology networks: sourcing abroad the most highly tacit capabilities', *Information Economics and Policy*, **11**, 101–23.

Cantwell, J.A. and G.D. Santangelo (2000), 'Capitalism, profits and innovation in the new techno–economic paradigm', *Journal of Evolutionary Economics*, **10**, 131–57.

Cappelen, A., J. Fagerberg and B. Verspagen (1999), 'Lack of regional convergence', in J. Fagerberg, P. Guerrieri and B. Verspagen (eds), *The Economic Challenge for Europe: Adapting to Innovation-Based Growth*, Cheltenham : Edward Elgar.

Caracostas, P. L. and L. Soete (1997), 'The building of cross-border institutions in Europe: towards a European system of innovation', in C. Edquist (ed.), *Systems of Innovation*, London: Pinter.

Carbonin, S. and R. Maglione (1987), 'Gli accordi internazionali nel settore delle tecnologie informatiche: i risultati di un'analisi empirica', *Economia e Politica Industriale*, (53), 131–58.

Caron, F. (1995), *Histoire Économique de la France XIXe-XXe siecle*, Paris: Armand Colin.

Casson, M.C. (1990), *Enterprise and Competitiveness*, Oxford: Clarendon Press.

Castells, M. (1985) (ed.), *High Technology, Space and Society*, Beverly Hills: Sage Publications.

Castells, M. and P. Hall (1994), *Technopoles of the World*, London and New York: Routledge.

Caves, R.E. (1982), *Multinational Enterprises and Economic Analysis*, Cambridge: Cambridge University Press.

Champion T., J. Mønnesland and C. Vandermotten (1996), 'The new regional map of Europe', *Progress in Planning*, **46**, Part 1, 1–89.

Chandler, A.D. (1990), *Scale and Scope. The Dynamics of Industrial Capitalism*, Cambridge, Massachussets: Harvard University Press.

Chandler, A.D. (1992), 'Corporate strategy, structure and control methods in the United States during the 20th century', *Industrial and Corporate Change*, **1** (2), 263–83.

Chesnais, F. (1988), 'Technical co-operation agreements between firms', *Strategic Technology International Review*, (4), 52–119.

Chesnais, F. (1996), 'Technological agreements, networks and selected issues in economic theory', in R. Coombs, A. Richards, P.P. Saviotti and V. Walsh (eds), *Technological Collaboration*, Cheltenham: Edward Elgar.

Christensen, J.F. (1998), 'The Dynamics of the diversified corporation and the role of central management of technology', *DRUID Working Papers*, No. 98–4.

Ciborra, C. (1991), 'Alliances as learning experiments: co-operation competition and change in hightech industries', in L.K. Mytelka (ed.), *Strategic Partnerships*, London: Pinter.

Clayton, K. and J.H. Johnson (1982), *Regional Disparities*, London: Macmillan.

Cohen, E. (1992), *Le colbertisme high-tech*, France: Edition Hachette.

Cohen, W.M. and D.A. Levinthal (1989), 'Innovation and learning; the two faces of R&D', *Economic Journal*, **99**, 569–96.

Cohen, W.M. and D.A. Levinthal (1990), 'Absorptive capacity: a new perspective on learning and innovation', *Administrative Science Quarterly*, **35**, 128–52.

Contractor, F.J. and P. Lorange (eds) (1988), *Cooperative Strategies in International Business*, Massachusetts: Lexington Books.

Cooke, P. and P. Wells (1991), 'Uneasy alliances: the spatial development of computing and communication market', *Regional Studies*, **25** (4), 345–54.

Coombs, R. and S. Metcalfe (1998), 'Distributed capabilities and the governance of the firm', *CRIC Discussion Papers*, No. 16.

Coombs, R., A. Richards, P.P. Saviotti and V. Walsh (1996), 'Introduction: technological collaboration and networks of alliances in the innovation process', in R. Coombs, A. Richards, P.P. Saviotti and V. Walsh (eds), *Technological Collaboration*, Cheltenham: Edward Elgar.

Courlet, C. and B. Soulage (1995), 'Industrial dynamics and territorial space'. *Enterpreneurship & Regional Development*, **7**, 309–27.

Cox, K.R. (1995), 'Globalisation, competition and the politics of local economic development', *Urban Studies*, **32** (2), 213–24.

Cowan, R. and D. Foray (1996), 'The changing economics of technological learning: implications for the distribution of innovative capabilities in Europe', in X. Vence-Deza and J.S. Metcalfe (eds), *Wealth from Diversity*, Dordrecht: Kluwer Academic Press.

Cowan, R. and D. Foray (1997), 'The economics of codification and the diffusion of knowledge', *Industrial and Corporate Change*, **6** (3), 595–622.

Cozzi, G., R. Camagni and F. Gambarotto (1988), 'Accordi di cooperazione, concorrenza dinamica e innovazioni organizzative nell'offerta di information technologies', *Economia e Politica Industriale*, (58), 215–31.

Dalum, B., C. Freeman, R. Simonetti, N. von Tunzelmann and B. Verspagen (1999), 'Europe and the information and communication technologies revolution', in J. Fagerberg, P. Guerrieri and B. Verspagen (eds), *The Economic Challenge for Europe: Adapting to Innovation-Based Growth*, Cheltenham: Edward Elgar.

Dasgupta, P. and P.A. David (1994), 'Toward a new economics of science', *Research Policy*, **23**, 487–521.

de Vylder, S. (1996) The rise and fall of the 'Swedish model', *UNDP HDRO Occasional Papers*, No. 26.

Delapierre, M. and J.B. Zimmerman (1991), 'Towards a new Europeanism: French firms in strategic partnerships', in L.K. Mytelka (ed.), *Strategic Partnerships*, London: Pinter.

Dierickx, I. and K. Cool (1989), 'Asset stock and sustainability of competitive advantage', *Management Science*, **35** (12), 1504–14.

Dodgson, M. (1989), *Technology Strategy and the Firm: Management and Public Policy*, Harlow: Longman.

Dosi, G. and F. Malerba (1996), 'Organisational learning and institutional embeddedness', in G. Dosi and F. Malerba (eds), *Organisation and Strategy in the Evolution of the Enterprise*, London: Macmillan Press.

Dosi, G., D.J. Teece and S.G. Winter (1992), 'Toward a theory of corporate coherence: preliminary remarks', in G. Dosi (ed.), *Technology and Enterprise in a Historical Perspective*, Oxford: Oxford University Press.

Dunning, J.H. (1993), *Multinational Enterprises and the Global Economy*, Wokingham: Addison-Wesley Publishers Ltd.

Dunning, J.H. (1994), 'Multinational enterprises and the globalisation of innovatory capacity', *Research Policy*, **23**, 67–88.

Dunning, J.H. (1995), 'Reappraising the eclectic paradigm in an age of alliance capitalism', *Journal of International Business Studies*, **26** (3), 461–91.

Dunning, J.H. (1996a), 'Globalisation, technological change and the spatial organisation of economic activity', *University of Reading Discussion Papers in International Investment & Business Studies*, No. 211.

Dunning, J.H. (1996b), 'The geography of the competitiveness of firms; some results of a new survey', *Transnational Corporations*, **5** (3), 1–30.

Dunning, J.H. (1997), *Alliance Capitalism and Global Business,* London: Routledge.

Dunning, J.H. and R.D. Pearce (1985), *The World's Largest Industrial Enterprises, 1962–1983*, Farnborough: Gower.

Dunning, J.H. and C. Wymbs (1999), 'The geographical sourcing of technology based assets by multinational enterprises', in D. Archibugi, J. Howells and J. Michie (1999) (eds) *Innovation Policy in a Global Economy*, Cambridge: Cambridge University Press.

Duysters, G. and J. Hagedoorn (1995a), 'Convergence and divergence in the international information technology industry', in J. Hagedoorn (ed.), *Technological Change and the World Economy; Convergence and Divergence in Technology Strategy*, Aldershot: Edward Elgar.

Duysters, G. and J. Hagedoorn (1995b), 'Strategic groups and inter-firm networks in international high-tech industries', *Journal of Management Studies*, **32** (3), 359–81.

Duysters, G. and J. Hagedoorn (1996), 'Internationalisation of corporate technology through strategic partnering: an empirical investigation', *Research Policy*, **25**, 1–12.

Duysters, G. and J. Hagedoorn (1998), Technological convergence in the IT industry: the role of strategic technology alliances and technological competencies', *International Journal of Economics of Business*, **5** (3), 355–68.

Dyer, J.H. and H. Singh (1998), 'The relational view: co-operative strategy and source of interorganisational competitive advantage', *Academy of Management Review*, **23** (4), 660–79.

Ernst, H. (1998), 'Industrial research as a source of important patents'. *Research Policy*, **27**, 1–15.

European Commission (1994), *The European Report on Science and Technology Indicators 1994*, Brussels.

European Commission (1997), *Building the European information society for us all*, Luxembourg: European Commission.

Eurostat (1995), *Nomenclature of Territorial Units Statistics*, Luxembourg.

Fagerberg, J. (1996), 'Heading for divergence?', *Journal of Common Market Studies*, **34** (3), 431–48.

Feldman, M.P. (1993), 'An examination of the geography of innovation', *Industrial and Corporate Change*, **2**, 451–70.

Feldman, M.P. (1994), *The Geography of Innovation*, Dordrecht: Kluwer Academic Press.

Feldman, M.P. and Audretsch, D.B. (1999), 'Innovation in cities: science-based diversity, spacialization and localized competition', *European Economic Review*, **43**, (409–29).

Feldman, M.P. and R. Florida (1994), 'The geographic sources of innovation: technological infrastructure and product innovation in the United States', *Annals of the Association of American Geographers*, **84** (2), 210–29.

Feller, I. (1975), 'Invention, diffusion and industrial location', in L. Collins and R. Walker (eds), *Location Dynamics of Manufacturing Activity*, London: John Wiley & Sons.

Florida, R. (1995), 'Toward the learning region', *Future*, **27** (5), 527–36.

Florida, R. (1997), 'The globalisation of R&D: results of survey of foreign-affiliated R&D laboratories in the USA', *Research Policy*, **26**, 85–103.

Fors, G. (1998), 'Locating R&D abroad: the role of adaptation and knowledge–seeking', in P. Braunerhjelm and K. Ekholm (eds), *The Geography of Multinational Firms*, Boston: Kluwer Academic Press.

Foss, N.J. and J.F. Christensen (1996), 'A process approach to corporate coherence', *DRUID Working Papers*, No. 96-7.

Freeman, C. (1982), *The Economics of Industrial Innovation*, London: Pinter.

Freeman, C. (1987), *Technology Policy and Economic Performance. Lessons From Japan*, London: Pinter.

Freeman, C. (1988), 'Japan: a new national system of innovation?', in G. Dosi, C. Freeman, R.R. Nelson, G. Silverberg and L.L.G. Soete (eds), *Technical Change and Economic Theory*, London: Pinter.

Freeman, C. (1995), 'The 'national system of innovation' in historical perspective', *Cambridge Journal of Economics*, **19** (1), 5–24.

Freeman, C. and J. Hagedoorn (1995), 'Convergence and divergence in the internationalisation of technology', in J. Hagedoorn (ed.), *Technical Change and the World Economy: Convergence and Divergence in Technology Strategies*, Aldershot: Edward Elgar.

Freeman, C. and C. Perez (1988), 'Structural crisis of adjustment: business cycles and investment behaviour', in G. Dosi, C. Freeman, R.R. Nelson, G. Silverberg and L.L.G. Soete (eds), *Technical Change and Economic Theory*, London: Pinter.

Fridenson, P. (1997), 'France: the relatively slow development of big business in the twentieth century', in A.D. Chandler, F. Amatori and T. Hikino (eds), *Big Business and the Wealth of Nations*, Cambridge: Cambridge University Press.

Frost, T. (1996), 'From exploitation to exploration: the geographic sources of subsidiary innovations and the evolutionary theory of the multinational enterprise', Paper presented at the EIBA Annual Conference, Stockholm, December.

Gambardella, A. and S. Torrisi (1998), 'Does technological convergence imply convergence in markets? Evidence from the electronic industry', *Research Policy*, **27** (5), 445–64.

Gerlach, G., (ed.) (1992), *Alliance Capitalism. The Social Organisation of Japanese Business*, Oxford: Oxford University Press.

Gertler, M.S. (1995), '"Being there": proximity, organisation and culture in the development and adoption of advanced manufacturing technologies', *Economic Geography*, **71** (1), 1–26.

Gooderham, P. and P. Heum (1997), 'Learning as a driver of internationalisation: the case of Norwegian companies', Paper presented at the EIBA Annual Conference, Stockholm, December.

Granstrand, O. (1996), 'International diversification and multitechnology corporations', Paper presented at the EIBA Annual Conference, Stockholm, December.

Granstrand, O., L. Håkanson and S. Sjölander (eds) (1992*)*, *Technology Management and International Business*, Chichester: Wiley.

Granstrand, O. and C. Oskarsson (1994), 'Technological diversification in "multi-tech" corporations', *IEEE Transactions on Engineering Management*, **41** (4), 355–64.

Granstrand, O., P. Patel and K.L.R. Pavitt (1997), 'Multi-technology corporation: why they have "distributed" rather than "distinctive core" competencies', *California Management Review*, **39**, 8–25.

Granstrand, O. and S. Sjölander (1990), 'Managing innovation in multi-technology corporations', *Research Policy*, **19**, 35–60.

Griliches, Z. (ed.) (1984), *R&D, Patents, and Productivity*, Chicago: University of Chicago.

Guimarães, P., O. Figueiredo and D. Woodward (1997), 'A regional analysis of foreign direct investment in Portugal', *Investigação – Trabalhos em Curso, Faculdade de Economia do Porto*, No. 77.

Hagedoorn, J. (1993a), 'Understanding the rationale of strategic technology partnering: internationalisation modes of co-operation and sectoral differences', *Strategic Management Journal*, **14**, 371–85.

Hagedoorn, J. (1993b), 'Strategic technology alliances and modes of co-operation in high-technology industries', in G. Grabher (ed.), *The Embedded Firm*, London: Routledge.

Hagedoorn, J. (1995a), 'A note on international market leaders and networks of strategic technology partnering', *Strategic Management Review*, **16**, 241–50.

Hagedoorn, J. (1995b), 'Strategic technology partnering during the 1980s: trends, networks and corporate patterns in non-core technologies', *Research Policy*, **24**, 207–31.

Hagedoorn, J. (1996), 'Trends and patterns in strategic technology partnering since the early seventies', *Review of Industrial Organisation,* **11**, 601–16.

Hagedoorn, J. (1998), 'Atlantic strategic technology alliances', in J. Hagedoorn (ed.), *The Struggle for World Markets – Competition and Cooperation between NAFTA and the European Union*, Cheltenham: Edward Elgar.

Hagedoorn, J. and R. Narula (1996), 'Choosing organisational modes of strategic technology partnering: international and sectoral differences', *Journal of International Business Studies*, second quarter, 264–84.

Hagedoorn, J. and J. Schakenraad (1990), 'Inter-firm partnerships and co-operative strategies in core technologies', in C. Freeman and L.L.G. Soete (eds), *New Explorations in the Economics of Technical Change*, London: Pinter.

Hagedoorn, J. and J. Schakenraad (1992), 'Leading companies and networks of strategic alliances in information technologies', *Research Policy*, **21**, 163–90.

Hagedoorn, J. and J. Schakenraad (1993a), 'Strategic technological partnering and international corporate strategy', in K.S. Hughes (ed.), *European Competitiveness*, Cambridge: Cambridge University Press.

Hagedoorn, J. and J. Schakenraad (1993b), 'A comparison of private and subsidised R&D partnerships in the European information technology industry', *Journal of Common Market Studies*, **31** (3), 373–90.

Håkanson, L. and R. Nobel (1998a), 'Technology characteristics and reverse technology transfer', Paper presented at the AIB Annual Conference, Vienna, October.

Håkanson, L. and R. Nobel (1998b) 'Organisational characteristics and reverse technology transfer', Paper presented at the EIBA Annual Conference, Jerusalem, December.

Hall, P. and P. Preston (1988), *The Carrier Wave*, London: Unwin Hyman.

Harhoff, D., F. Narin, F.M. Scherer and K. Vopel (1999), 'Citation frequency and the value of patented innovation', *Review of Economics and Statistics,* **81** (3), 511–15.

Harrigan, K.R. (1988), 'Strategic alliances and partner asymmetries', in F.J. Contractor and P. Lorange (eds), *Cooperative Strategies in International Business*, Massachusetts: Lexington Books.

Harrison, B., M.R. Kelley and J. Gant (1996), 'Innovative firm behavior and local milieu: exploring the intersection of agglomeration firm effects, and technological change', in *Economic Geography*, **72** (3), 233–58.

Hart, P.E. (1971), 'Entropy and other measures of concentration', *Journal of the Royal Statistics Society*, **134**, 74–85.

Hart, P.E. and S.J. Prais (1956), 'The analysis of business concentration', *Journal of the Royal Statistics Society*, Series A, **134**, 73–85.

Hast, A. (ed.) (1991), *International Directory of Company Histories*, Chicago and London: St James Press.

Hedlund, G. (1986), 'The hypermodern MNC: a heterarchy?', *Human Resource Management*, **25**, 9–25.

Hedlund, G. (1992), 'A model of knowledge management and the global N-form corporation', Paper presented at the EIBA Annual Conference, Reading, December.

Hedlund, G. and J. Ridderstråle (1995), 'International development projects', *International Studies of Management Organisation*, **25** (1–2), 158–84.

Hedlund, G. and D. Rolander (1990), 'Action in heterarchies – new approaches to managing the MNCs', in C.A. Barlett, Y. Doz and G. Hedlund (eds), *Managing the Global Firm*, London: Routledge.

Hepworth, M. (1986), 'The geography of technological change in the information economy', *Regional Studies*, **20** (5), 407–24.

Holmström, B. and J. Roberts (1998), 'The boundaries of the firm revisited', *Journal of Economic Perspectives*, **12** (4), fall, 73–94.

Howells, J. (1999), 'Regional Systems of Innovation', in D. Archibugi, J. Howells and J. Michie (eds), *Innovation Policy in a Global Economy*, Cambridge: Cambridge University Press.

Howells, J. and J. Michie (1997a), 'The globalisation of technology: perspects and prospects', in J. Howells and J. Michie (eds), *Technology, Innovation and Competitiveness*, Cheltenham: Edward Elgar.

Howells, J. and J. Michie (1997b), 'Technological competitiveness in an international arena', in J. Howells and J. Michie (eds), *Technology, Innovation and Competitiveness*, Cheltenham: Edward Elgar.

Howells, J. and M. Wood (1993), *The Globalisation of Production and Technology*, London and New York: Belhaven Press.

Humbert, M. (1995), 'Globalisation and innovation', *Working Papers in European Industrial Policy*, Research Centre for Industrial Strategy, Department of Commerce, The Birmingham Business School.

Iammarino, S. and J. Michie (1998), 'The political economy of the globalisation of technology – some implications for competition and collaboration', *International Journal of the Economics of Business*, **5** (3), 335–53.

Iammarino, S., M.R. Prisco and A. Silvani (1995), 'Geographic statistics', *Research Evaluation*, **5** (3), 189–206.

Iammarino, S., M.R. Prisco and A. Silvani (1998), 'The geography of production and innovation: how regional "styles" play in the global scenario', *The Regional Science Review*, **18**, 31–45.

Iammarino, S. and G.D. Santangelo (2000), 'FDI and Regional Attractiveness in the EU integration process: some evidence for the Italian regions', *European Urban and Regional Studies*, **7** (1), 5–18.

Inkpen, A.C. (1998), 'Learning and knowledge acquisition through international strategic alliances', *Academy of Management Executive*, **12** (4), 69–80.

Isard, W. (1956), *Location and Space Economy: a general theory relating to industrial location, market areas, land use, trade, and urban structure*, Cambridge, Massachussets: MIT Press.

Ivarsson, I. (1996), Integrated International Production. Göteborg, *Department of Geography, University of Göteborg*, Series B, No. 90.

Jaffe, A.B., M. Trajtenberg and R. Henderson (1993), 'Geographical localisation of knowledge spillovers, as evidenced by patent citations', *Quarterly Journal of Economics*, **58** (3), 577–98.

Jenkins, B. (1991), 'Strategic partnership in telecommunications: the role of states in determining comparative advantage', L.K. Mytelka (ed.), *Strategic Partnerships. States, Firms and International Competition*, London: Pinter.

Jowett, P. and M. Rothwell (1986), *The Economics of Information Technology*, London: Macmillan.

Justman, M. and M. Teubal (1996), 'Strategic technology policy for new industrial infrastructure: creating capabilities and building new markets', in X. Vence-Deza and J.S. Metcalfe (eds), *Wealth from Diversity*, Dordrecht: Kluwer Academic Press.

Keeble, D., C. Lawson, H. Lawton Smith, B. Moore and F. Wilkinson (1997), 'Internationalisation processes, networking and local embeddedness in technology-based small firms', *ESRC Centre for Business Research, University of Cambridge Working Papers*, No. 53.

Kitson, M. and J. Michie (1996), 'The political economy of globalisation', Paper presented at the Euroconference, Rome, April.

Klevorick, A.K., R.C. Levin, R.R. Nelson and S. Winter (1993), 'On the sources and significance of interindustry differences in technological opportunities', Yale University Cowels Foundation Discussion Papers, No. 1052.

Kline, S.J. and N. Rosenberg (1986), 'An overview of innovation', in R. Landau and N. Rosenberg (eds), *The Positive Sum Strategy*, Washington: National Academy Press.

Knox, P. and J. Agnew (1989), *The Geography of the World Economy*, London: Edward Arnold.

Kodama, F. (1992a), 'Japan's unique capability to innovate: technology fusion and its international implications', in T.S. Arrison, C.F. Bergsten, M.E. Graham and M.C. Harris (eds), *Japan's Growing Technological Capability: Implication for the US Economy*, Washington D.C.: National Academy Press.

Kodama, F. (1992b), 'Technology fusion and the new R&D', *Harvard Business Review*, July–August, 70–8.

Kogut, B. (1988), 'A study of the life cycle of joint ventures', in F.J. Contractor and P. Lorange (eds), *Cooperative Strategies in International Business*, Massachusetts: Lexington Books.

Kogut, B. (1990), 'International sequential advantages and network flexibility', in A.C. Barlett, Y. Doz and G. Hedlund (eds), *Managing the Global Firm*, London: Routledge.

Krugman, P. (1991a), *Geography and Trade*, Cambridge, Massachussets: MIT Press.

Krugman, P. (1991b), 'Increasing returns and economic geography', *Journal of Political Economy*, **99** (31), 483–99.

Krugman, P. (1995), *Development, Geography and Economic Theory*, Cambridge, Massachussets: The MIT Press.

Krugman, P. (1998), 'Space: the final frontier', *Journal of Economic Perspectives*, **12** (2), 161–74.

Kuemmerle, W. (1996), 'Home-based and investment into research and development abroad – an investigation into the international allocation of research activity by multinational enterprises', *Harvard Business School Working Papers*, No. 96-063.

Kuemmerle, W. (1997a), 'Building effective R&D capabilities abroad', *Harvard Business Review*, March–April, 61–70.

Kuemmerle, W. (1997b), 'Knowledge creation and exploitation in foreign environments – an investigation into the drivers of foreign direct investment in R&D by multinational companies', Harvard Business School, *mimeo.*

Kuemmerle, W. (1999), 'The drivers of foreign direct investments into research and development: an empirical investigation', *Journal of International Business Studies*, **30** (1), 1–24.

Latham III, W.R. (1976), 'Needless complexity in the identification of industrial complexes', *Journal of Regional Science*, **16** (1), 45–55.

Lawson, C. (1999), 'Towards a competence theory of the region', *Cambridge Journal of Economics*, **23**, 151–66.

Lazonick, W. (1992), 'Business organisation and competitive advantage: capitalist transformations in the twentieth century', in G. Dosi, R. Giannetti and P.A. Torinelli (eds), *Technology and Enterprise in a Historical Perspective*, Oxford: Oxford University Press.

Lemelin, A. (1982), 'Relatedness in the Patterns of Interindustry Diversification'. *The Review of Economics and Statistics*, **64**, 646–57.

Leonard, D. and S. Sensiper (1998), 'The role of tacit knowledge in group innovation', *California Management Review*, **40** (3), 112–32.

Leyton-Brown, D. (1994), 'The Political Economy of North American Free Trade', in R. Stubbs and G.R.D. Underhill (eds), *Political Economy and the Changing Global Order*, London: Macmillan.

Lichtenberg, F.R. (1994), 'R&D collaboration and specialization in the European Community', *Centre for International Business Education and Research Working Papers*, Columbia University, No. 94/95-01.

Loasby, B.J. (1991), *Equilibrium and Evolution. An exploration of connecting principle in economics*, Manchester and New York: Manchester University Press.

Loasby, B.J. (1994), 'Organisational capabilities and interfirm relations', *Macroeconomica*, **45**, 248–65.

Loasby, B.J. (1998), 'The organisation of capabilities', *Journal of Economic Behavior & Organisation*, **35**, 139–60.

Loinger, G. and V. Peyrache (1988), 'Technological clusters and regional economic restructuring', in P. Aydalot and D. Keeble (eds), *High Technology Industry and Innovative Environments: the European Experience*, London: Routledge.

Lösch, A. (1954), *The Economics of Location*, New Haven: Yale University Press.

Loveridge, R. and M. Pitt (1990), 'Introduction: defining the field of technology and strategy', in R. Loveridge and M. Pitt (eds), *Strategic Management of Technological Innovation*, Chichester: Wiley.

Magrini, S. (1998), 'Modelling Regional Economic Growth: the Role of Human Capital and Innovation', London School of Economics, PhD thesis.

Maillat, D. (1995), 'Territorial dynamic, innovative milieus and regional policies'. *Enterpreneurship & Regional Development*, **7**, 157–65.

Malecki, E.J. (1985), 'Industrial and corporate organization in high technology industries', *Economic Geography*, **61**, 345–69.

Malecki, E.J. (1991), *Technology and Economic Development – The Dynamics of Local, Regional and National Change*, New York: Longman Scientific & Technical.

Malecki, E.J. (1994), 'High technology and local economic development', *Journal of American Planning Association*, **50** (1), 262–69.

Malerba, F., F. Lissani and S. Torrisi (1997), *Computer and Office Machinery – Firms' External Growth & Technological Diversification*, EIMS Publications, European Commission.

Malerba, F. and L. Orsenigo (1996), 'The dynamics and evolution of industries', *Industrial and Corporate Change*, **5** (1), 51–87.

Malerba, F. and L. Orsenigo (1997), 'Technological regimes and sectoral patterns of innovative activities, *Industrial and Corporate Change*, **6** (1), 83–117.

Malerba, F. and S. Torrisi (1996), 'The dynamics of market structure and innovation in the western European software industry', in D.C. Mowery (ed.), *The International Computer Software Industry*, New York and Oxford: Oxford University Press.

Malmberg, A. (1996), 'Industrial geography: agglomeration and local milieu', *Progress in Human Geography*, **20** (3), 392–403.

Malmberg, A., Ö. Sölvell and I. Zander (1996), Spatial clustering, local accumulation of knowledge and firm competitiveness', *Geografiska Annaler*, **78B** (2), 85–97.

Mariti, P. and R.H. Smiley (1983), 'Co-operative agreements and the organisation of industry', *The Journal of Industrial Economics*, **XXI** (4), 437–51.

Markides, C.C. (1995a), *Diversification, Refocusing and Economic Performance*, Cambridge, Massachussets: MIT Press.

Markides, C.C. (1995b), 'Diversification, restructuring and economic performance', *Strategic Management Review*, **16**, 101–18.

Martin, R. (1999), 'Critical survey: the new "geographical turn" in economics – some critical reflections', *Cambridge Journal of Economics*, **23**, 65–91.

Maskell. P. (1996), 'Local embeddness and pattern of international specialisation', Paper presented at the EIBA Annual Conference, Stockholm, December.

Maurseth, P.B. and B. Verspagen (1998), 'Knowledge spillovers in Europe and its consequences for systems of innovation', *Eindhoven Center for Innovation Studies Working Papers*, No. 98-001.

McCann, P. (1995), 'Rethinking the economics of location and agglomeration', *Urban Studies*, **32** (3), 563–77.

McDonald, J.M. (1995), 'R&D and the directions of diversification', *The Review of Economics and Statistics*, **67**, 583–90.

McKerm, B. (1993), 'An evolutionary approach to strategic management in the international firm', in P. Lorange, B. Chakravarthy, J. Roos and A. Van de Ven (eds), *Implementing Strategic Process: Change, Learning and Cooperation*, Oxford: Blackwell.

Merges, R.P. (1996), 'A comparative look at property rights and software industry', in D.C. Mowery (ed.), *The International Computer Software Industry*, New York and Oxford: Oxford University Press.

Metcalfe, J.S. (1996), 'Economic dynamics and regional diversity – some evolutionary ideas', in X. Vence-Deza and J.S. Metcalfe (eds), *Wealth from Diversity*, Dordrecht: Kluwer Academic Press.

Metcalfe, J.S. (1998), *Evolutionary Economics and Creative Restructuring*, Routledge: London.

Mitchell, G.R. (1986), 'New approach for the strategic management of technology', in M. Horwitch (ed.), *Technology in Modern Corporation*, New York: Pergamon Press.

Molot, M.A. (1994), 'The Canadian State in the International Economy', in R. Stubbs and G.R.D. Underhill (eds), *Political Economy and the Changing Global Order*, London: Macmillan.

Montgomery, C.A. and S. Hariharan (1991), 'Diversified expansion by large established firms', *Journal of Economic Behavior & Organization*, **15**, 71–89.

Morris, P.R. (1990), *A History of the World Semiconductor Industry*, London: Peter Peregrinus Ltd.

Mowery, D.C. (1996), *The International Computer Software Industry – A Comparative Study of Industry Evolution and Structure*, New York and Oxford: Oxford University Press.

Mowery, D.C., J.E. Oxley and B.S. Silverman (1997), 'Convergent and divergent technological development in strategic alliances', Paper presented at the conference on 'Internationalisation of Corporate R&D', University of Quebec, August.

Mytelka, L.K. and M. Delapierre (1988), 'The alliance strategies of European firms in the information technology industry and the role of ESPRIT', in J.H. Dunning and P. Robson (eds), *Multinationals and the European Community*, Oxford: Basil Blackwell.

Nakamura, M., J.M. Shaver and B. Yeung (1996), 'An empirical investigation of joint venture dynamics: evidence from US–Japan joint ventures', *International Journal of Industrial Organisation*, **14**, 521–41.

Narula, R. (1999), 'Explaining the growth of strategic R&D alliances by European firms', *Journal of Common Market Studies*, **37** (4), 711–22.

Narula, R. (2001), 'In-house R&D, outsourcing or alliances? Some strategic and economic consideration', in F. Contractor (ed.), *The Evaluation of Intangible Assets in Global operations*, Westport CT and London: Quorum Books.

Narula, R. and J.H. Dunning (1998), 'Explaining international R&D alliances and the role of governments', *International Business Review*, **7**, 377–97.

Narula, R. and J. Hagedoorn (1997), 'Globalisation, organisational modes and the growth of international strategic technology alliances', *MERIT Working Papers*, No. 2/97-017.

Narula, R. and J. Hagedoorn (1999), 'Innovating through strategic alliances: moving toward international partnerships and contractual agreements', *Technovation*, **19**, 283–94.

Nelson, R.R. (1984), *High-Technology Policy*, Washington: American Enterprise Institute for Public Policy Research.

Nelson, R.R. (1991), 'Why do firms differ, and how does it matter?', *Strategic Management Review*, **12**, 61–74.

Nelson, R.R. (1992), 'What is "commercial" and what is "public" about technology, and what should be?', in N. Rosenberg, R. Landau and D.C. Mowery (eds), *Technology and the Wealth of Nations,* Stanford: Stanford University Press.

Nelson, R.R. (ed.) (1993), *National Innovation Systems: A Comparative Analysis*, Oxford and New York: Oxford University Press.

Nelson, R.R. (1995), 'Why should managers be thinking about technology policy?', *Strategic Management Journal*, **16**, 581–88.

Nelson, R.R. and S.G. Winter (1977), 'In search of a useful theory of innovation', *Research Policy*, **6**, 37–76.

Nelson, R.R. and S.G. Winter (1982), *An Evolutionary Theory of Economic Change*, Cambridge, Massachussets: Harvard University Press.

Nobel, R.R. and J. Birkinshaw (1998), 'Innovation in multinational corporations: control and communication patterns in international R&D operations', *Strategic Management Journal*, **19**, 479–96.

Norton, R.D. (1992), 'Agglomeration and competitiveness: from Marshall to Chinits', *Urban Studies*, **29** (2), 155–70.

Oakey, R. (1985), 'High-technology industries and agglomeration economies', in P. Hall and A. Markusen (eds), *Silicon Landscapers*, Boston: Allen & Unwin.

Oakey, R. and Y. Cooper (1989), 'High technology industry, agglomeration and the potential for peripheral sited small firms', *Regional Studies*, **23**, 347–60.

Oakley, B.W. (1984), *Co-operation in Information Technology Research*, London: Birkbeck College.

O'Farrell, P. (1986), 'Entrepreneurship and regional development; some conceptual issues', *Regional Studies*, **20** (6), 565–74.

Paci, R. and S. Usai (2000), 'Technological enclaves and industrial districts. Analysis of the regional distribution of innovative activity in Europe', *Regional Studies*, **34** (2), 97–114.

Padoan, P.C. (1997), 'Technology accumulation and diffusion: is there a regional dimension?', *Working Papers*, No. 41, Università di Roma 'La Sapienza'.

Papanastassiou, M. and R.D. Pearce (1994), 'Host-country determinants of the market strategies of US companies' overseas subsidiaries', *Journal of the Economic Business*, **1** (2), 199–217.

Papanastassiou, M. and R.D. Pearce (1997), 'Technology sourcing and the strategic roles of manufacturing subsidiaries in the UK: local competencies and global competitiveness', *Management International Review*, **37** (1), 5–25.

Patel, P. (1995), 'Localised production of technology for global markets', *Cambridge Journal of Economics*, **19**, 141–53.

Patel, P. and K.L.R. Pavitt (1987), 'Is Western Europe losing the technological race?', *Research Policy*, **16**, 59–85.

Patel, P. and K.L.R. Pavitt (1991a), 'Europe's technological performance', C. Freeman, M.L. Sharp and W. Walker (eds), *Technology and the future of Europe: Global competition and the Environment in the 1990s*, London: Francis Pinter.

Patel, P. and K.L.R. Pavitt (1991b), 'Large firms in the production of the world's technology: an important case of non-globalisation', *Journal of International Business Studies*, **22**, 1–21.

Patel, P. and K.L.R. Pavitt (1994), 'National innovation systems: why they are important, and how they might be measured and compared', *Economics of Innovation and New Technology*, **3** (1), 77–95.

Patel P. and K.L.R. Pavitt (1996), 'Uneven technological development', in X. Vence-Deza and J.S. Metcalfe (eds), *Wealth from Diversity*, Dordrecht: Kluwer Academic Press.

Patel, P. and K.L.R. Pavitt (1997), 'The technological competencies of the world's largest firms: complex and path-dependent but not much variety', *Research Policy*, **26**, 141–56.

Pavitt, K.L.R. (1985), 'Patent statistics as indicators of innovative activity: possibilities and problems', *Scientometrics*, **7** (1–2), 77–99.

Pavitt, K.L.R. (1988), 'Use and abuse of patent statistics', in A.H. van Raan (ed.), *Handbook of Quantitative Studies of Science Policy*, Amsterdam: North-Holland.

Pavitt, K.L.R. (1998), 'Technologies, products and organisation in the innovating firm: what Adam Smith tells us and Joseph Schumpeter doesn't', *Industrial and Corporate Change*, **7** (3), 433–52.

Pavitt, K.L.R., M. Robson and J. Townsend (1989), 'Accumulation, diversification and organisation in UK companies, 1945–1983', in M. Dodgson (ed.), *Technology Strategy and the Firm: Management and Public policy*, Essex: Longman Group UK Limited.

Pearce, R.D. (1983), *The Growth and Evolution of Multinational Enterprise*, Aldershot: Edward Elgar.

Pearce, R.D. (1997a), *Global Competition and Technology*, London: Macmillan Press.

Pearce, R.D. (1997b), 'Decentralised R&D and strategic competitiveness: globalised approaches to generation and use of technology in MNEs', Paper presented at the CIRST Conference, Montréal, August.

Pearce, R.D. and M. Papanastassiou (1996), 'R&D networks and innovation: decentralised product development in multinational enterprises', *R&D Management*, **26**, October, 315–33.

Pearce, R.D. and A.T. Tavares (1998), 'Strategies of multinational subsidiaries in a context of regional trading blocs', University of Reading Discussion Papers in International Investment & Management, No. 257.

Penrose, E. (1959), *The Theory of the Growth of the Firm*, Oxford: Basil Blackwell.

Piore, M.J. and C.F. Sabel (1984), *The Second Industrial Divide*, NewYork: Basic.

Piscitello, L. (1998), Corporate Diversification, Coherence, and the Dialectic Relationship between Technological and Product Competencies, Politecnico di Milano, PhD Thesis.

Porter, M.E. and M.B. Fuller (1986), 'Coalitions and global strategy', in M. Porter (ed.), *Competition in Global Industries*, Boston: Harvard Business School Press.

Powell, W.W. (1998), 'Learning from collaboration', *Californian Management Review*, **40** (3), 228–40.

Quévit, M. (1992), 'The regional impact of the internal market a comparative analysis of traditional industrial regions and lagging regions', *Regional Studies*, **26** (4), 349–60.

Quévit, M. (1996), 'The regional impact on the internal market: analysis for lagging regions', in X. Vence-Deza and J.S. Metcalfe (eds), *Wealth from Diversity*, Dordrecht: Kluwer Academic Press.

Richardson, G.B. (1972), 'The organisation of industry', *The Economic Journal*, **82**, 883–96.

Ridderstråle, J. (1992), 'Developing product development: holographic design for successful creation in the MNC', Paper presented at the EIBA Annual Conference, Reading, December.

Ridderstråle, J. (1996), *Global Innovation – Managing International Innovation Projects at ABB and Electrolux*, Stockholm: Institute of International Business.

Rosenberg, N. (1976), *Perspectives on Technology*, Cambridge and New York: Cambridge University Press.

Rosenberg, N. (1982), *Inside the Black Box: Technology and Economics*, Cambridge: Cambridge University Press.

Rosenberg, N. (1996), 'Uncertainty and technological change', in R. Landau, T. Taylor and G. Wright (eds), *The Mosaic of Economic Growth*, Stanford: Stanford University Press.

Rozenblat, C. and D. Pumain (1993), 'The location of multinational firms in the European urban systems', *Urban Studies*, **30** (10), 1691–709.

Rugman, A.M. (1987), *Outward Bound: Canadian Direct Investment in the United States*, Toronto: Home Institute and National Planning Association.

Sahal, D. (1981), *Patterns of Technological Innovation*, Canada: Addison-Wesley Publishing Company Inc.

Sahal, D. (1985), 'Technological guideposts and innovation avenues', *Research Policy*, **14**, 61–82.

Santangelo, G.D. (1996), 'The Impact of Information Technology on the Activities of Multinational Corporations', University of Warwick, MA dissertation.

Santangelo, G.D. (1997), 'The IT revolution and Europe: the European lag and reaction. An analysis of ESPRIT', Department of Political Studies, University of Catania, *Jean Monnet Working Papers in Comparative and International Politics*, No. 09.97.

Santangelo, G.D. (1998), 'Corporate technological specialisation in the European information and communications technology industry', *International Journal of Innovation Management*, **2** (3), 339–66.

Santangelo, G.D. (2000a), 'Inter-European regional dispersion of corporate research activity in information and communication technology: the case of German, Italian and UK regions', *International Journal of the Economics of Business*, **7** (3), 275–95.

Santangelo, G.D. (2000b), 'Corporate strategic technological partnerships in the European information and communications technology industry', *Research Policy*, **29** (9), 1015–31.

Santangelo, G.D. (2001), 'The impact of the information technology revolution on the internationalisation of corporate technology', *International Business Review*, **10** (6), pp. 701–26.

Saviotti, P.P. (1996), *Technological Evolution, Variety and the Economy*, Aldershot: Edward Elgar.

Saxenian, A. (1994), *Regional Advantage*, Cambridge, Massachussets: Harvard University Press.

Scherer, F.M. (1983), 'The propensity to patent', *International Journal of Industrial Organisation*, **1**, 107–28.

Schmenner, R.W. (1977), 'Urban industrial location: an evolutionary model', *Journal of Regional Science*, **17** (2), 179–94.

Schmookler, J. (1966), *Invention and Economic Growth*, Cambridge, Massachussets: Harvard University Press.

Scott, A.J. (1988), *New Industrial Space,* London: Pion Limited.

Scott, A.J. (1992), 'The role of large producers in industrial districts: a case study of high technology systems houses in southern California', *Regional Studies*, **26** (3), 265–75.

Scott, A.J. and M. Storper (1986), 'High Technology Industry and Regional Development: A Theoretical Critique and Reconstruction', The 17th Normal Wilkinson Memorial Lecture.

Scott, J.T. and G. Pascoe (1987), 'Purposive diversification of R&D in manufacturing', *The Journal of Industrial Economics*, **36** (2), 193–205.

Sharp, M. and C. Shearman (1987), *European Technological Collaboration*, London: Routledge & Kegan Paul.

Silverman, B.S. (1999), 'Technological resources and the direction of corporate diversification: toward an integration of the resource-based view and transaction cost economics', *Management Science*, **45** (8).

Soete, L. (1987), 'The impact of technological innovation on international trade patterns: the evidence reconsidered', *Research Policy*, **16**, 101–30.

Soete, L. and S. Wyatt (1983), 'The use of foreign patenting as an internationally comparable science and technology output indicator', *Scientometrics*, **5** (1), 31–54.

Sölvell, Ö. and M. Bengtsson (2000), 'Innovative performance in industries – the role of industry, structure, climate of competition and cluster strength', in J.H. Dunning (ed.), *Regions, Globalization and the Knowledge Based Economy*, Oxford: Oxford University Press.

Sölvell, Ö. and J. Birkinshaw (2000), 'Multinational enterprises in the knowledge driven economy: leveraging global practises', in J.H. Dunning (ed.), *Regions,*

Globalization and the Knowledge Based Economy, Oxford: Oxford University Press.

Stafford, D.C. and R.H.A. Purkis (1989), *Macmillan Directory of Multinationals*, Basingstoke: Macmillan Publishers Ltd.

Stiglitz, J.E. (1987), 'Learning to learn, localized learning and technological progress', in P. Dasgupta and P. Stoneman (eds), *Economic Policy and Technological Performance*, Cambridge: Cambridge University Press.

Stiglitz, J.E. (1999), 'The Economics of the Knowledge Driven Economy', Paper presented at the CEPR/DTI Conference, London.

Storper, M. (1997), *The Regional World*, New York: The Guilford Press.

Storper, M. and A.J. Scott (1995), 'The wealth of regions', *Future*, **27** (5), 505–26.

Stuart, T.E. and J.M. Podolny (1996), 'Local search and the evolution of technological capabilities', *Strategic Management Journal*, **17**, 21–38.

Stubbs, O. and P. Saviotti (1997), 'Science and Technology Policy', in M.J. Artis and N. Lee (eds), *The Economics of the European Union. Policy and Analysis*, Oxford: Oxford University Press.

Svetličič, M. (1996), 'Challenges of globalisation and regionalisation in the World Economy', *Global Society*, **10** (2), 107–23.

Swann, P. and M. Prevezer (1996), 'A comparison of the dynamics of industrial clustering in computing and biotechnology', *Research Policy*, **25**, 1139–57.

Tavares, A.T. and R. Pearce (1998), 'Regional economic integration process and the strategic (re)positioning of MNEs' subsidiaries: a conceptual investigation', *University of Reading Discussion Papers in International Investment & Management*, No. 254.

Teece, D.J. (1998), 'Capturing value from knowledge assets: the new economy, markets for know-how, and intangible assets', *California Management Review*, **40** (3), 1–25.

Teece, D.J., R. Rumelt, G. Dosi and S. Winter (1994), 'Understanding corporate coherence – theory and evidence', *Journal of Economic Behavior & Organization*, **23**, 1–30.

Thomas, M.D. (1986), 'Growth and structural change: the role of technical innovation', in A. Amin and J. Goddard (eds), *Technological Change, Industrial Restructuring and Regional Development*, London: Unwin Hyman.

Ullman, E.L. (1958), 'Regional development and the geography of concentration', *Papers and Proceedings of the Regional Science Association*, **IV**, 179–98.

Urban, S. and S. Vendemini (1992), *European Strategic Alliances*, Oxford: Blackwell.

Van Tulder, R. and G. Junne (1988), *European Multinationals in Core Technologies*, Chichester: John Wiley & Sons.

Venables, A.J. (1994), 'Economic integration and industrial agglomeration', *The Economic and Social Review*, **26** (1), 1–17.

Vence-Deza, X. (1996), 'Innovation, regional development and technology policy: new spatial trends in industrialization and the emergence of regionalization of technology policy', in X. Vence-Deza and J.S. Metcalfe (eds), *Wealth from Diversity*, Dordrecht: Kluwer Academic Press.

Verspagen, B. (1997a), 'Science and Technology Infrastructure in the European Union', Paper presented at the workshop of the TSER project 'Technology, Economic Integration and Social Cohesion', November.

Verspagen, B. (1997b), 'European "regional clubs": do they exist, and where are they heading? On economic and technological differences between European region', *MERIT Working Papers*, No. 2/97-010.

Verspagen, B. (1997c), 'Estimating international technology spillovers using technologies flow matrices', *Weltwirtschaftliches-Archiv*, **133** (2), 226–48.

Vertova, G. (1998a), 'Technological similarity in national pattern of specialisation in a historical perspective', *Technology Analysis and Strategic Management*, **10** (4), 437–49.

Vertova, G. (1998b), 'Historical Evolution of National Systems of Innovation and National Technological Specialisation', University of Reading, PhD thesis.

Vertova, G. (1999), 'Stability in national patterns of technological specialisation: some evidence from patent data', *Economics of Innovation and New Technology*, **8** (4), 331–54.

von Tunzelmann, G.N. (1995), *Technology and Industrial Progress: the Foundations of Economic Growth*, Aldershot: Edward Elgar.

von Tunzelmann, G.N. (1999), '"Convergence" and corporate change in the electronics industry', " in A. Gambardella and F. Malerba (eds), *The Organisation of Economic Innovation in Europe*, Cambridge: Cambrdige University Press.

Walsh, V. (1988), 'Technology and the Competitiveness of Small Countries: Review', in C. Freeman, B-Å. Lundvall (eds), *Small Countries Facing Technological Revolutio,* London: Pinter.

Weber, M.J. (1984), *Industrial Location*, Beverly Hills: Sage Publications.

Williamson, O.E. (1990), 'The firm as a nexus of treaties: an introduction', in M. Aoki, B. Gustafsson and O. Williamson (eds), *The Firm as a Nexus of Treaties*, London and Newbury Park: Sage Publications.

Winter, S.G. (1987), 'Knowledge and competence as strategic assets', in D. Teece (ed.), *The Competitive Challenge. Strategies for Innovation and Renewal*, Cambridge: Ballinger.

Wymbs, C.D. (1998), 'How New Jersey's localized knowledge hub affects the global telecommunication industry', Baruch College, *mimeo*.

Yoffie, D.B. (ed.) (1997), *Competing in the Age of Digital Convergence*, Boston: Harvard Business School Press.

Young, S., N. Hood and E. Peters (1994), 'Multinational enterprises and regional economic development', *Regional Studies*, **28** (7), 657–77.

Zander, I. (1994), 'The Tortoise Evolution of the Multinational Corporation – Foreign technological activity in Swedish multinational firms 1890–1990', PhD dissertation.

Zander, I. (1996), 'The evolution of international innovation networks – ASEA/ABB in the period 1890–1990', Paper presented at the EIBA Annual Conference, Stockholm, December.

Zander, I. (1997a), 'Technological diversification in the multinational corporation – historical evolution and future prospects', *Research Policy*, **26**, 209–27.

Zander, I. (1997b), 'Technological renewal in the multinational corporation – an evolutionary perspective' Stanford University, *mimeo*.

Zander, I. (1997c), 'How do you mean "global"? A taxonomy of innovation networks in the multinational corporation', *Research Policy*, **28** (2–3), 195–213.

Zander, I. (1998), 'The formation of international innovation networks in the multinational corporation – an evolutionary perspective', Stockholm School of Economics, *mimeo*.

Zander, I. and Ö. Sölvell (1997), 'Internationally integrated innovation – an unexplored aspect of the multinational corporation', *IIB Research Paper 97/4*, Stockholm School of Economics.

Index